Real Life, Real Progress for Children with Autism Spectrum Disorders

Strategies for Successful Generalization in Natural Environments

edited by

Christina Whalen, Ph.D., BCBA
Jigsaw Learning

·P A U L·H·
BROOKES
PUBLISHING CO.®

Baltimore • London • Sydney

Paul H. Brookes Publishing Co.
Post Office Box 10624
Baltimore, Maryland 21285-0624
USA

www.brookespublishing.com

Typeset by Broad Books, Baltimore, Maryland.
Manufactured in the United States of America by
Sheridan Books, Inc., Chelsea, Michigan.

The individuals described in this book are composites or real people whose situations are masked and are based on the authors' experiences. In all instances, names and identifying details have been changed to protect confidentiality.

Library of Congress Cataloging-in-Publication Data

Real life, real progress for children with autism spectrum disorders:
   strategies for successful generalization in natural environments/edited
   by Christina Whalen
      p.   cm.
Includes bibiliographical references and index.
ISBN-13: 978-1-55766-954-4 (pbk.)
ISBN-10: 1-55766-954-6 (pbk.)
1. Autistic children—Education—United States.   I. Whalen, Christina.
II. Title.
LC4718.R43 2009
371.94—dc22   2009004455

British Library Cataloguing in Publication data are available from the British Library.

2013   2012   2011   2010   2009

10   9   8   7   6   5   4   3   2   1

Contents

v

About the Editor

Christina Whalen, Ph.D., BCBA, President and Chief Science Officer, Jigsaw Learning, 2815 Eastlake Avenue East, Suite 300, Seattle, Washington 98102

Dr. Whalen is a licensed psychologist and Board Certified Behavior Analyst specializing in autism and related disorders. She is one of the founders of TeachTown, Inc. (http://www.drchris.teachtown.com), and is now Co-founder and President and Chief Science Officer of Jigsaw Learning (http://www.jig-sawlearning.com; a merged company of TeachTown, Inc., and Animated Speech Co.). She received her Ph.D. at the University of California, San Diego, and did her postdoctoral fellowship at the University of California, Los Angeles. She also worked at Autism Spectrum Therapies in Los Angeles and at the University of Washington Autism Center as the Early STAART Treatment and Training Director.

Dr. Whalen has more than 15 years of experience in research and clinical practice with children with autism and their families. She has developed and supervised home programs, educated and trained parents and teachers, consulted with school districts, taught college and graduate courses in psychology and education, presented at numerous professional conferences, participated in fund-raising activities for various autism organizations, and published in professional scientific journals. She is also a chapter author in *Universal Usability: Designing Computer Interfaces for Diverse Users* (edited by Jonathan Lazar; Wiley, 2007), a book about how technology can help people with special needs. Dr. Whalen served on a task force for the California Blue Ribbon Commission for Autism, acted as the ABA Liaison for the California Association for Behavior Analysis (Cal-ABA), and is now the Chair of the Technology Special Interest Group for the Association for Behavior Analysis (ABA).

Dr. Whalen resides in Millbrae, California, near San Francisco. She is married and has a 6-year-old boy.

Contributors

Anne Bernard, Research and Clinical Coordinator, Autism and Neurodevelopment Clinic, University of California, San Francisco, California 94143. In addition to her research on diagnosis and intervention strategies for autism spectrum disorders, Ms. Bernard is currently coordinating a magnetic source imaging study on sensory processing disorders.

Andy Bondy, Ph.D., Co-founder, Pyramid Educational Consultants, Inc., 13 Garfield Way, Suite 1, Newark, Delaware 19713. Dr. Bondy has more than 35 years of experience in applied behavior analysis and autism. He directed a statewide program for students with autism for 14 years and co-developed the Picture Exchange Communication System. He also co-founded (with his wife, Lori Frost) Pyramid Educational Consultants, which provides parent and staff training around the world.

Shannon Cernich, Ph.D., BCBA, Director of Implementation and Training, Jigsaw Learning, 2815 Eastlake Avenue East, Suite 300, Seattle, Washington 98102. Dr. Cernich has more than 10 years of experience working with children and adults with autism spectrum disorders and special needs as well as with their educators and caregivers. She is a Board Certified Behavior Analyst and has a Ph.D. in psychology. Her goal is to work with her team to utilize technology to help 100,000 children with special needs in the next 5 years, and she has met her 1-year benchmark.

Sabrina D. Daneshvar, Ph.D., BCBA, Program Coordinator, Autism Spectrum Therapies, 1526 Brookhollow Drive, Suite 70, Santa Ana, California 92705. Dr. Daneshvar received her Ph.D. in applied developmental psychology from Claremont Graduate University with a concentration in behavioral treatment of developmental disabilities. She is a Board Certified Behavior Analyst and a program coordinator with Autism Spectrum Therapies. Her expertise includes early intervention, parent education, behavior support, consultation, and staff development.

Carol Davis, Ed.D., Associate Professor of Special Education, University of Washington, Box 353600, Seattle, Washington 98195. Dr. Davis's research interests include examining effective instructional practices that facilitate skill acquisition and promote positive behavior of students with moderate to profound disabilities in inclusive settings, identifying variables that contribute to the use of effective strategies by teachers in these settings, and developing systems to support students with severe disabilities to have access to the general education curriculum within the public school setting.

Anna Dvortcsak, M.S., CCC-SLP, Private Practice, 4110 South East Hawthorne Boulevard #420, Portland, Oregon 97214. Ms. Dvortcsak, a licensed speech and language pathologist, specializes in parent-mediated intervention for children with autism spectrum disorders. In 2004, Ms. Dvortcsak founded Dvortcsak Speech and Language Services (DSLSI), which provides individual and group training to families with children with autism and related disorders, individualized speech and language services, and training to professionals working with children with autism and related disorders. She also consults with school districts, private practices, and hospitals to train staff to use naturalistic treatment strategies to enhance children's engagement, imitation, language, and play skills and to use parent-mediated interventions.

Lauren Franke, Psy.D, Private Practice, 1600 Pacific Coast Highway, Suite C, Seal Beach, California 90740. As a licensed clinical psychologist and language pathologist, Dr. Franke has spent the last 25 years in private and clinical practice with an emphasis on the diagnosis and treatment of language disorders, developmental disabilities, autism spectrum disorders, learning disorders, and attention-deficit/hyperactivity disorder. She also consults with school districts providing training to professionals and parents regarding diagnosing developmental disorders and treatment strategies for expressive language development and improving language comprehension and social-pragmatic skills.

William D. Frea, Ph.D., BCBA, Chief Clinical Officer, Autism Spectrum Therapies, 6001 Bristol Parkway, Suite 200, Culver City, California 90230. Dr. Frea is the co-founder of Autism Spectrum Therapies (http://www.autismtherapies .com), an agency providing comprehensive applied behavior analysis services to individuals with autism. He and his agency specialize in intensive behavioral interventions, positive behavior supports, and social skills across the life span. Autism Spectrum Therapies also works closely with school districts to develop state-of-the-art autism programs.

Lori Frost, Co-founder, Pyramid Educational Consultants, Inc., 13 Garfield Way, Suite 1, Newark, Delaware 19713. Ms. Frost is Vice-President and Co-founder of Pyramid Educational Consultants, Inc., as well as a coauthor of the *Picture Exchange Communication System (PECS) Training Manual*. Ms. Frost has been the driving force behind creating PECS, a unique system that allows children with limited communication abilities to initiate communication with teachers, parents, and peers. She has a wealth of background in functional communication training and applied behavior analysis.

Carol Gray, President and Consultant to Individuals with Autism Spectrum Disorders, The Gray Center for Social Learning and Understanding, 4123

Embassy Drive Southeast, Kentwood, Michigan, 49546. Ms. Gray is an author, speaker, and consultant who works on behalf of individuals with autism spectrum disorders. She developed the Social Story approach early in 1991 and is noted for the development of other instructional strategies and her groundbreaking articles on bullying and loss and learning. She is the recipient of the Barbara Lipinski Award for her international contribution to the education and welfare of individuals on the autism spectrum.

Brooke Ingersoll, Ph.D., BCBA, Assistant Professor of Psychology, Michigan State University, 105B Psychology Building, East Lansing, Michigan 48824. Dr. Ingersoll is an assistant professor at Michigan State University, where she heads the Autism Research Laboratory. Her research is focused on social-communication development and interventions aimed at improving social-communication deficits in children with autism. She is a licensed psychologist and a Board Certified Behavior Analyst.

Robert H. LaRue, Ph.D., BCBA, Assistant Professor and Assistant Director of Research and Training, Douglass Developmental Disabilities Center, Rutgers University, 151 Ryders Lane, New Brunswick, New Jersey 08901. Dr. LaRue received his doctorate in biological and school psychology from Louisiana State University and completed a predoctoral internship and a postdoctoral fellowship with the Kennedy Krieger and Marcus Institutes at The Johns Hopkins School of Medicine and Emory University. He is Assistant Director of Research and Training at The Douglass Developmental Disabilities Center. He has coauthored articles in peer-reviewed journals as well as book chapters and has presented at national and international conferences.

Dominic W. Massaro, Ph.D., Professor, University of California, Santa Cruz, Department of Psychology, Santa Cruz, California 95060. Dr. Massaro is Professor of Psychology and Computer Engineering, Director of the Perceptual Science Laboratory, and Founding Chair of Digital Arts and New Media M.F.A. program at the University of California, Santa Cruz. He has been a Guggenheim Fellow, a University of Wisconsin Romnes Fellow, a James McKeen Cattell Fellow, and a National Institute of Mental Health Fellow. His research uses a formal experimental and theoretical approach to the study of speech perception, reading, psycholinguistics, memory, cognition, learning, and decision making.

Annie McLaughlin, M.T., Doctoral Student, Experimental Education Unit, University of Washington, Box 353600, Seattle, Washington 98195. Ms. McLaughlin has a master's of teaching in special education from The University of Virginia with a specialization in working with people with developmental disabilities, learning disabilities, and emotional/behavior disorders. She is currently working on her Ph.D. in severe disabilities at the University of Washington. Her classroom and research experiences focus on students with severe disabilities, autism, and challenging behavior.

Ronit M. Molko, Ph.D., BCBA, Founder, Autism Spectrum Therapies, 6001 Bristol Parkway, Suite 200, Culver City, California 90230. Dr. Molko is a Board Certified Behavior Analyst and clinical psychologist, specializing in the treatment of children with autism and related disorders. She is co-founder of Autism Spectrum Therapies (http://www.autismtherapies.com), an agency that specializes in intensive behavioral interventions, positive behavior supports, and social skills for individuals with autism across the life span. Autism Spectrum Therapies also works closely with school districts to develop state-of-the-art autism programs.

Daniel Openden, Ph.D., BCBA, Vice President/Clinical Services Director, Southwest Autism Research & Resource Center (SARRC), 300 North 18th Street, Phoenix, Arizona 85006. Dr. Openden is Faculty Associate in the Division of Curriculum & Instruction at Mary Lou Fulton College of Education at Arizona State University. He has worked extensively with families with children with autism spectrum disorders on both federal- and state-funded research projects; provided consulting and training for school districts across the country; presented research at regional, state, and national conventions; and been published in peer-reviewed journals and book chapters in the field. Dr. Openden has expertise in developing training programs for teaching parents and professionals to implement Pivotal Response Treatment (PRT) and is currently an associate editor for the *Journal of Positive Behavior Interventions*.

Nancy E. Rosenberg, Ph.D., Teaching Associate, Experimental Education Unit, University of Washington, 4000 15th Avenue Northeast, Seattle, Washington 98195. Dr. Rosenberg received her Ph.D. in special education from the University of Washington with a particular focus in autism. She currently teaches classes for both educators and parents around issues related to autism and consults with families and school districts for these children. Dr. Rosenberg is also the parent of a son with autism.

Laura Schreibman, Ph.D., Distinguished Professor of Psychology, University of California, San Diego (UCSD), 9500 Gilman Drive, La Jolla, California 92093. Dr. Laura Schreibman directs the UCSD Autism Intervention Research Program, a federally funded research program focusing on the experimental analysis and treatment of autism. A co-developer of Pivotal Response Training, her general research interests include naturalistic behavioral intervention strategies, development of individualized treatment protocols, analysis of language and attentional deficits, generalization of behavior change, parent training, and issues of assessment. She is the author of three books and more than 120 research articles and book chapters.

Ilene S. Schwartz, Ph.D., Professor and Chair of Special Education, University of Washington, Box 357925, Seattle, Washington 98195. Dr. Schwartz is the director of the Norris and Dorothy Haring Center for Applied Research and Training in Education at the University of Washington. She has an active research program in the area of effective programming for young children with autism. Dr. Schwartz is especially interested in developing and evaluating programs that promote inclusion in general education and provide positive social outcomes for children and in developing and evaluating programs that are sustainable.

Bryna Siegel, Ph.D., Adjunct Professor, Director, Autism Clinic, Co-director, Autism Neurodevelopment Center, 401 Parnassus Avenue, University of California, San Francisco (UCSF), California 94143. Dr. Siegel founded and directs the UCSF Autism Clinic. She has been involved with autism research for the past 25 years and has authored numerous books, chapters, and scientific papers. Her work has focused on operationalizing a definition for autism as specific autistic learning disabilities and autistic learning styles that can be treated with developmental curricula administered using behavioral methodologies.

Aubyn C. Stahmer, Ph.D., BCBA, Research Scientist, Psychologist, Rady Children's Hospital, 3020 Children's Way, MC 5033, San Diego, California 92123. Dr. Stahmer is a research scientist and clinical psychologist at Rady Children's Hospital and the Child and Adolescent Services Research Center. She has published many scholarly articles on inclusion and early intervention services in the area of autism. Her current interests include the study of early intervention systems for children with autism and the translation of evidence-based practices into community settings.

Jessica Suhrheinrich, Ph.D., Postdoctoral Fellow, University of California, San Diego, 9500 Gilman Drive, La Jolla, California 92093. Ms. Suhrheinrich has been implementing behavioral interventions with children on the autism spectrum for more than 10 years. Her research interests include training therapists, parents, and special education teachers to implement behavioral interventions. Currently, Dr. Suhrheinrich is a postdoctoral fellow at the University of California, San Diego.

Manya Vaupel, M.Ed., BCBA, Curriculum Director, Jigsaw Learning, 2815 Eastlake Avenue East, #300, Seattle, Washington 98102. Ms. Vaupel is an internationally recognized Board Certified Behavior Analyst and has a master's degree in early childhood special education with a specialized focus in applied behavior analysis, remedial reading, and early literacy. She has worked with children with autism spectrum disorders ages 8 months to 21 years since 1994 and continues to build comprehensive, data-based, and individualized programs that meet the specific needs of this population in schools, homes, and community settings.

Mary Jane Weiss, Ph.D., BCBA, Director of Research and Training, Douglass Developmental Disabilities Center, Rutgers University, 151 Ryders Lane, New Brunswick, New Jersey 08901. Dr. Weiss is an associate research professor at

Rutgers University. Her clinical and research interests center on defining best practice applied behavior analysis (ABA) techniques, on identifying the specific utilities of various instructional methodologies within ABA, on evaluating the impact of ABA in learners with autism spectrum disorders, and in maximizing family members' expertise and adaptation. She has written numerous articles and four books on autism and is a regular presenter at regional and national conferences.

Foreword

It is about time someone wrote a book about generalization in autism spectrum disorders (ASDs). This is a topic that is generally not discussed but is of great importance to consider when planning any type of service or intervention strategy.

Generalization is one of the three common characteristics of ASDs that I have observed in almost every person on the spectrum that I have ever met. These common characteristics are as follows:

1.   Communication or the difficulty in communicating

It does not matter if the person seems to have strong verbal skills (like someone with Asperger's syndrome) or is on the nonverbal end of the spectrum. Everyone on the spectrum has difficulty in communicating and verbally expressing him- or herself. Many people with ASDs describe the intense physical demands it takes for them to be able to carry on a conversation. We, too, often underestimate and devalue those with ASDs who cannot verbally express themselves—this is a terrible mistake. I have yet to meet a person with ASD who, when given the opportunity or the ability or the means to open his or her communicative powers, shows that there is much, much more to him or her as an individual than we could have ever imagined. It is a discrimination that needs to be removed to think that people with ASDs, if they cannot talk, have nothing to say.

All behavior is communication. Those who work with people with ASDs must understand this so as to truly understand and become sensitive to what the individual may be trying to communicate. In finding the means and patience in allowing people with ASDs to communicate, it can liberate their intellect and emotions so that we can truly see what unique and wonderful gifts they have as people. As I always mention in my presentations, "What we see in a person with ASD is usually not what we get . . . because there is so much more positively to them and so much potential than we can ever imagine if we can only open up their communication avenues."

2.   Abilities or the disparities in their abilities

An individual with ASD may be a genius in math but cannot care for him- or herself or attend to his or her most basic of life skills. A person with ASD may have a tremendous ability to memorize and speak in great detail on a particular interest but cannot hold a conversation or discuss abstract ideas. The examples of the variance in the skill levels of people with ASDs are as numerous as those who have the condition.

In this common characteristic, we need to focus our attention on individuals with ASD's strengths and nurture those abilities. It is when we do that, that we can develop a sense of accomplishment and success within them and accordingly provide them with an anchor so that they can find the support necessary to either overcome or build into strength those areas of weaknesses. Focus on the strengths, and the rest will improve.

3.   Generalization or the lack thereof

It seems as though people on the autism spectrum are born without a "generalization gene." For example, most people learn through observing and experiencing their environment. Through these observations, they learn certain skills and functions, how to interact and relate to others, and how to take these learned abilities to matrix into or craft new seamless skills and experiences; this is our ability to generalize. Those on the spectrum typically lack this ability—every nuance, every minute detail stands alone and has its own distinction. In other words, connections and bridges of these experiences and observations are not made.

To create these connections requires much patience, repetition, time, intensity, and individualization. For example, for a toddler, every detailed aspect of using a fork to feed him- or herself may have to be broken down into a series of tasks that may have to be individually mastered before the entire act of using a fork is accomplished. For an adolescent, it may mean developing a strategy to take his or her focused interest and relate it to more abstract and interactive activities. And for an adult on the spectrum, it may be finding his or her passion and honing it to be an employment placement.

Regardless of the situation, much needs to be done with an individual with ASD to create the "body of work" that provides enough similar experiences so he or she can find the similarities to connect these various sequences together. These connections provide confidence and success and reinforce additional opportunities for gained experiences, which further build more shared knowledge. And through this work, hopefully, individuals with ASD will have the abilities to transition easier, understand others, expand their interests, adapt to their environment, acquire broader skills, and live successfully in the world.

I would argue that the three common characteristics—abilities, communication, and generalization—present the strongest case for therapies (behavioral and/or educational) to be intensive, specialized, and individualized programs for all with autism. Taken together, these aspects differentiate ASD from all other conditions.

The disparity in ability is best addressed when we identify the strengths of individuals and build upon those to give them a sense of accomplishment. Through this, they can improve upon their weaknesses as well. Secondly, as I mentioned previously, all behavior is communication. When we observe people with autism exhibiting a behavior, it is a way for them to express themselves to us. We need to be cognizant of what it is that they are communicating and provide greater understanding and sensitivity by making it easier for them to communicate. Lastly, there is no "short cut" to teaching generalization. When a person with autism masters one certain skill set, we must go through the same steps to teach the individual another skill set—and another and another. After the individual has mastered a number of similar skill sets, he or she will be able to bridge the gap or generalize between these new acquired abilities.

Much has been written about disparities and abilities and an even a greater amount about communication difficulties in people with autism. I applaud the authors and contributors of this book for finally discussing the other important common characteristic of autism—generalization—and helping us to build stronger services and techniques to address the challenges of teaching generalization so that we can improve the lives of those with autism.

Lee Grossman
President and CEO
Autism Society of America
Bethesda, Maryland

Preface

Learning to work with children with autism spectrum disorders (ASDs) taught me how important generalization is to a child's success. Without it, you simply have a child who has learned to respond to certain cues, but one who does not seem to understand his or her own responses. I have seen too many children with years of intervention, a long list of "mastered" skills, and no real life skills. Programs that carefully plan for and measure generalization result in children who understand their words and actions and children who are better able to assimilate into their surroundings. However, planning for and measuring generalization is not necessarily an easy thing to do, and not everyone does it.

Once I initiated my plans for using videos and computers to teach children with ASDs, the issue of generalization became so much more significant. My critics and my conscience highlighted the fact that the use of computers to teach children with ASDs could be problematic for generalization to the natural environment. So, in the design of my software, I carefully planned for generalization and became even more aware of how significant this is to a child's success. In the Chapter 6 appendix, there are activities that supplement a computer program, TeachTown: Basics, as well as data sheets for tracking generalization to naturalistic activities.

I spent many hours thumbing through the literature on generalization and realized that a book was needed with this focus. I have been strongly influenced by the researchers that I worked with over the years—many of whom are authors in this book—who recognized and acted on the fact that without generalization, treatment has very little value.

In this book, various interventions and treatment settings are discussed with a focus on how the intervention or treatment setting incorporates generalization. Research is discussed in each chapter, and specific strategies are offered for increasing generalization. The authors in this book are revered in the research community, but more importantly, they are advocates for child success and believe that generalization is the key. I hope that you will find the chapters enlightening and practical and that upcoming interventions will plan for and highlight generalization so that children can show real progress that has real meaning in their everyday lives.

Acknowledgments

I developed my passion and respect for generalization in my first experiences with autism spectrum disorders (ASDs) through the wisdom and guidance of Laura Schreibman and Aubyn Stahmer at the University of California, San Diego (UCSD). I also learned a great deal from Karen Pierce, Michelle Sherer, Amy Anderson, Michelle Sullivan, Brooke Ingersoll, Jamie Winter, Aaron Ilan, Mike Taffe, Rob Duncan, Mark Becker, and too many others to list; all were my fellow graduate students at UCSD and some of the smartest people I have ever met.

I learned how to better measure generalization in my work with Connie Kasari at the University of California, Los Angeles. I learned to apply these principles in homes and schools when I worked with Bill Frea and Ronit Molko at Autism Spectrum Therapies. Sally Rogers taught me that a child's success is the responsibility of the people working with the child, and Geri Dawson at the University of Washington taught me how important research is to creating effective treatment programs. My colleagues at the University of Washington, especially Manya Vaupel and Felice Orlich, were extremely supportive and taught me many things that have been embedded into the TeachTown program and into this book.

Each of the authors in this book has also inspired me, and I was thrilled to have every one of them contribute to this book. I hope that those who read this will learn as much as I have from their amazing insight and intellect.

I am fortunate to work with a team of people who are incredibly creative, zealous, and knowledgeable. You have all taught me to be a better leader and a better person. Thank you all for your support and motivation. Your work is so important, and you are helping children with special needs every day and should be so proud of your accomplishments. Cheers to my great friends and team: Dan Feshbach, Walter Schwartz, Shannon Cernich, Joel Walden, Jeanette Ryan, Kevin MacDonald, Eric Dashen, Thomas Roxstrom, Ed Tang, Manya Vaupel, Liz Ralston, Barbara Gilbert, Glenn Chapin, Stephanie Trinh, and Jennifer Kahler. Special thanks to David Lockhart, Paul Fielding, and Asif Rahman for their extra help with data analysis and to Mya Kramer, Dina Berman, and Michelle Norris for their help with marketing. I would also like to thank Brad McGuire, Sven Liden, Lars Liden, Sally Vilardi, Sascha Broomberg, Scott Kennedy, Lara Schneider, and Eric Dallaire for their contributions to making TeachTown a reality and changing the lives of so many people. I am grateful to the leadership and financial support from our team of investors and to the Department of Education (SBIR and Stepping Stones for Innovative Technology) and the National Center for Technology Innovation for their grant support in various projects.

All of the wonderful, compassionate, and very bright parents whom I have worked with over the years have also taught me so much, and their energy is inspiring. The children with ASDs are, of course, the biggest inspiration to me, and I hope that each of them will have the opportunity to learn and love learning and that what they learn will make them happy and successful in life.

I would also like to acknowledge my family—Eileen Parr, Jerry Parr, Ellen Long, Patrick Whalen, Kelli Caracci, Betty Dallaire, Richard Dallaire, Tricia Dallaire, and Robert Mouck—who are always there for me when I need them. I would especially like to thank my husband and friend, Eric Dallaire, for the many sacrifices he has made over the years so that I could pursue my dreams. I would also like to thank my son, Brendan, for always making me proud and making me laugh. I am so lucky to have you in my life.

This book is dedicated to Indiana Jones, Luke Skywalker, Ironman,
Superman, Batman, Spiderman, Yoda, Flash, Harry Potter, Mario, Luigi, Sonic,
and to my amazing little boy, Brendan Michael Dallaire,
who aspires each day to be all of them, but you are so much more.

1

Generalization and Autism Spectrum Disorders

Daniel Openden, Christina Whalen, Shannon Cernich, and Manya Vaupel

---

Autism is a complex neurobiological disorder that includes core deficits in three primary areas: language and communication, social interaction, and repetitive and restrictive interests and behaviors (American Psychiatric Association, 1994). In 1943, Dr. Leo Kanner first coined the term *autism* to describe a group of children who displayed similar patterns of behavior. At around the same time, Dr. Hans Asperger described comparable characteristics, although in a milder form, that are now known as Asperger syndrome. Today, autism is most commonly referred to as an *autism spectrum disorder* (ASD) to highlight the varying degrees of impairment, symptoms, and characteristics across three related disorders: autism, Asperger syndrome, and pervasive developmental disorder-not otherwise specified (PDD-NOS). Together, these three disorders and two others—Rett syndrome and childhood disintegrative disorder—fall under the umbrella of pervasive developmental disorders.

Statistics from the Centers for Disease Control and Prevention (2007) indicate that about 1 in every 150 children in the United States may be affected with an ASD, making ASDs more common than pediatric cancer, diabetes, and acquired immunodeficiency syndrome (AIDS) combined. Diagnoses of ASDs occur across all racial, ethnic, and social groups and are 4 times more prevalent in boys than in girls. Autism is assumed to be present at birth. Although research has increasingly suggested that genetics play a key role in its development, the impact of the environment and its interaction with genetic susceptibility continue to be studied. The causes of ASDs therefore remain largely unknown. Furthermore, although there is much debate about whether the incidence of autism is truly on the rise and represents an epidemic increase, it is clear that more children than ever are being diagnosed with ASDs, which has important implications for the delivery and implementation of effective treatments.

ASDs can be reliably diagnosed by age 2 years (Lord et al., 2006), although research has continued to improve earlier identification of autism to as young as 6 months. No medical test exists for ASDs, and diagnoses are primarily made based on behavioral symptoms. Developmental screenings for autism should occur during 18-, 24-, and 30-month well-child visits, followed by more comprehensive diagnostic evaluations. Diagnostic tools usually rely on a combination of parent descriptions and direct observation of the child's behavior. The gold standard for accurately assessing ASDs is a combination of the Autism Diagnostic Interview–Revised (Tadevosyan-Leyfer et al., 2003) and the Autism Diagnostic Observation Schedule–Generic (Lord et al., 2000). The importance of accurate and early identification of ASDs cannot be overstated; the best prognostic outcomes have generally been associated with early identification and intervention.

TREATMENT FOR AUTISM SPECTRUM DISORDERS

No two children with ASDs are exactly alike. Therefore, it is important to individualize treatment to meet the unique needs of the child and family. There is no shortage of treatment and therapy options for children with ASDs. However, with the increasing prevalence of ASDs has come a simultaneous rise in the number of treatments, many of which have little or no scientific evidence supporting their efficacy. Although efforts such as the National Autism Center's (2007) National Standards Project are underway to help families and professionals better identify evidence-based intervention components and comprehensive treatments, and new research on treatments continues to emerge, scientifically validated treatments have generally been based on applied behavior analysis (ABA).

Simpson (2005) and Simpson et al. (2005) categorized treatments for autism in two ways. First, treatments were defined as interpersonal, skill based, cognitive, physiological/biological/neurological, or other. Next, each treatment was classified as a scientifically based practice, a promising practice, a practice with limited supporting information, or a practice that was not recommended. Of the many treatments reviewed, only four were classified as scientifically based practices, all of which were based on the principles of ABA, including discrete trial training (DTT), Pivotal Response Training (PRT), and Learning Experiences: An Alternative Program for Preschoolers and Parents.

Although treatments based on ABA rely on the same fundamental learning principles, the implementation of various ABA intervention approaches differs. The terms *DTT* and *ABA* often are used interchangeably, which is a common but significant misunderstanding. While the field of autism treatment and intervention is greatly indebted to Ivar Lovaas and colleagues—some of the first researchers to experiment with and investigate the efficacy of ABA procedures with children with autism—DTT is a systematic curriculum based on the principles of ABA. Under the umbrella of ABA-based treatments are a number of interventions that use the same ABA principles but are implemented differently. For instance, while DTT generally includes highly structured learning trials that focus on individual target behaviors, PRT focuses on key areas of responding that, when targeted for intervention, often produce collateral improvements in untargeted behaviors. Incidental teaching, like PRT, takes advantage of incidental learning opportunities that occur mostly in natural settings and environments and primarily focuses on eliciting verbal social communication. Picture Exchange Communication System (PECS), on the other hand, is also designed to be implemented in the natural environment but teaches children to exchange a picture as the primary means to communicate and eventually augments verbal language. Although these intervention approaches are distinguished both by name and the differences in how they are implemented, they each manipulate antecedents and consequences to increase desired behaviors and reduce undesirable behaviors.

Although the evidence supporting ABA-based interventions is substantial, little evidence compares comprehensive treatments, making it difficult to determine which treatment is most effective. Also, growing evidence indicates that a number of interventions—as opposed to comprehensive approaches—may be effective components of a child's treatment program. For instance, evidence supporting video modeling and video self-modeling for teaching social skills and other adaptive behaviors has begun to emerge (Bellini & Akullian, 2007), yet comprehensive approaches have not typically included video self-modeling as part of the curriculum. Furthermore, the gap in quickly translating research to real-world practice has led many families with children with ASDs to experiment with treatments that are unsupported by research, yet those families often report positive outcomes. As our understanding of both ASDs and how children with ASDs respond to treatments has improved, researchers have begun studying characteristics and behavioral phenotypes that may help to predict how children may respond to various treatments (Sherer & Schreibman, 2005). In addition, individualized assessment is one area in which behavior analysts may be particularly helpful in designing and evaluating appropriate interventions for children with ASDs. Using single-subject research methodology, clinicians and parents can systematically examine an individual's response to an intervention and determine the most appropriate course of treatment (Horner et al., 2005).

In the absence of data that compares comprehensive treatments, many reports on treatment for children with ASDs have identified critical components of effective interventions (Dawson & Osterling, 1997; Iovannone, Dunlap, Huber, & Kincaid, 2003; Koegel, Openden, Fredeen, & Koegel, 2006; National Research Council, 2001). Early intervention, family involvement, treatment intensity, a structured curriculum that focuses on communication and social interaction, intervention in natural environments, and involvement with typically developing peers are among the components that have been recommended to be present within a comprehensive treatment program for a child with autism. Yet, one component may be the most critical because it should almost always be planned for and measured in each behavior targeted for intervention: generalization.

GENERALIZATION

The importance of planning for generalization was identified by the National Research Council (2001) as critical to the design of treatment programs for children with ASDs. Clinically, generalization of skills across settings and/or people is an area in which many children with autism have historically struggled. It is not clear whether the difficulty with generalization is due specifically to the disorder; the nature, delivery, or quality of the instruction or intervention; or some combination of the two. However, a child's ability not only to learn a behavior but also to generalize and use that behavior or skill with different people and in different environments may be one of the best indicators of the significance of the skill, the quality of the teaching, and broader outcomes for the child. Thus, planning for generalization for children with ASDs should not occur once a new behavior has already been learned; rather, interventions should be designed with generalization in mind a priori. If generalization is considered at the beginning stages of designing interventions, then intervention may be more likely to include functional, socially adaptive target behaviors and therefore improve quality of life for children with autism and their families.

Generalization Basics

The recommended practices for intervention inform us that systematic and intensive individualized instruction provides the most effective and efficient outcomes when teaching new skills to children with ASD and other special needs (Smith, Groen, & Wynn, 2000). Some individuals with special needs will require instruction in a controlled training environment, whereas others may benefit from more naturalistic approaches to learning. In either case, individualized goals should be systematically implemented—and often embedded—within daily activities. Individual progress should be well documented through ongoing data collection and analysis with clear expectations, effective prompting and fading procedures, and reinforcement to promote future occurrence of the newly learned behaviors and skills. But after training, what is the next step? What do you do once an individual has mastered a goal in a training environment? How can a skill be meaningful to a child if he or she can only demonstrate it in one environment, with one particular person, or with only specific materials? A simple answer to these questions is generalization. When working with a child with ASD or other disabilities, all skills learned in a training environment must be generalized (Liberty & Billingsley, 1988).

Simply stated, generalization is the occurrence of a behavior in the presence of a novel stimulus. Stimulus generalization refers to when a behavior occurs appropriately when new materials, environments, and/or people require or elicit a desired response. Natural settings such as the student's home, school, and community are critical environments for teaching the child in order to ensure stimulus generalization. The student must be able to use learned skills in different environments and with different people. Stimulus generalization largely includes the desired behavior in the presence of any variation of the setting. For instance, when teaching a child to respond to greetings in the training environment, the student should also be taught to respond to greetings at home, in school, in the community, with different people, and upon hearing variations of the greetings (e.g., a child says, "Hi," when he hears either "Hey, Charlie," "Hey there," "Hey, buddy," or "What's up?").

Response generalization also refers to any variation of the student's behavior or response to particular stimuli. For example, in the training setting, if a student learned to respond to the greeting of "Hi, Charlie" by saying, "Hi," back to the listener but now is demonstrating the ability to reciprocate greetings in various ways (e.g., "Hey," "Hi, Suzie," or "Hi, how are you?"), then the student has demonstrated response generalization.

Finally, maintenance of treatment effects is a critical component of generalization. Although stimulus and response generalization are critical for a child's success, generalization should also be demonstrated over time. Thus, newly learned skills or behaviors should be meaningful and functional for the student so that they are likely to improve the student's quality of life. For Charlie to be truly successful, he must not only learn to greet people in a variety of ways and in a variety of environments, but he should also continue his generalization of greetings as he gets older and the greetings delivered by his peers change (e.g., a preschooler may say, "Hi, Charlie," whereas a teenager may say, "Yo, Chuck!").

When an individual can demonstrate a newly learned behavior independently, spontaneously, and appropriately over time in a variety of settings, with similar and novel materials, with numerous people, and in a variety of ways, one can consider the behavior generalized. A trained or learned skill is said to have generalized if it is observed over time, appears in a wide variety of environments, and produces functionally equivalent variations of the behavior (Baer, Wolf, & Risley, 1968).

Generalization of newly acquired skills is not always demonstrated when applying behavior analytic approaches to learning. Difficulties with generalization are frequently reported in ASDs and have important implications for educational practices. Historically, instruction was deemed to be a failure if generalization was not observed. Individuals with ASDs often will not spontaneously apply behaviors learned in one setting to other fairly similar settings. However, if a particular teaching strategy was effective in one setting, it is often effective in another setting. Baer et al. (1968) suggested that implementation of an effective procedure in the training environment should be applied across relevant settings until widespread generalization is observed. Thus, unless generalization is specifically addressed, children with ASDs may fail to generalize newly acquired skills. For maximal effectiveness, generalization should be planned and built into programming rather than be expected to naturally occur (Baer et al., 1968). Generalization of trained skills has been and very likely will remain a fundamental concern of ABA-based interventions (Stokes & Baer, 1977).

In 1968, Baer et al. explicitly indicated that behavior analysts should recognize the importance of specifically planning for generalization of skills. Stokes and Baer (1977) reviewed the literature and identified many methodologies for planning and assessing for generalization. They concluded that researchers and clinicians alike should systematically design interventions that include programming for generalization. Haring, Liberty, White, and Billingsley (1988) presented a decision rule system for selecting generalization strategies. Stokes and Osnes (1989), in response to the enduring lack of planning and systematic programming for generalization in the existing literature, provided additional information and methods for explicitly planning for generalization. Table 1.1 cross-references some of the various systems for generalization planning and assessment with the articles in which they are referenced.

Why Is Generalization Important?

ABA has provided a wealth of procedures for increasing and decreasing specific behaviors in children with autism. However, if these behaviors do not generalize to novel situations, they often have little or no social significance. Imagine a student who consistently raises his hand to ask a question or make a comment when with his behavior therapist but never does so in his classroom when classmates are present. Without generalization to a group setting, hand raising has little value for the student. A young adult who uses the toilet at home has learned a valuable skill from the point of view of her caregivers. However, if she requires diapers outside of her home, then her options for employment or recreation are likely limited by the lack of generalization of toileting behaviors. Unfortunately, the lack of attention to generalization is often common in schools or clinical programs.

Generalization has both advantages and disadvantages. If every desired behavior had to be trained in every possible environment with every possible set of materials and with every individual in a child's life, the costs—both in time and resources—would be astronomical. If a student had to be retrained to write his

Table 1.1.   Various systems for generalization planning and assessment

Reference	Strategy
Liberty and Billingsley (1988)	Alter generalization contingencies
	Amplify instructed behavior
	Eliminate training reinforcers
	Eliminate training stimuli
	Increase proficiency
	Program natural reinforcers
	Reinforce at natural schedules
	Reinforce generalized behavior
	Teach self-reinforcement
	Teach to solicit reinforcement
	Train in the target situation
	Use natural consequences
	Vary stimuli
Stokes and Baer (1977)	Mediate generalization
	Program common stimuli
	Train and hope
	Train loosely
	Train sufficient exemplars
	Train to generalize
	Use indiscriminable contingencies
	Use natural maintaining contingencies
	Use sequential modification
Stokes and Osnes (1989)	Contact natural reinforcers

name each time he used a new pencil or pen, for example, practitioners would be unlikely to say that he could write his name. Fortunately, generalization can be successfully integrated into the instruction or methodology.

Stimulus generalization can be both an advantage and disadvantage. Stimulus generalization is particularly useful when it occurs across individuals. The child who greets peers and store clerks as well as familiar adults with, "Hello," and a smile has an advantage socially over the child who only greets familiar adults in this manner. Many positive social interactions often follow an appropriate greeting. Sometimes, a slight prompt is all that is needed for generalization to occur across individuals; however, more often than not, specific programming for generalization is necessary.

Sometimes generalization occurs in a problematic manner, such as with stimulus generalization. For instance, a young child may call a male stranger "da-da", which is an example of overgeneralization (Sulzer-Azaroff & Mayer, 1991). In another example, a young boy had a tantrum when he was not given an apple that he requested at the food court of a mall. The apple was artificial and part of a display, but the boy was upset that his appropriate requesting did not result in access to an apple. In this situation, it would have been highly desirable to teach discrimination of real versus fake apples immediately. However, because the display was out of reach, the boy was not able to touch and smell the fake apple, which would have allowed him to discover his error in overgeneralizing all objects that looked like apples as edible apples. According to Sulzer-Azaroff and Mayer (1991), "Remedying unwanted generalization adds to the cost of changing behavior, because then we need to teach new discriminations. So it is best prevented in the first place" (p. 501) by teaching tight stimulus control and including generalization in the initial phases of learning.

Response overgeneralization can also result in undesired generalization. Some behaviors need to be performed in exactly the same manner each time. For instance, dialing the phone number of a close friend must be done in the same order each time or you will call the wrong person. Thus, planning for generalization and for discrimination (i.e., decreasing overgeneralization) are both important.

Sometimes generalization simply does not occur. Frequently, parents, teachers, and clinicians will utter in dismay, "But he knows this," when a child fails to generalize to a slightly novel situation. The mindset of "train and hope" must be replaced with specific programming for generalization when training and treating children with autism (Stokes & Baer, 1977).

Programming for generalization is particularly important when working with children with autism. Many people have raised concerns that children with ASDs who have received intensive behavior intervention always respond the same way whether they are interacting with familiar or unfamiliar children or adults. This perception likely occurs because of a lack of response generalization. A child may be trained to say, "Hello, nice to meet you," and extend her hand when meeting strangers. If the child greets a preschool classmate in this manner, however, the peer (and some observing adults) may label the child as "weird." It is extremely important to teach children with autism a variety of responses for only slightly different social situations.

Research on Generalization

The notion that generalization is something that needs to be explicitly taught and planned for in treatment is not new (Osnes & Lieblein, 2003); however, intervention research and practices have not advanced nearly enough in terms of generalization. In 1977, half of the applied literature on generalization focused on the train-and-hope category (Stokes & Baer, 1977). By 1989, more studies were discussing generalization, but the field was still desperately in need of more studies that examined planning for generalization (Stokes & Osnes, 1989). Many intervention studies do not report generalization, and those that do typically do not discuss how they programmed for it (Singh, Deitz, Epstein, & Singh, 1991).

Researchers are now making more of an effort to incorporate assessment for generalization and to find more functional relationships between treatment and generalization, but they need to further investigate highly discriminable interventions that demonstrate durability over time or continue to show generalization when the intervention is withdrawn (Osnes & Lieblein, 2003). In addition, with the exception of some ABA interventions such as PRT (e.g., Ingersoll & Schreibman, 2006; Koegel et al., 2006; Whalen, Schreibman, & Ingersoll, 2006), few studies report changes in collateral behaviors (i.e., behaviors that are not directly targeted in the intervention; Singh et al., 1991).

Many studies have examined stimulus generalization by measuring generalization to different people. For example, Stewart, Van Houten, and Van Houten (1992) found that withdrawn adults living in a residential center for individuals with psychosis and mental disorders increased the social interaction of other withdrawn residents when they served as peer therapists. However, these increases did not generalize to other residents until the introduction of a multiple peer therapist condition. In the field of autism, Carr and Kologinsky (1983) trained six children with autism who exhibited poor communication skills to use their sign repertoire to make spontaneous requests of adults. They used multiple exemplar training (i.e., multiple examples) to facilitate stimulus generalization.

While less common, several studies have measured response generalization. For example, Charlop-Christy and Daneshvar (2003) taught perspective taking to children with autism by using video modeling. They defined perspective taking as "the ability to determine mental states of others in order to explain or predict behavior" (p. 12). They observed generalization of perspective taking across untrained similar stimuli as well as response generalization. MacDuff, Krantz, and McLanahan (1993) specifically programmed for response generalization when teaching four boys with autism to independently follow photographic activity schedules. They included a resequencing phase for three of the four boys to promote generalization of the use of the photographic activity schedules to novel sequences. During the generalization phase, two of the six original activities were replaced with two similar but novel leisure activities for each boy. The boys were able to generalize to the novel activities, as well as to new sequences of activities.

Clinically, programming for generalization is considered a critical component of recommended practices, yet there are a limited number of studies that have systematically investigated procedures on *how* to program generalization. Some approaches, such as PRT, specifically describe strategies for increasing generalization (e.g., interspersing maintenance tasks, using natural reinforcers) and describe aspects of the intervention that are most likely to result in successful generalization of newly learned behaviors (e.g., Koegel et al., 2006).

Furthermore, few studies have examined maintenance of newly acquired skills over time. In one study, functional communication skills were taught to three students and were maintained for 18–24 months after the intervention was implemented (Durand & Carr, 1991). Most studies, however, do not include data on maintenance of intervention effects because it is often difficult to keep in touch with participants or sustain a research relationship. Future research should establish relationships that may decrease the possibility of losing communication with participants, such as by working with clinics or schools that often see children for many years. Maintenance of skills in these environments is often overlooked because of staff turnover, students leaving programs or moving, or lack of resources to follow students over time. Nevertheless, maintenance is a critical outcome measure that should be targeted and measured by both researchers and practitioners.

The assessment of collateral behaviors is still not common practice, but several studies have included these measures. In one study, joint attention skills were taught to children with ASDs using PRT (Whalen & Schreibman, 2003). A follow-up study reanalyzed the videotapes and assessments of these same children. Not only was the intervention effective in increasing joint attention behaviors that generalized to different providers and different stimuli, but collateral changes were also observed (Whalen et al., 2006). Specifically, children demonstrated positive changes in language, social interaction, play, and imitation, as well as decreases in inappropriate behaviors.

Other studies have shown that teaching children to use sign language resulted in decreases in inappropriate behaviors (Horner & Budd, 1985). Collateral changes in language, pretend play, and joint attention were also reported in a study that targeted imitation (Ingersoll & Schreibman, 2006). Assessing collateral behavior change is a significant aspect of generalization. If an intervention not only teaches a particular skill but also addresses multiple deficits and/or affects other skills simultaneously, the intervention is likely to make a more meaningful, sustained impact on the individual's quality of life.

Generalization research has revealed several important factors that have influenced the design of new interventions and modifications to existing treatment approaches. For instance, Chandler, Fowler, and Lubeck (1992) studied preschool children's social skills and found the following treatment strategies to be most common: addressing functional target behaviors (i.e., exploiting current functional contingencies), specifying a fluency criterion (i.e., incorporating functional mediators), using indiscriminable contingencies (i.e., training diversely), and using mediation techniques (i.e., incorporating functional mediators). These strategies have increasingly been used in clinical practice, particularly in interventions designed to teach new behaviors to children with autism.

Landrum and Lloyd (1992) reviewed social behavior research conducted with children with emotional and/or behavior disorders. In the studies they reviewed, four used train-and-hope methods, three taught relevant behaviors and used sequential modification (i.e., exploited current functional contingencies), and two used training with sufficient exemplars (i.e., trained diversely). Although this is an improvement from the research in the 1980s in which train and hope was the most common strategy, it is anticipated—and hoped—that the next review of generalization will reveal more sophisticated strategies for the incorporation and measurement of generalization.

Generalization Strategies

Although some students with autism may require highly structured teaching, it is not always necessary to structure teaching interactions in a strictly controlled and well-ordered manner. Naturalistic ABA instruction supports the likelihood of generalization, assists in maintaining the child's natural motivation, and can facilitate increased participation in inclusive activities (McEachin & Leaf, 1999).

Generalization over time to new materials, places, and people may happen naturally, but it is not likely to occur without planning. Therefore, it is important to have strategies for times when more rigorous planning for generalization is necessary. It is helpful to start the treatment process with a basic checklist for generalization, which will help plan for generalization goals and determine what strategies may need to be implemented for further generalization programming. The checklist in Figure 1.1 will help you to assess generalization challenges in your programming.

The following section provides some guidelines to promote generalization and simple strategies that the therapist or caregiver can implement to make teaching

Antecedent and setting considerations (See the strategies guide section for ideas for modifying the setting, antecedent strategies, and possible solutions to anything not checked off.)

Item	Date completed
1. Skill has been completed with various sets of objects and pictures	
_____ Program completed with objects	_____
_____ Program used objects in natural environment	_____
_____ Program completed with photos	_____
_____ Program used photographs in books, magazines, other natural materials	_____
_____ Program used with videos, TV shows, movies, and so forth.	_____
2. Skill is demonstrated with family, peers, and other people in natural settings and cues	
_____ Program completed with different teachers and therapists	_____
_____ Program completed out of the work table or chair	_____
_____ Program completed in various rooms and locations	_____
_____ Program completed at school, home, community	_____
_____ Program done with family members	_____
_____ Program done with peers	_____
3. Therapist/teacher has incorporated multiple exemplars	
_____ Program completed with preferred/nonpreferred items and activities	_____
_____ Program completed with various teaching styles	_____
_____ Student responds to various instructional cues and discrimination instructions	_____
_____ Program completed in various levels of structure	_____
_____ Student can discriminate mixed and varied instruction	_____

Response considerations (See the strategies guide section for ideas for modifying the response and behavior and what's expected from your student.)

Item	Date completed
1. Student's behavior is fluent, functional, and meaningful	
_____ Skill is fluent in training setting	_____
_____ Skill is functional and meaningful in generalization setting	_____
_____ Skill is demonstrated independently/appropriately in natural setting	_____
2. Student's behavior is effective	
_____ Skill is allowing student to access natural reinforcers	_____
_____ Skill is demonstrated spontaneously	_____

Consequence considerations (See the strategies guide section for ideas for modifying the consequences and reinforcement.)

Item	Date completed
1. Sudent is reinforced by naturally occurring reinforcers and natural reinforcement schedules	
_____ Skill is exhibited in natural settings with natural reinforcers	_____
_____ Skill is exhibited with thinned schedules of reinforcement	_____
_____ Student responds to natural consequences	_____
2. Team approaches and self-management	
_____ Student's educational team is trained and involved	_____
_____ Student will solicit social approval of desired behavior	_____
_____ Student exhibits spontaneous generalized behavior	_____
_____ Student demonstrates self-reinforcement	_____

Figure 1.1. Generalization checklist. (*Source:* Liberty & Billingsley, 1988.)

Table 1.2.   Summary of strategies for improving generalization

Antecedent strategies
Use interesting, preferred, and functional activities and items.
Exaggerate and vary affect when interacting with your students.
Vary your instructions.
Vary your teaching environments and settings.
Watch carefully for mastery of skills.
Intersperse tasks.
Teach using multiple types of stimuli.
Use stimuli that are routinely found in the natural environment.
Use natural language.
Train in natural settings as much as possible.

Response strategies
Increase your student's proficiency in the newly acquired goal.
Amplify the target response or make the target response more obvious.

Consequence strategies
Eliminate training reinforcers completely and thin your reinforcement schedule.
Use varied and natural reinforcers.
Plan for consistency of caregiver responses in the natural environment.
Reinforce only generalized behavior.
Program for naturally occurring consequences.
Teach your student to solicit reinforcement in structured and natural settings.
Teach self-reinforcement.

Sources: Liberty & Billingsley (1988); Stokes & Baer (1977); Stokes & Osnes (1989).

more natural, fun, and generalizable. These strategies can be used in conjunction with the generalization checklist in Figure 1.1 to accomplish further generalization planning and programming. For additional information on the following strategies, see Stokes and Baer (1977), Liberty and Billingsley (1988), and Stokes and Osnes (1989).

STRATEGIES GUIDE: TOWARD IMPROVING GENERALIZATION

See Table 1.2 for a quick guide of strategies presented in this section.

Antecedent Strategies

When planning for and teaching generalization, consider the following strategies:

- **Use interesting, preferred, and functional activities and items.**

Students are more likely to engage in an activity when there is natural reinforcement associated with the activity. For example, if you want to teach turn taking in board games, find out what board games the children are playing at school. This way, if there is a group of children playing a particular game, your student will already know how to play and can then join the group.

- **Exaggerate and vary affect when interacting with your students.**

Your students are the first ones to notice if something is boring. If you are not interested, they may not be either. Your student may not pick up on various moods or feelings if you are subtle. Often, students with ASDs have a delay in affect and have difficulty picking up on the affective states of others. Therefore, as a therapist, it is important to exaggerate your affect so that students may then notice various types of affect in others and better demonstrate affect themselves in different social situations. For example, if you find a missing puzzle piece while doing a puzzle with your student and want to show her that you are happy about it, exaggerate your happiness so that it is clear to her that you are happy about it. Say, "Yeah! I found the piece that goes here!" with a big smile on your face while looking at the child. Reciprocally, when she finds a missing piece, model the same reaction and wait for her to have the opportunity to display her affective response. It is also critical to vary your affective responses as people are not always going to be happy all the time and your time with your student is a good time to model and teach appropriate affect in various situations. This applies to negative emotions as well. For instance, if you are playing a video game with your student and your character gets knocked out of the game, you can model an appropriate affective response such as saying, "Oh no! Not again!" and frowning, but then also demonstrate a return to neutral affect by getting back into the game and saying, "Oh well, I'll try it again."

- **Vary your instructions.**

The same question can be asked in many ways (e.g., "What is it?" "What do you see?" "Tell me what this is." "Tell me about this!"). It is important for students with ASDs to know how to respond to a variety of instructions, questions, and comments to optimize generalization.

- **Vary your teaching environments and settings.**

Try different rooms of the house, go outside, go to the park, or go grocery shopping. Remember to incorporate the daily routines and settings of the child's family. If a child can only raise his or her hand in the therapy room at home, then the skill will not be very functional for the child. He or she will also need to raise his or her hand in the classroom, so it is important that instruction occurs in the classroom as well.

- **Watch carefully for mastery of skills.**

Students will get bored easily if they are expected to continue to work on the same skill over and over again, especially if they have already demonstrated that they have learned it. Once a student masters a skill, immediately move it into generalization (see Figure 1.1). Teach the skill with new materials, in new settings, and with new people and assess whether the child maintains the skill over time.

- **Intersperse tasks.**

Mix and vary your materials, instructions, goals, and activities. The student should learn to discriminate his or her response based on the question or instruction and then respond appropriately.

- **Teach using multiple types of stimuli.**

Sometimes it is necessary to use all possible stimuli that are appropriate for your student. For example, teach your student all varieties of fasteners on pants (e.g., snaps, zippers, buttons, hook and loop closures, belts, drawstrings) so that he or she is independent in every setting with his or her own clothing. However, in some cases it is not possible to teach all stimuli. In cases such as teaching every kind of dog, you may need to just have multiple exemplars (i.e., many examples, but not all) to teach the concept of *dog*.

- **Use stimuli that are routinely found in the natural environment.**

Optimize generalization by using stimuli from the natural environment in the training environment whenever possible.

- **Use natural language.**

Think of language and instructions that the students would typically expect during the activity outside of the training environment and in natural settings or situations. Then, when the student is working with other people or in natural environments, he or she is more likely to engage appropriately in the activity.

- **Train in natural settings as much as possible.**

If the behavior that you are working on with your student is only appropriate in a limited number of situations, then it is likely going to be more efficient and effective if you just work directly in those environments. For example, teaching grocery shopping is much more effective in the grocery store than it is in a mock grocery store. Similarly, if you are working on a play activity, try it on the floor rather than the worktable. If you are looking at books, try doing so on a beanbag chair or in a reading corner rather than just at a desk. By doing this, you will likely be able to determine what other skills need to be worked on when you are in the natural setting, which will help with future treatment plan goals.

Response Strategies

When working toward generalization, you can use the following techniques to help maximize your student's success in everyday life:

- **Increase your student's proficiency in the newly acquired goal.**

If the student has recently mastered a goal in the training environment but is not exhibiting that skill in the natural environment, try increasing your student's performance of the target skill in the training environment (e.g., improving student's response time). Increasing a student's proficiency in the training environment ensures a stronger response, which will then provide a better chance at success in the natural environment. For example, when babies have become proficient at crawling from one place to another, it is often quite difficult for them to make the transition to walking. Because they often fall down and get frustrated, they are more likely to just crawl to the desired item or location. But, after working with a baby in the training setting (e.g., short jaunts between mom and dad), you will likely see a quick transition to walking in other environments because the baby has built up confidence and proficiency in the training setting with mom and dad.

- **Amplify the target response or make the target response more obvious.**

You will need to analyze whether the target response is reliably providing access to the natural reinforcers found in the generalization setting. If you find that the target response is not providing access to reinforcement, then you will need to change the target response in a way that will ensure access to natural reinforcers. For example, if your student is not getting a listener's attention by simply saying the listener's name, then teach the child to tap the listener on the arm while saying the listener's name.

Consequence Strategies

After your student responds to generalization training, you can use the following techniques to address consequences and reinforcement:

- **Eliminate training reinforcers completely and thin your reinforcement schedule.**

In the training and acquisition environment, eliminate training reinforcers or any reinforcers that are considered to be artificial (i.e., not directly related to the desired behavior). Compare what should reinforce the behavior naturally with what is reinforcing the behavior in the training setting. Gradually fade out the artificial reinforcers while thinning your reinforcement schedule so that it better reflects what is found in natural settings.

- **Use varied and natural reinforcers.**

Natural reinforcers are directly and functionally related to the activity or desired behavior. For example, if a student loves to swing, try teaching all of the language associated with swinging (e.g., "push me," "my turn," "go higher," "get down," "underdog," "spin me"). Because the consequences associated with these requests are naturally reinforcing, appropriate requests during a swinging activity are likely to increase.

- **Plan for consistency of caregiver responses in the natural environment.**

It is helpful if everyone involved in the student's treatment plan (e.g., parents, caregivers, extended family, school staff) receives training and information on how to effectively respond to your student across settings. For example, everyone will know to answer the student's most commonly asked question (e.g., "When were you born?") only if the student asks an appropriate social question first (e.g., "What did you do this weekend?" or "Having a good day?") in order to increase the frequency of appropriate social questions from the student.

- **Reinforce only generalized behavior.**

Sometimes it is necessary to systematically plan to only reinforce behavior that has not been demonstrated before. For example, if you are trying to teach your student to explore more playground equipment, you may need to only provide reinforcement when the student tries a new piece of equipment.

- **Program for naturally occurring consequences.**

Often, a student's target behavior is not necessarily observed due to subtleties in social interactions and natural reinforcers are provided by the event itself. For example, the possibility of a social punisher motivates most adults to avoid engaging in certain inappropriate behaviors (e.g., being frowned at if we bump someone with our grocery cart, our conversation partner interrupting us if we dominate the conversation too much, someone hanging up on us if we are being rude on the telephone or walking away if we are being disrespectful). These are natural consequences to inappropriate behavior and may need supplemental training so that your student understands that other people typically do not respond well to these types of behaviors.

- **Teach your student to solicit reinforcement in structured and natural settings.**

Teach your student to follow a target behavior with an additional behavior that will normally elicit social approval both in the structured and less structured setting. In a structured environment such as playing a board game, your student may easily give up his or her turn for another student if he or she has learned to consistently and spontaneously seek desired praise from the teacher. You will also need to train in less structured settings such as taking turns riding bikes at recess and seeking reinforcement from playground staff.

- **Teach self-reinforcement.**

If reinforcement is sparse or unidentifiable in the generalization setting, consider teaching your student to self-reinforce for accuracy of his or her own behavior. Remember that self-reinforcement can be difficult, and portability is key. Often, just the training involved in teaching self-reinforcement increases the proficiency of the target behavior. For instance, an older student is learning to stay on task on his job. He carries a vibrating timer that is pre-programmed to vibrate at varying times throughout his work session before his first break. At each intermittent timing, he checks in with himself to determine if he is on task (i.e., he was taught to ask himself each time the timer went off, "Am I on task?"). If he decides that he was on task, he gives himself a star on his "on task chart." At the end of his work session, he adds up his stars and if he has enough stars, he buys himself a soda to drink during his break. It is important to note that before this program was implemented in the workplace, the student first learned how to self-reinforce his own behavior with his instructor during his one-to-one work. The program was then introduced in his classroom with his teacher before moving it to his job setting.

FUTURE DIRECTIONS

Future studies should include generalization measures beyond train and hope to improve interventions for ASDs and to advance the science and application of generalization. Specifically, generalization should be built into the intervention by including multiple exemplars, training in various settings, training with various people (including peers), and training using multiple strategies (e.g., on the computer, during play, in the classroom). Researchers should carefully measure the effects of these generalization strategies on various interventions and use this data to improve existing treatments. Strategies for measuring generalization should be provided to parents, teachers, aides, and anyone working with a person with ASD.

It is important to emphasize the importance of including generalization as a critical component of teaching to parents, therapists, teachers, and other professionals who provide intervention for children with autism. After all, problems with generalization have less to do with autism than they do with teaching. That is, perhaps the most significant predictor of whether a behavior will generalize is the quality of the instruction and whether it specifically programs for generalization. An individual with autism's quality of life is largely dependent on his or her ability to successfully generalize newly learned skills, particularly those skills that allow the individual to live and participate in the community. Therefore, those who work with individuals with ASDs bear the burden, responsibility, and opportunity to ensure that interventions systematically include a plan and assessment for generalization. This book was developed with the intention of highlighting the important features of generalization in various treatment approaches and providing a scientific background, as well as practical solutions, for making generalization a part of everyday life.

REFERENCES

American Psychiatric Association. (1994). *Diagnostic and statistical manual of mental disorders* (4th ed.). Washington, DC: Author.

Baer, D., Wolf, M., & Risley, T. (1968). Some current dimensions of applied behavior analysis. *Journal of Applied Behavior Analysis, 1*, 91–97.

Bellini, S., & Akullian, J. (2007). A meta-analysis of video modeling and video self-modeling interventions for children and adolescents with autism spectrum disorders. *Exceptional Children, 73*(3), 264–287.

Carr, E.G., & Kologinsky, E. (1983). Acquisition of sign language by autistic children: II. Spontaneity and generalization effects. *Journal of Applied Behavior Analysis, 16*, 297–314.

Centers for Disease Control and Prevention. (2007). Prevalence of autism spectrum disorders: Autism and developmental disabilities monitoring network, 14 sites, United States 2002. *Morbidity and Mortality Weekly Report 2007, 56*(SS01), 12–28.

Chandler, L.K., Fowler, S.A., & Lubeck, R.C. (1992). An analysis of the effects of multiple setting events on the social behavior of preschool children with special needs. *Journal of Applied Behavior Analysis, 25*, 249–263.

Charlop-Christy, M., & Daneshvar, S. (2003). Using video modeling to teach perspective taking to children with autism. *Journal of Positive Behavior Interventions, 5*, 12–21.

Dawson, G., & Osterling, J. (1997). Early intervention in autism: Effectiveness and common elements of current approaches. In M.J. Guralnick (Ed.), *The effectiveness of early intervention: Second generation research* (pp. 307–326). Baltimore: Paul H. Brookes Publishing Co.

Durand, V.M., & Carr, E.G. (1991). Functional communication training to reduce challenging behavior: maintenance and application in new settings. *Journal of Applied Behavior Analysis, 24*(2), 251–264.

Haring, N.G., Liberty, K.A., White, O.R., & Billingsley, F.F. (1988). *Generalization: Strategies and solutions for students with severe handicaps.* Seattle: University of Washington Press.

Horner, R.H., & Budd, C. (1985). Acquisition of manual sign use: Collateral reduction of maladaptive behavior, and factors limiting generalization. *Education and Training of the Mentally Retarded, 20*(1), 39–47.

Horner, R.H., Carr, E.G., Halle, J., McGee, G., Odom, S., & Wolery, M. (2005). The use of single-subject research to identify evidence-based practice in special education. *Exceptional Children, 71*(2), 165–179.

Ingersoll, B., & Schreibman, L. (2006). Teaching reciprocal imitation skills to young children with autism using a naturalistic behavioral approach: Effects on language, pretend play, and joint attention. *Journal of Autism and Developmental Disorders, 36*, 487–505.

Iovannone, R., Dunlap, G., Huber, H., & Kincaid, D. (2003). Effective educational practices for students with autism spectrum disorders. *Focus on Autism and Other Developmental Disabilities, 18*, 150–165.

Kanner, L. (1943). Autistic disturbances of affective contact. *Nervous Child, 2*, 217–250.

Koegel, R.L., Openden, D., Fredeen, R.M., & Koegel, L.K. (2006). An overview of Pivotal

Response Treatment. In R.L. Koegel & L.K. Koegel (Eds.), *Pivotal Response Treatments for autism: Communication, social, and academic development* (pp. 3–30). Baltimore: Paul H. Brookes Publishing Co.

Landrum, T., & Lloyd, J. (1992). Generalization in social behavior research with children and youth who have emotional or behavioral disorders. *Behavior Modification, 16,* 593–616.

Liberty, K., & Billingsley, F. (1988). Strategies to improve generalization. In N.G. Haring (Ed.), *Generalization for students with severe disabilities: Strategies and solutions.* Seattle: University of Washington Press.

Lord, C., Risi, S., DiLavore, P.S., Shulman, C., Thurm, A., & Pickles, A. (2006). Autism from 2 to 9 years of age. *Archives of General Psychiatry, 63*(6), 694–701.

Lord, C., Risi, S., Lambrecht, L., Cook, E.H., Leventhal, B.L., DiLavore, P.C., et al. (2000). The Autism Diagnostic Observation Schedule-Generic: A standard measure of social and communication deficits associated with the spectrum of autism. *Journal of Autism and Developmental Disorders, 30*(3), 205–230.

MacDuff, P., Krantz, P., & McLanahan, L. (1993). Teaching children with autism to use photographic activity schedules: Maintenance and generalization of complex response chains. *Journal of Applied Behavior Analysis, 26,* 89–97.

McEachin, J., & Leaf, R. (1999). The autism partnership curriculum for discrete trial teaching with autistic children. In R. Leaf & J. McEachin (Eds.), *A work in progress: Behavior management strategies and a curriculum for intensive behavioral treatment of autism* (pp.127–344). New York: DRL Books.

National Autism Center. (2007). *National Standards Project.* Retrieved from http://www.nationalautismcenter.org/about/national.php.

National Research Council, Committee on Educational Interventions for Children with Autism, Division of Behavioral and Social Sciences and Education. (2001). *Educating children with autism.* Washington, DC: National Academies Press.

Osnes, P., & Lieblein, T. (2003). An explicit technology of generalization. *Behavior Analyst Today, 3,* 364–374.

Sherer, M.R., & Schreibman, L. (2005). Individual behavioral profiles and predictors of treatment effectiveness for children with autism. *Journal of Consulting and Clinical Psychology, 73*(3), 525–538.

Simpson, R.L. (2005). Evidence-based practices for students with autism spectrum disorders. *Focus on Autism and Other Developmental Disorders, 20*(3), 140–149.

Simpson, R.L., de Boer-Ott, S.R., Griswold, D.E., Myles, B.S., Byrd, S.E., Ganz, J.B., et al. (2005). *Autism spectrum disorders: Interventions and treatments for children and youth.* Thousand Oaks, CA: Corwin Press.

Singh, N., Deitz, D., Epstein, M., & Singh, J. (1991). Social behavior of students who are seriously emotionally disturbed: A quantitative analysis of intervention studies. *Behavior Modification, 15,* 74–94.

Smith, T., Groen, A.D., & Wynn, J.D. (2000). Randomized trial of intensive early intervention for children with pervasive developmental disorder. *American Journal on Mental Retardation, 105*(4), 269–285.

Stewart, G., Van Houten, R., & Van Houten, J. (1992). Increasing generalized social interactions in psychotic and mentally retarded residents through peer-mediated therapy. *Journal of Applied Behavior Analysis, 25,* 335–339.

Stokes, T.F., & Baer, D.M. (1977). An implicit technology of generalization. *Journal of Applied Behavior Analysis, 10,* 349–367.

Stokes, T.F., & Osnes, P.G. (1989). An operant pursuit of generalization. *Behavior Therapy, 20,* 337–355.

Sulzer-Azaroff, B., & Mayer, G. (1991). Extending behavior: Generalization training. In *Behavior analysis for lasting change* (pp. 499–515). Fort Worth, TX: Holt, Rinehart & Winston.

Tadevosyan-Leyfer, O., Dowd, M., Mankoski, R., Winklosky, B., Putnam, S., McGrath, L., et al. (2003). A principal components analysis of the Autism Diagnostic Interview–Revised. *Journal of the American Academy of Child and Adolescent Psychiatry, 42*(7), 864–872.

Whalen, C., & Schreibman, L. (2003). Joint attention training for children with autism using behavior modification procedures. *Journal of Child Psychology and Psychiatry and Allied Disciplines, 44*(3), 456–468.

Whalen, C., Schreibman, L., & Ingersoll, B. (2006). Collateral changes in language, play, imitation, and social initiations following joint attention training for preschool children with autism. *Journal of Autism and Developmental Disorders, 36*(5), 655–664.

I

Popular Autism Interventions and Generalization Strategies

2

Enhancing Generalization of Treatment Effects via Pivotal Response Training and the Individualization of Treatment Protocols

Laura Schreibman, Aubyn C. Stahmer, and Jessica Suhrheinrich

A large body of research supports the effectiveness of behavioral interventions for the treatment of children with autism spectrum disorders (ASDs); in fact, treatments based on a behavioral model are the only treatments empirically validated as leading to substantial improvement in many of these children (e.g., National Research Council, 2001; Schreibman, 2005). However, the same research technology that has allowed for the development of these treatments has also allowed us to continually self-evaluate our methods and improve them as noted limitations are identified. The early behavioral interventions involved a highly structured teaching format called *discrete trial training* (DTT); these interventions gave us the first successful tools to teach individuals with autism (e.g., Baer, Peterson, & Sherman, 1967; Lovaas, 1987; Lovaas, Berberich, Perloff, & Schaeffer, 1966; Maurice, Green, & Luce, 1996; Metz, 1965; Schroeder & Baer, 1972). For the first time, we had a set of procedures allowing many children with ASDs to learn rather extensive behavioral repertoires. Yet, as effective as these early interventions proved to be, continued study and evaluation exposed several limitations to their effectiveness (e.g., Schreibman, 2005).

The major limitations of these early treatment strategies related to issues of generalization. Thus, behaviors learned via the highly structured treatments often 1) did not generalize to other people, situations, and settings (stimulus generalization); 2) were not accompanied by changes in related behaviors (response generalization); and 3) often did not maintain over time (maintenance). Other problems included a lack of spontaneity in responding, robotic responding, and prompt dependency. In addition, the specific structure of DTT made it more difficult for clinicians and parents to learn; thus, it was less available to those who would

Preparation of this chapter and some of the research herein was supported by U.S. Public Health Service Research Grant #39434 from the National Institute of Mental Health.

benefit from it. These serious issues proved to be a hindrance in the global generalization of the treatment effects, threatening the use of a powerful clinical strategy.

Another problem was that the highly structured nature of the teaching interactions was quite different from the natural interactions one has with children. The teaching procedures were often not pleasant for the treatment provider (e.g., parent, teacher, clinician) and not very fun for the child, which often resulted in escape- and avoidance-motivated behaviors such as tantrums and attempts to leave the teaching situation. Thus, this highly structured form of treatment was not very attractive to either the child or therapist (Schreibman, Kaneko, & Koegel, 1991).

While one approach to these limitations has been to add specific generalization-enhancing procedures to the basic DTT model, probably the most helpful approach has been the development of "naturalistic" behavioral interventions. Many clinical researchers throughout the United States have developed behavioral strategies that, while still adhering to proven behavioral principles, are more naturalistic in their implementation (e.g., Hart & Risley, 1968; Kaiser, Yoder, & Keetz, 1992; McGee, Krantz, & McClannahan, 1985; McGee, Morrier, & Daly, 1999). The purpose of all these naturalistic interventions is to directly increase the generalization of treatment effects and increase the acceptability of the protocols for both child and treatment provider.

Pivotal Response Training (PRT) is the type of naturalistic treatment we study and implement, as well as what we will be presenting in this chapter (Koegel, O'Dell, & Koegel, 1987; Koegel et al., 1989; Schreibman & Ingersoll, 2005). Essentially, the focus of PRT is on two pivotal behaviors that are hypothesized to affect a wide array of other specific behaviors. The pivotal behaviors in PRT are *motivation* and *responsivity* to multiple cues in the environment. Children with autism are renowned for problems with motivation, and the early literature on behavioral treatment describes attempts to motivate these children to learn. One can assume that an increase in child motivation to participate in the therapeutic process would be pivotal in that it would assist in the learning of any number of new skills.

Similarly, responsivity to multiple environmental cues is another area known to be problematic for children with ASDs. Specifically, a deviant attentional pattern called *stimulus overselectivity* has been identified in individuals with autism. Stimulus overselectivity is characterized by the failure to use simultaneous environmental cues. Because most learning requires response to such simultaneous cues (e.g., seeing a toy car and hearing the label *car*), a deficit in this area of attention would seriously impede the learning process. Indeed, this is what happens with many children with autism. In fact, stimulus overselectivity has been directly implicated in the failure to learn and the failure to generalize learned behaviors for many of these children (see Schreibman, 1988, for a review).

To enhance the pivotal behavior of motivation, several specific treatment components are used, including the following (see Koegel et al., 1989, for a more detailed description of specific procedures).

1. Child choice and shared control

To maximize the child's interest in the learning situation, he or she is given a great deal of input in determining the specific stimuli and the nature of the learning interaction. A variety of materials (e.g., toys, games, snacks) are presented, and the child is allowed to select an activity or object about which the learning interaction will take place. Throughout the session, the therapist is alert to the child's changing interests and allows the child to change to another preferred activity. During the teaching interaction, the therapist and child take turns with the materials and activity, thus sharing control. This allows the child to become accustomed to the back-and-forth nature of verbal and social interaction while also allowing opportunities for the therapist to model appropriate and/or more sophisticated responses.

2. Interspersing maintenance tasks

To enhance motivation by keeping the overall success and reinforcement level high, previously mastered tasks are interspersed frequently among new (acquisition) tasks that are more difficult for the child.

3. Direct/natural reinforcers

Direct, rather than indirect, reinforcers are used. Direct reinforcers are consequences that are directly related to the response they follow. A direct reinforcer for the verbal response "car" might be access to a toy car as opposed to a food or token reinforcer. Access to a toy car is a direct and natural consequence of saying "car," whereas food is not.

4. Reinforcement of attempts

To maximize reinforcement and therefore enhance the child's motivation to respond, therapists reinforce all reasonable attempts made by the child to respond. Thus, reinforcers are contingent upon attempts that may not be completely correct or as good as previous attempts but are within a broader range of correct responses.

5. Responsivity to multiple cues

Research has indicated that, for many children with autism who are overselective in their responding, training on a series of successive conditional discriminations teaches them to respond to simultaneous multiple cues. A *conditional discrimination* is one that requires response to multiple cues (e.g., Koegel & Schreibman, 1977; Schreibman, Charlop, & Koegel, 1982). For example, asking a child to go get her red sweater is a conditional discrimination task because the child undoubtedly has more than one red item of clothing and more than one sweater. Correct responding depends on attention to both color and object. To enhance the child's responsivity to multiple cues, the therapist presents the child with tasks involving conditional discriminations. As the child learns to respond on the basis of multiple cues, his or her attention is more normalized, allowing for more environmental cues to become functional. Because stimulus control of behavior is no longer as restricted, enhanced generalization should result.

These components of PRT have been highly successful as an intervention package for children with autism (e.g., Delprato, 2001; Humphries, 2003; Koegel & Koegel, 2006). Spoken language has been the primary target behavior in the majority of the research on PRT, and it has been well documented that this technique is very effective at increasing spoken communication in children with ASDs (e.g., Delprato, 2001; Koegel & Koegel, 2006; Laski, Charlop, & Schreibman, 1988). Using PRT for children with ASDs has resulted in profound language improvements. In fact, when compared with other more structured techniques, PRT has been found to be more effective for increasing verbalizations and contingent language use. PRT has been shown to be effective for improving a variety of language functions including speech imitation, labeling, question asking, spontaneous speech, conversational communication, and rapid acquisition of functional speech in previously nonverbal children (see Delprato, 2001, and Koegel & Koegel, 2006, for reviews). In addition to gains in language skills, PRT has been used to teach a variety of skills, including symbolic play and sociodramatic play (Stahmer, 1995,1999; Thorp, Stahmer, & Schreibman, 1995), peer social interaction (Pierce & Schreibman, 1995, 1997), self-initiations (Koegel, Carter, & Koegel, 2003), and joint attention (Bruinsma, 2005).

RESEARCH SUPPORTING GENERALIZATION OF SKILLS THROUGH PIVOTAL RESPONSE TRAINING

The research supporting the effectiveness of PRT highlights the ability of children learning via PRT to generalize new skills. Because generalization was a primary concern of the developers of PRT, there is a sound body of research supporting generalization of skills through PRT. Generalization of skills can be broken down into response generalization, stimulus generalization, and maintenance of skills.

Response generalization refers to changes in behavior that are related to targeted behaviors (i.e., collateral changes). PRT has been found to increase response generalization of behavior change in children with ASDs. Research shows that when social initiation skills are targeted through PRT, children exhibit a decrease in disruptive behavior (Oke & Schreibman, 1990). More specifically, when social initiations in the form of questions were targeted through PRT, children increased their overall use of verbs and question asking (Koegel et al., 2003). Improving the joint attention skills of children with autism has been a focus of several research studies of PRT. Studies show that when children's joint attention skills are targeted through PRT, the children exhibit positive changes in social initiation, positive affect, imitation skills, play skills, and spontaneous language (Whalen, Schreibman, & Ingersoll, 2006). In addition, when the ability to respond to joint attention bids was targeted though PRT, children showed response generalization in their ability to initiate joint attention bids (Rocha, Schreibman, & Stahmer, 2007). Finally, children who were specifically taught symbolic play skills showed response generalization in the form of improved social skills, other play skills, and language skills (Stahmer, 1995). When PRT, in conjunction with DTT, was used to teach joint attention skills to children with autism, the children showed concomitant gains in social-behavioral initiations, participation in routines, eye contact, and language (Vismara & Lyons, 2007). Overall, there is strong support for response generalization as a result of teaching through PRT.

Stimulus generalization occurs when skills that are learned under one set of circumstances can be used correctly with new people, in new settings, and with new materials. Stimulus generalization should occur with multiple stimuli (e.g., teacher, environment, materials, instructional cues). PRT has been effectively used to promote stimulus generalization.

PRT has been shown to effectively generalize to multiple treatment providers (e.g., parents, teachers, peers). Children who learned new skills while working with highly trained clinicians were able to use these skills with their parents as well. For example, children with ASDs have been taught to use joint attention skills, language skills, and symbolic play by working directly with professional clinicians. The same children exhibited stimulus generalization of these skills when working with their parents (L. Koegel, Camarata, Menchaca, & Koegel, 1998; Sherer & Schreibman, 2005; Vismara & Lyons, 2007) or siblings (Laski et al., 1988).

Another example of generalization across multiple teachers includes training children with ASDs and selected peers to engage in appropriate social play behavior. Later, the children with ASDs demonstrated generalization of newly taught social skills with other peers who did not participate in the training (Harper, Symon, & Frea, 2007; Oke & Schreibman, 1990; Pierce & Schreibman, 1997). These results demonstrate the ability of children with ASDs to generalize skills across treatment providers when using PRT.

Another important element of stimulus generalization involves varying the teaching environment or setting. Although PRT was developed in a laboratory setting, this naturalistic behavioral intervention has been shown to lead to generalization of skills to other environments. Many research studies have demonstrated that children learning through PRT in a clinical setting can generalize skills they have learned to playrooms (Laski et al., 1988; Sherer & Schreibman, 2005) or their home environment (Ingersoll & Schreibman, 2006; L. Koegel et al., 1998; Koegel et al., 2003; Laski et al., 1988; Rocha et al., 2007; Thorp et al., 1995). In addition, children who were taught in one classroom at school generalized to other classrooms or settings at their school site (R. Koegel, Camarata, Koegel, Tall, & Smith, 1998; Pierce & Schreibman, 1997). Finally, stimulus generalization can occur with instructional materials and activities. A strong body of research demonstrates how children learning through PRT with specific materials can later use the skills they have learned with new toys or activities (L. Koegel et al., 1998; Pierce & Schreibman, 1997; Sherer & Schreibman, 2005; Stahmer, 1995; Thorp et al., 1995).

Maintenance of skills is a final form of generalization that refers to a child's ability to demonstrate skills after training or teaching ends. Children with ASDs who are learning via PRT have effectively maintained skills they have learned. Specifically, children who were taught to use symbolic play skills continued to use these advanced play skills 3 months after teaching ended (Stahmer, 1995). Children who learned to respond to joint attention bids maintained this appropriate social behavior after 3 months without additional instruction (Rocha et al., 2007; Whalen & Schreibman, 2003). Also, their ability to initiate joint attention bids (which was not directly targeted) increased during training and was maintained (Whalen & Schreibman, 2003).

Together, response generalization, stimulus generalization, and maintenance of skills have been strongly supported by research on PRT. These findings are encouraging because only when skills are exhibited across environments and people, as well as over time, will they be truly functional for children. Response generalization is ultimately the greatest encouragement associated with PRT. Children benefiting from response generalization are learning new skills that are not targeted through direct teaching, which leads to a reduction in the overall time needed to educate children with ASDs. See Appendices 2.1 and 2.2 for examples of a probe to test for generalization of new skills after PRT use.

CHILD DEVELOPMENT AND PIVOTAL RESPONSE TRAINING

PRT has been used with children of a variety of age ranges. In earlier studies, children with ASDs often received initial diagnoses in early elementary school; work with parents and children using PRT began soon after. Now that children are receiving diagnoses at younger and younger ages, PRT can be used with toddlers at risk for autism. When using PRT, it is important to consider a child's chronological age; overall developmental level; and existing communication, play, and social skills.

When determining specific goals for an individual child, the use of a developmental assessment can be helpful. It is best to choose a developmentally relevant activity (i.e., an activity that a child is ready to learn) to improve motivation and reduce failure. Research on play and autism has shown that children more quickly learn activities for which they are developmentally ready (Lifter, Sulzer-Azaroff, Anderson, Coyle, & Cowdery, 1993). For example, if a 3-year-old child is at a 12-month level of communication development, PRT acquisition goals might include sound imitation and early word imitation for highly familiar words; PRT maintenance skills might include babbling and reaching toward a preferred toy. Alternatively, a 10-year-old child with language skills at the 5-year level might be learning appropriate conversational skills, how to ask and answer questions, and appropriate pronoun usage.

Topics of conversation and materials should be age appropriate whenever possible. For example, a 10-year-old child should learn to talk about video games, sports, or the latest music rather than exclusively toy trains or playdough—even if developmentally the child may still enjoy these younger toys. This approach will facilitate positive social interaction with the child's peers; however, a balance is important to capture the child's motivation. New activities and topics can be interspersed with preferred ones to encourage the child to try new things. For preschool children, toys that cross levels by providing opportunities for both cause-and-effect play and higher-level symbolic play can encourage play and language complexity using PRT.

PRT can be used to teach specific language skills. Gabe's example shows how components of PRT can be incorporated into a naturally occurring interaction to target language.

Gabe is thirsty and walks into the kitchen, where his mom is making dinner. He carries his juice cup over to his mom and says, "More." Gabe's mom pours a small amount of juice into his cup and waits while he drinks it. Then, she holds the juice bottle up again and presents a verbal cue, "More juice." Gabe responds by saying, "More ju." His mom pours more juice into his cup and praises his attempt to use a new language skill. Next time, his mom waits patiently until Gabe responds on his own with "ju."

PRT can also be used to teach specific play skills. Observe how components of PRT were incorporated for Monica into a naturally occurring interaction to target play.

Monica enjoys spinning the wheels of cars and trains, but she doesn't play appropriately with these toys. Monica's therapist, Jane, knows that Monica enjoys playing with vehicles, but she wants to teach her more complex play skills. While Monica is spinning the wheels of a train, Jane interrupts her play by putting her own hand on the train to get Monica's attention. Then Jane says, "On the track," and models how the train should go around the track. She hands the train back to Monica and repeats, "On the track," as an instruction to Monica.

Monica places the train on the track, and Jane gently helps her to push it around the track. Because Monica follows Jane's instruction, Jane lets Monica play with the train any way she wants, even if she is spinning the wheels. As Monica gets better at playing, longer appropriate play sequences will be expected.

Finally, PRT can be used to teach social skills. Notice how the components of PRT were used to facilitate appropriate social skills for several students during a group activity.

Mark teaches first grade and has several children in his class who have trouble taking turns. During an art activity, Mark chooses to work with a group of three children on appropriate turn taking. Anthony, Miguel, and Claire sit with Mark at a table, and Mark gives them each a large piece of paper for painting. He holds a handful of paintbrushes in front of him but does not present any verbal cues. Anthony requests, "Paintbrush, please," so Mark gives him a brush. Miguel reaches for the paintbrushes and says, "My paintbrush," so Mark gives him a brush. Claire signs BLUE and says, "Buh," so Mark hands her the blue paintbrush.

Now, Mark opens one paint tray and explains, "We're taking turns. It's my turn." He dips the brush and makes several strokes on his paper, then he waits for the students to request a turn. Claire bangs the table, so Mark helps her to form the sign for "my turn." After she attempts to make the sign, Mark lets Claire use the paint. While Claire paints, Mark praises the boys for waiting and asks, "Whose turn is it?" Anthony and Miguel both reach for the paint, so Mark reminds them to ask for a turn. Anthony says, "I want a turn," so Mark moves the paint toward Anthony and thanks the other two children for waiting. Then, he holds the paint up to Miguel and models, "My turn." Miguel repeats, "My turn," so Mark gives him the paint.

ACTIVITIES AND TIPS FOR IMPROVING GENERALIZATION OF SKILLS THROUGH PIVOTAL RESPONSE TRAINING

As noted, PRT is naturally conducive to promoting generalization of skills. The following factors, however, contribute to the overall success of a PRT program (see also Appendix 2.3).

1. *Use PRT with varied teachers, in varied settings, and with varied materials.* We have discussed the research supporting generalization of skills through PRT. We measure this stimulus generalization by teaching under one set of circumstances and then assessing a child's skill under another set of circumstances. However, if you want to dramatically increase the likelihood that your child will respond to PRT under a wide variety of circumstances, you can intentionally teach to increase generalization. You should

   • Use multiple teachers (mom, dad, older sister, babysitter, teacher, speech therapist)

   • Teach in multiple settings (bedroom, dinner table, playground, grocery store, classroom, lunchroom)

   • Teach with varied materials

2. *Use teaching materials that interest the child and are readily available in the environment.* Because the child's motivation is a key component of PRT, it is important

to ensure the child is motivated to maximize learning. When choosing materials, observe the child in free play and note the child's reaction when you take a toy away. A strong reaction from the child indicates a preference for the toy. Also consider any nontoy objects that the child enjoys. Good toys for children at the manipulative play level include noisy toys, toys with lights, spinning toys, cars that go down ramps, Koosh balls, bubbles, puzzles, and games such as Crocodile Dentist and Ants in the Pants. Good toys for children who are beginning to use representation play and have phrase speech include a garage with cars, play food with pots and pans, a doctor's kit, a dollhouse, and dolls with movable parts. Remember to

- Use developmentally appropriate materials to encourage play skills and keep children motivated

- Ensure that materials are well organized and easy to access (or visible and easy to request)

3. *Anticipate when PRT can be used throughout the day.* PRT was developed to fit naturally into the daily routine of a family, thereby increasing the ease of use of the strategies and the number of teaching opportunities throughout the day. You should

- Develop routines and use PRT to require your student to request the next steps (e.g., put on the student's shoes and get his or her backpack, then wait for him or her to initiate a request to go to the car or bus)

- Intentionally remove important pieces of an activity to encourage communication (e.g., put out a cup without juice and wait for your student to request juice at breakfast; get paper out for coloring, but "forget" the crayons)

- Use environmental arrangement to encourage communication (e.g., place favorite toys or foods out of the student's reach; use containers that are clear but difficult to open)

After you begin using PRT with your student, you may develop questions. Some common questions that parents and teachers ask are discussed in the following sections.

Where Do I Begin If My Student Is Not Using Verbal Communication?

Many children who have a young chronological or young developmental age benefit from PRT. If your student does not use verbal communication yet, you can focus on other communication skills. Target eye contact, reaching, pointing, gestures, or sign language by making the student's access to desired items contingent on the use of one of these skills.

What Should I Do If My Student Is Not Motivated to Work with Me?

Because motivation is a key component of PRT, it is important to correctly identify what interests and motivates the student. The first step is gathering information.

Observe your student while he or she is playing alone with a variety of toys or activities. What does the student play with most often? Then, systematically take away one toy at a time and notice the student's reaction. Does he or she hardly notice when you remove one toy but cry or protest when other toys are removed? These reactions are good indicators of what the student likes. In addition, share information with other caregivers. Generate a list of preferred activities (e.g., swinging, tickles), toys (e.g., train set, markers, farm animals), and foods (e.g., apple juice, Goldfish crackers, banana) based on the observations of the student's parents, teachers, and babysitters, among others.

You can also increase how motivating an object is by making it available for limited periods of time. For example, if your student has a few preferred toys or foods, plan to use them during PRT exclusively. The student will look forward to working with you because he or she will have access to some favorite things.

LIMITATIONS TO THE PIVOTAL RESPONSE TRAINING APPROACH

Just as limitations to a highly structured approach became apparent in the light of research, so did some limitations to PRT. Fortunately, these limitations are not substantial, and we have other treatment options to help in those instances when a naturalistic approach such as PRT may not be the most effective. Certain behaviors may not lend themselves to a naturalistic approach because there is no intrinsic reinforcer and the child would seldom or never choose them. Thus, behaviors such as toilet training, household chores, and certain academic tasks may require a different approach. Although it certainly is possible to be creative and adapt some of these behaviors to naturalistic strategies (e.g., make a household chore "fun" for the child), sometimes it just will not be successful. In such circumstances, it may be appropriate to use a more highly structured approach such as DTT or the general principles of applied behavior analysis.

Another potential limitation is when we address a behavior that requires prerequisite skills not yet in the child's repertoire. For example, when working on expressive language, the child may learn words and even phrases with PRT, but articulation may remain a problem. Work on articulation also can be addressed with PRT, but faster acquisition of articulation may be achieved via DTT using a "drill" format. Research, however, has demonstrated that although DTT may be effective in the training of articulation skills, these skills do not generalize well unless taught via a naturalistic strategy such as PRT (R. Koegel et al., 1998). Thus, it is important to make the transition from DTT to PRT to promote generalization of this skill.

Another limitation to PRT is one that applies to all treatment interventions for children with ASDs: substantial improvement is not achieved for all children. Although behavioral interventions are the only ones empirically demonstrated to be effective for this population, there is significant variability in treatment outcomes: Some children show substantial improvement, some children improve to a lesser degree, and some children show little or no improvement. Given the heterogeneity of the population with ASDs, this result is not surprising. A way to enhance our use of these procedures is needed so that the overall effectiveness is improved.

FUTURE DIRECTIONS

To increase the overall effectiveness of our interventions, we need to develop strategies that will allow us to individualize the treatment, tailoring it to the needs of a specific child. The well-documented heterogeneity in treatment outcomes indicates that other variables interact with a specific treatment and affect the child's response to that treatment. These other variables likely include child characteristics, family variables, and cultural variables, among others. An understanding of how these other variables interact with treatment will likely allow us to determine a priori the best behavioral intervention for a child.

In an early attempt to determine the characteristics of children most likely to benefit from PRT, Sherer and Schreibman (2005) identified and tested a behavioral profile to determine its ability to predict PRT treatment responders and nonresponders. Based on known treatment outcomes in a sample of children who had received PRT treatment, these investigators found that those children who showed the best treatment response engaged in more toy contact, more social approach behavior, less social avoidance behavior, less nonverbal stereotypy, and more verbal stereotypy than those children who showed a poor response to PRT. In the subsequent prospective portion of this study, six children with ASDs, ages 4–6 years, were matched on mental age, language, and symptom severity. Three of the children matched the nonresponder profile, and three matched the responder profile. All six children received a course of intensive PRT treatment. As predicted, those children matching the responder profile showed significant gains in language, social, and play behaviors, while the children matching the nonresponder profile did not improve. This study represents a first step toward tying specific behavioral characteristics to response to a particular intervention (in this case, PRT), but two questions remained. First, is the behavioral profile specific to PRT or will it predict response to any intervention? Also, can the profile be refined to determine which (if not all) specific behaviors are required for the predictive profile?

In a subsequent preliminary study, Schreibman, Stahmer, Cestone-Barlett, and Dufek (2008) identified six children with ASDs who met the nonresponder profile of the original Sherer and Schreibman (2005) study, except three of the children had less social avoidance than those original nonresponders and three of the children had more toy contact than the original nonresponders. Thus, the effect of toy contact and avoidance as requirements for the profile could be assessed. In addition, the children were also given DTT to assess the profile's predictive ability for this form of treatment. Results of this investigation suggest that toy contact is more important in the prediction than social avoidance. In addition, the profile did not predict response to DTT, thus supporting the view that the predictive profile is specific to PRT.

These studies are only the start of a long line of research that needs to tie PRT treatment responsiveness to important variables in order to predict outcome. Ideally, in the future we will know enough about how child behaviors and other variables interact with treatment so that we will be in a position to have prescriptive treatments tailored to individual children. Importantly, continued assessment of these variables should be implemented so treatment can be changed as the child's needs change.

Another important and related future line of research must focus on determining how different behavioral treatments can be combined into a more effective overall treatment program. As noted previously, it may be the case that certain behaviors do not lend themselves to best be taught via PRT. Research needs to be conducted on identifying which behaviors are best taught via which treatments and how these interventions might be best combined to achieve maximum outcome.

Of course, when we describe treatments as being effective, we mean that they lead to generalized behavioral gains. Thus, it is important that all of our assessments of behavior change include measures of stimulus and response generalization as well as treatment durability (i.e., maintenance of skills). Without generalized treatment effects, we cannot claim to have anything more than limited success.

REFERENCES

Baer, D.M., Peterson, R.F., & Sherman, J.A. (1967). The development of imitation by reinforcing behavioral similarity to a model. *Journal of the Experimental Analysis of Behavior, 10*, 405–416.

Bruinsma, Y. (2005). Increases in the joint attention behavior of eye gaze alternation to share enjoyment as a collateral effect of Pivotal Response Treatment for three children with autism. *Dissertation Abstracts International: Section B: The Sciences and Engineering, 65*(9-B), 4811–4882.

Delprato, D.J. (2001). Comparisons of discrete-trial and normalized behavioral intervention for young children with autism. *Journal of Autism and Developmental Disorders, 31*, 315–325.

Harper, C., Symon, J., & Frea, W. (2007). Recess is time-in: Using peers to improve social skills in children with autism. *Journal of Autism and Developmental Disorders, 38*, 815.

Hart, B.M., & Risley, T.R. (1968). Establishing use of descriptive adjectives in the spontaneous speech of disadvantaged preschool children. *Journal of Applied Behavior Analysis, 1*, 109–120.

Humphries, T.L. (2003). Effectiveness of Pivotal Response Training as a behavioral intervention for young children with autism spectrum disorders. *Bridges, 2*, 1–10.

Ingersoll, B., & Schreibman, L. (2006). Teaching reciprocal imitation skills to young children with autism using a naturalistic behavioral approach: Effects on language, pretend play, and joint attention. *Journal of Autism and Developmental Disorders, 36*, 487–505.

Kaiser, A.P., Yoder, P.J., & Keetz, A. (1992). Evaluating milieu teaching. In S.F. Warren & J. Reichle (Vol. & Series Eds.), *Communication and language intervention series: Vol. 1. Causes and effects in communication and language intervention* (pp. 9–47). Baltimore: Paul H. Brookes Publishing Co.

Koegel, L., Camarata, S., Menchaca, M., & Koegel, R. (1998). Setting generalization of question-asking by children with autism. *American Journal on Mental Retardation, 102*, 346–357.

Koegel, L., Carter, C., & Koegel, R. (2003). Teaching children with autism self-initiations as a pivotal response. *Topics in Language Disorders, 23*, 134–145.

Koegel, R., Camarata, S., Koegel, L., Tall, A., & Smith, A. (1998). Increasing speech intelligibility in children with autism. *Journal of Autism and Developmental Disorders, 28*, 241–251.

Koegel, R.L., & Koegel, L.K. (2006). *Pivotal Response Treatments for autism: Communication, social, and academic development*. Baltimore: Paul H. Brookes Publishing Co.

Koegel, R.L., O'Dell, M.C., & Koegel, L.K. (1987). A natural language teaching paradigm for nonverbal autistic children. *Journal of Autism and Developmental Disorders, 17*, 187–200.

Koegel, R.L., & Schreibman, L. (1977). Teaching autistic children to respond to simultaneous multiple cues. *Journal of Experimental Child Psychology, 24*, 299–311.

Koegel, R.L., Schreibman, L., Good, A., Cerniglia, L., Murphy, C., & Koegel, L. (1989). *How to teach pivotal behaviors to children with autism: A training manual*. Santa Barbara: University of California.

Laski, K., Charlop, M., & Schreibman, L. (1988). Training parents to use the natural language paradigm to increase their autistic children's speech. *Journal of Applied Behavioral*

Analysis, 21, 391–400.

Lifter, K., Sulzer-Azaroff, B., Anderson, S.R., Coyle, J.T., & Cowdery, G.E. (1993). Teaching play activities to preschool children with disabilities: The importance of developmental considerations. *Journal of Early Intervention, 17,* 139–159.

Lovaas, O.I. (1987). Behavioral treatment and normal educational and intellectual functioning in young autistic children. *Journal of Consulting and Clinical Psychology, 55,* 3–9.

Lovaas, O.I., Berberich, J.P., Perloff, B.F., & Schaeffer, B. (1966). Acquisition of imitative speech by schizophrenic children. *Science, 151,* 705–707.

Maurice, C., Green, G., & Luce, S.C. (Eds.). (1996). *Behavioral intervention for young children with autism: A manual for parents and professionals.* Austin, TX: PRO-ED.

McGee, G.G., Krantz, P.J., & McClannahan, L.E. (1985). The facilitative effects of incidental teaching on preposition use by autistic children. *Journal of Applied Behavior Analysis, 18,* 17–31.

McGee, G.G., Morrier, M.J., & Daly, T. (1999). An incidental teaching approach to early intervention for toddlers with autism. *Journal of The Association for Persons with Severe Handicaps, 24,* 133–146.

Metz, J.R. (1965). Conditioning generalized imitation in autistic children. *Journal of Experimental Child Psychology, 4,* 389–399.

National Research Council. (2001). *Educating children with autism.* Washington, DC: National Academies Press.

Oke, J., & Schreibman, L. (1990). Training social initiation to a high-functioning autistic child: Assessment of collateral behavior change and generalization in a case study. *Journal of Autism and Developmental Disorders, 20,* 479–497.

Pierce, K., & Schreibman, L. (1995). Increasing complex social behaviors in children with autism: Effects of peer-implemented Pivotal Response Training. *Journal of Applied Behavior Analysis, 28,* 285–295.

Pierce, K., & Schreibman, L. (1997). Multiple peer use of Pivotal Response Training to increase social behaviors of classmates with autism: Results from trained and untrained peers. *Journal of Applied Behavioral Analysis, 30,* 157–160.

Rocha, M., Schreibman, L., & Stahmer, A.C. (2007). Effectiveness of training parents to teach joint attention in children with autism. *Journal of Early Intervention, 29,* 154–172.

Schreibman, L. (1988). *Autism.* Thousand Oaks, CA: Sage Publications.

Schreibman, L. (2005). *The science and fiction of autism.* Cambridge, MA: Harvard University Press.

Schreibman, L., Charlop, M.H., & Koegel, R.L. (1982). Teaching autistic children to use extra-stimulus prompts. *Journal of Experimental Child Psychology, 33,* 475–491.

Schreibman, L., & Ingersoll, B. (2005). Behavioral interventions to promote learning in individuals with autism. In F.R. Volkmar, R. Paul, A. Klin, & D. Cohen (Eds.), *Handbook of autism and pervasive developmental disorders* (3rd ed., pp. 882–896). Hoboken, NJ: John Wiley & Sons.

Schreibman, L., Kaneko, W.M., & Koegel, R.L. (1991). Positive affect of parents of autistic children: A comparison across two teaching techniques. *Behavior Therapy, 22,* 479–490.

Schreibman, L., Stahmer, A.C., Cestone-Barlett, V., & Dufek, S. (2008). Brief report: Toward refinement of a predictive behavioral profile for treatment outcome in children with autism. *Research in Autism Spectrum Disorders, 3,* 163–172.

Schroeder, G.L., & Baer, D.M. (1972). Effects of concurrent and serial training on generalized vocal imitation in retarded children. *Developmental Psychology, 6,* 293–301.

Sherer, M.R., & Schreibman, L. (2005). Individual behavioral profiles and predictors of treatment effectiveness for children with autism. *Journal of Consulting and Clinical Psychology, 73,* 525–538.

Stahmer, A.C. (1995). Teaching symbolic play skills to children with autism using Pivotal Response Training. *Journal of Autism and Developmental Disorders, 25,* 123–141.

Stahmer, A.C. (1999). Using Pivotal Response Training to facilitate appropriate play in children with autistic spectrum disorders. *Child Language Teaching and Therapy, 15,* 29–40.

Thorp, D., Stahmer, A.C., Schreibman, L. (1995). Effects of sociodramatic play training on children with autism. *Journal of Autism and Developmental Disorders, 25,* 265–282.

Vismara, L., & Lyons, G. (2007). Using perseverative interests to elicit joint attention behaviors in young children with autism: Theoretical and clinical implications of understanding motivation. *Journal of Positive Behavioral Interventions, 9,* 214–228.

Whalen, C., & Schreibman, L. (2003). Joint attention for children with autism using behavioral modification procedures. *Journal of Child Psychology and Psychiatry, 44,* 456–468.

Whalen, C., Schreibman, L., & Ingersoll, B. (2006). The collateral effects of joint attention training on social initiations, positive affect, imitation, and spontaneous speech for young children with autism. *Journal of Autism and Developmental Disorders, 36,* 655–664.

Chapter 2
Appendices

APPENDIX 2.1.

Sample Pivotal Response Training: Generalization Probe Form

Child: John

Skill domain: Expressive Language

Skill target: Requesting "help"

To ensure a skill target is functional for your student, you must know if he or she can use this skill in a variety of circumstances. Identify three different materials, settings, and teachers for the purpose of probing the skill listed above. The materials you choose should be highly preferred by the child.

Materials
1) putting straw in juice box
2) playing DVD
3) blowing bubbles

Setting
1) family room
2) back yard
3) park

Teacher
1) Mom
2) Tanya (babysitter)
3) Marco (therapist)

Indicate the date and the circumstances in which you will probe the skill. Circle the number that corresponds with the specific materials, setting, or teacher listed above. Circle the child's response to the probed skill target as Correct (C), Incorrect (I), or No Response (NR).

Date	Materials			Setting			Teacher			Child Response		
6/05/08	**①**	2	3	**①**	2	3	**①**	2	3	**Ⓒ**	I	NR
6/06/08	1	2	**③**	1	2	**③**	1	2	**③**	C	I	**Ⓝ̲Ⓡ̲**
6/06/08	**①**	2	3	1	**②**	3	1	2	**③**	**Ⓒ**	I	NR
6/07/08	**①**	2	3	1	**②**	3	1	**②**	3	C	**Ⓘ**	NR
6/09/08	1	**②**	3	**①**	2	3	1	**②**	3	C	**Ⓘ**	NR
6/10/08	**①**	2	3	1	2	**③**	**①**	2	3	C	I	**Ⓝ̲Ⓡ̲**
6/11/08	**①**	2	3	**①**	2	3	1	2	**③**	**Ⓒ**	I	NR
6/12/08	1	**②**	3	**①**	2	3	**①**	2	3	**Ⓒ**	I	NR
	1	2	3	1	2	3	1	2	3	C	I	NR
	1	2	3	1	2	3	1	2	3	C	I	NR

(continued)

(continued)

Date	Materials			Setting			Teacher			Child Response		
	1	2	3	1	2	3	1	2	3	C	I	NR
	1	2	3	1	2	3	1	2	3	C	I	NR
	1	2	3	1	2	3	1	2	3	C	I	NR
	1	2	3	1	2	3	1	2	3	C	I	NR
	1	2	3	1	2	3	1	2	3	C	I	NR
Total												

Summary:

The probes show good progress toward generalization; however, John gives no response when at the park. In addition, John is responding incorrectly with his babysitter. These are areas that may need to be more specifically targeted.

APPENDIX 2.2.

Pivotal Response Training: Generalization Probe

Child: _____

Skill domain: _____

Skill target: _____

To ensure a skill target is functional for your student, you must know if he or she can use this skill in a variety of circumstances. Identify three different materials, settings, and teachers for the purpose of probing the skill listed above. The materials you choose should be highly preferred by the child.

Materials   1) _____

2) _____

3) _____

Setting   1) _____

2) _____

3) _____

Teacher   1) _____

2) _____

3) _____

Indicate the date and the circumstances in which you will probe the skill. Circle the number that corresponds with the specific materials, setting, or teacher listed above. Circle the child's response to the probed skill target as Correct (C), Incorrect (I), or No Response (NR).

Date	Materials			Setting			Teacher			Child Response		
	1	2	3	1	2	3	1	2	3	C	I	NR
	1	2	3	1	2	3	1	2	3	C	I	NR
	1	2	3	1	2	3	1	2	3	C	I	NR
	1	2	3	1	2	3	1	2	3	C	I	NR
	1	2	3	1	2	3	1	2	3	C	I	NR
	1	2	3	1	2	3	1	2	3	C	I	NR
	1	2	3	1	2	3	1	2	3	C	I	NR
	1	2	3	1	2	3	1	2	3	C	I	NR
	1	2	3	1	2	3	1	2	3	C	I	NR
	1	2	3	1	2	3	1	2	3	C	I	NR

(continued)

(continued)

Date	Materials			Setting			Teacher			Child Response		
	1	2	3	1	2	3	1	2	3	C	I	NR
	1	2	3	1	2	3	1	2	3	C	I	NR
	1	2	3	1	2	3	1	2	3	C	I	NR
	1	2	3	1	2	3	1	2	3	C	I	NR
	1	2	3	1	2	3	1	2	3	C	I	NR
	1	2	3	1	2	3	1	2	3	C	I	NR
	1	2	3	1	2	3	1	2	3	C	I	NR
	1	2	3	1	2	3	1	2	3	C	I	NR
	1	2	3	1	2	3	1	2	3	C	I	NR
	1	2	3	1	2	3	1	2	3	C	I	NR
Total												

Summary:

_____

_____

_____

APPENDIX 2.3.

Targeting Generalization of Skills
Using Pivotal Response Training (PRT)

PRT generalization goals	Specific suggestions
Use PRT with varied teachers, in varied settings, and with varied materials.	Use multiple teachers (e.g., mom, dad, older sister, babysitter, teacher, speech therapist). Teach in multiple settings (e.g., bedroom, dinner table, playground, grocery store, classroom, lunchroom). Teach with varied materials.
Use teaching materials that interest the child and are readily available in the environment.	Materials should be well organized and easy to access or visible and easy to request. When choosing materials, observe the child in free play and note the child's reaction when you take a toy away. If the child reacts strongly, it indicates a preference for the toy. Identify nontoy objects and activities the child enjoys. Use developmentally appropriate materials to encourage play skills and keep children motivated. Good toys for children at the manipulative play level include noisy toys, toys with lights, spinning toys, cars that go down ramps, Koosh balls, bubbles, puzzles, and games such as Crocodile Dentist and Ants in the Pants. Good toys for children who are beginning to use representational play and have phrase speech include garage with cars, play food or pots and pans, doctor kit, dollhouse, and dolls with movable parts.
Anticipate when PRT can be used throughout the day.	Develop routines and use PRT to require your student to request the next steps (i.e., put on shoes and get your student's backpack, then wait for him to initiate a request to go to the car or bus). Intentionally remove important pieces of an activity to encourage communication (e.g., during breakfast put out a cup without juice and wait for your student to request juice, or get paper out for coloring but "forget" the crayons). Use environmental arrangement to encourage communication (e.g., place favorite toys or foods out of the student's reach, or use containers that are clear but difficult to open).

3

Enhancing the Generalization of Skills Taught Through Discrete Trial Instruction

Mary Jane Weiss and Robert H. LaRue

Learners with autism spectrum disorders (ASDs) manifest a number of characteristics that impede their ability to learn. The most widely accepted criteria for autism are contained in the *Diagnostic and Statistical Manual of Mental Disorders, Fourth Edition, Text Revision* (American Psychiatric Association, 2000). According to this resource, autism has three central defining characteristics:

1. Qualitative impairment in reciprocal social interaction

2. Qualitative impairment in verbal and nonverbal communication and in imaginative ability

3. Markedly restricted and repetitive repertoire of behavior, activities, and interests

The ways in which these characteristics are manifested, however, are highly variable. While some individuals with autism lack interest in social interaction, others are affectionate and attached to others. Some individuals with autism lack vocal language ability, whereas others use vocal speech communicatively. Even when speech is used to communicate, there are often unusual aspects to the speech or the vocalization output may lag behind the child's communicative potential. For example, a child may only request for one highly desired item and not be able to hold conversations or may converse only about topics of special interest. Restricted behaviors and interests may manifest themselves as body rocking or hand flapping. Alternately, restricted behaviors may be evidenced by adhering to rituals or routines or becoming fixated on a single toy or conversational topic.

About 75% of children with autism have developmental delays (APA, 2000). Development tends to be nonuniform or scattered, with clear strengths and weaknesses evident. Behavioral challenges are common, occurring in about 90% of individuals with autism (Smith, McAdam, & Napolitano, 2007). At least 10%–20% of individuals with autism exhibit severe behavior problems such as aggression and self-injury (Lovaas, 1987; Smith et al., 2007).

The current diagnostic criteria for Asperger syndrome (also called Asperger's disorder) highlight impairments in nonverbal communication and in social interaction with an absence of delays in cognitive or language skills (APA, 2000). However, individuals with Asperger syndrome do experience a variety of problems in communication and interaction, such as poor reciprocal conversational abilities, difficulties in comprehending abstract language, and perseveration on topics of special interest that interfere with true reciprocity. Individuals classified as having pervasive developmental disorder-not otherwise specified (PDD-NOS) generally exhibit features of autism but fail to meet the full diagnostic criteria for autism.

In recent years, many clinicians and researchers have discussed autism, PDD-NOS, and Asperger syndrome as a spectrum. Criteria are not yet reliable for distinguishing between these groups. It may be that the same disorder essentially varies in presentation and severity along the continuum (Wing, 1988), but the concept of a continuum seems to have utility.

BEHAVIORAL TREATMENT OF AUTISM SPECTRUM DISORDERS: EARLY AND SEMINAL RESEARCH

Behavior analytic treatment of children with autism began in the 1960s. Ferster and DeMyer (1962) first demonstrated that behavioral principles could be used to increase appropriate behavior in children with autism. At the time, this was a radical idea because autism was viewed as essentially unchangeable. In the years that followed, behavioral intervention was demonstrated to be effective at increasing skills (e.g., Wolf, Risley, & Mees, 1964) and in reducing challenging behaviors (e.g., Lovaas, Freitag, Gold, & Kassorla, 1965). Applied behavior analysis (ABA) was shown to be very effective at increasing skills and remediating deficits.

Children with autism have been shown to be capable of learning and altering their behavior. Studies showed that certain procedures worked better in helping children with autism learn than did others (e.g., Lovaas, Schreibman, Koegel, & Rehm, 1971). In particular, individuals with autism learned well by a form of teaching in which there were clear instructions, repetition and practice, and immediate reinforcement for correct responses. *Discrete trial instruction* (DTI; also called *discrete trial training*) uses repetition and sequenced instruction to build a variety of skills in students with autism (Lovaas, 1981; Lovaas, Koegel, Simmons, & Long, 1973; Smith, 1993). It has been effective in teaching a wide variety of foundation and essential skills in a structured, formal context. Intensive applications of ABA intervention have relied mainly on DTI.

Lovaas's (1987) study is clearly the most ambitious and most extensive in the existing literature, and the gains documented are by far the most impressive (McEachin, Smith, & Lovaas, 1993). Lovaas (1987) compared a group of children younger than age 4 who received 40 hours of intervention (largely DTI) per week for 2 or more years with groups of children who received either fewer hours of such intervention or no intervention. Following intensive intervention, nearly half of the children in the intensive intervention group were able to be placed in general education classes without assistance and had intelligence quotients (IQs) in the average range. Other researchers have also found that early intensive behavioral intervention results in significant gains for some children (e.g., Green,

Brennan, & Fein, 2002; Smith, 1999). Again, these studies relied heavily on the use of DTI in programming.

Overall, when ABA is implemented by qualified practitioners, there is clear consensus that it leads to important improvements. In fact, dramatic improvements are seen in about 50% of children who receive such intervention (Sallows & Graupner, 2005). More research is still needed to identify essential elements and intensity levels of intervention and how such variables impact outcome. Because outcome remains quite variable, researchers are seeking more reliable predictors of how children respond to intensive intervention. Nevertheless, intensive ABA intervention that relies heavily on DTI has been shown to be dramatically effective.

DISCRETE TRIAL INSTRUCTION

Within DTI, the assessment of skill acquisition has historically focused on the student attaining a set mastery criterion. In general, clinicians have focused on percent correct (usually 80% or 90%) as an indicator of mastery (e.g., Anderson, Taras, & O'Malley Cannon, 1996; Leaf & McEachin, 1999). Typically, some consistency in the demonstration of the skill has also been required, such as achieving the target percent correct across several different sessions, days, or clinicians.

Advantages of a DTI approach include efficiency, applicability to a wide range of skills, and simplicity of staff training. It is generally easy to train staff in the implementation of DTI, to plan next steps in curricular sequencing within a DTI approach, and to evaluate progress in an objective manner. Disadvantages of a DTI approach to instruction include an exclusive emphasis on responsivity and limited generalizability.

DTI focuses on responsivity rather than initiation. A child who receives only DTI may respond but not initiate. In extreme cases, the child may await instructions instead of responding to his or her own internal states or environmental cues. Responsivity, however, is a tremendously important skill. A procedure that builds responsiveness in learners with ASDs is important. It may simply be the case that initiation skills need to be built using other instructional methods. Generalizability of skills learned within DTI is limited, especially in comparison to skills taught more naturalistically. However, DTI can be altered to help with this issue.

Effective elements of DTI include errorless learning procedures (e.g., Etzel & LeBlanc, 1979; Lancioni & Smeets, 1986; Terrace, 1963; Touchette & Howard, 1984) and task variation and interspersal (e.g., Dunlap, 1984; Mace et al., 1988; Winterling, Dunlap, & O'Neill, 1987; Zarcone, Iwata, Hughes, & Vollmer, 1993). *Errorless learning* involves the prevention and interruption of errors. It is designed to ensure that children do not make and repeat errors or form error patterns in their responses. To prevent errors, clinicians generally use a most-to-least prompt hierarchy in teaching new skills. A child is first assisted with a great deal of intrusive support. For example, a child learning to touch his or her head might be guided hand over hand to respond appropriately to the instruction, "Touch your head." As the child begins to understand the response expected, support is faded. The same child may be helped to touch his or her head by simply beginning to help him or her make the movement toward the head (but letting go before contact is made) or by gesturing toward the child's head. Eventually, the child is expected to respond independently. In errorless procedures, prompts are given immediately—right along with the instruction—to ensure that the child makes the correct response.

Task interspersal involves the mingling of new targets with mastered material, mixing new material with things the child already knows how to do well. Task interspersal has been shown to increase correct performance. This strategy diverges from historical applications of DTI, which often utilized blocks of identical target trials. Children were often asked to do the very same action (e.g., touch head) 10 or 20 times in a row. This practice was associated with a number of outcomes that were not ideal, including learner boredom, high levels of frustration, and automatic responding. Some learners tired of the repetition; an inference of boredom was usually made when teachers observed off-task behaviors and poor quality responses. Alternately, some learners had trouble tolerating the continuous presentation of challenging instructions, especially when the task was difficult or nonpreferred. In these cases, challenging behaviors sometimes erupted. Perhaps most importantly, some learners simply stopped attending to the vocal instructions and began responding "automatically," based on the feedback received on the first instruction (e.g., touching their head again after learning that "touch head" was the current response being taught, sometimes even before the instruction was given). Task interspersal procedures correct each of these problems by ensuring that the learner must first hear the instruction before responding to the teacher, as well as by mixing difficult and easy tasks together to increase attention and reduce frustration. Furthermore, task interspersal procedures better train individuals for future educational environments, where variability in demands is the norm.

DISCRETE TRIAL INSTRUCTION AND THE PROMOTION OF GENERALIZATION

State-of-the-art clinical application of DTI procedures generally involves mixing new and mastered material as well as preventing and interrupting errors. In addition, several other changes are commonly seen in current applications, which have implications for the generalization of skills (see Table 3.1). In the early days of DTI, it was common for individuals to use a particular tone of voice when giving instructions, which was presumed to help the learner to focus on the demand. However, it did not prepare learners to respond to the naturalistic ways in which others make requests. Sometimes a child who had received extensive DTI intervention failed to

Table 3.1.   State-of-the-art characteristics of discrete trial instruction

Fast-paced instruction

Use of interspersal and errorless learning procedures

Use of natural tone of voice

Variability of wording in instructions

Teaching in the context of daily routines

Teaching conducted across environments

Involvement of peers in training

Involvement of family members in training

Use in combination with naturalistic teaching procedures

respond unless that particular tone of voice was used. Furthermore, an instruction was commonly delivered in only one way, with wording that was kept constant during all instructional sessions (e.g., a child might learn to follow the instruction "throw away," but would not be familiar with or responsive to synonymous instructions such as "find the garbage" or "put this in the trash can"). "Translation" was therefore required on a continual basis, which had serious implications for both integration and independence.

Today, there is an emphasis on integrating variability in instruction from the earliest stages. Naturalistic tones are preferred because they transfer more readily to the natural environment. In addition, variability in phrasing of instructions is preferred at all stages of instruction, whenever a learner can tolerate variability. These procedures enhance the utility of skills learned and reduce the likelihood of dependence on adults. Other changes in the application of DTI include an emphasis on increased pacing to build the number of learning opportunities and teaching in the context of functional daily routines.

There is consumer confusion about the utility of DTI. As more naturalistic teaching procedures have gained popularity, DTI has become less popular. However, DTI remains very useful for teaching a wide variety of skills to children with ASDs; its utility should not be obscured by the recent emphasis on more naturalistic approaches. DTI works well for teaching skills requiring repetition; teaching skills that are not intrinsically motivating; and building solid repertoires of tacting, imitation, and receptive skills (e.g., Sundberg & Partington, 1998, 1999).

In addition, DTI is much more effective if used with strategies for effective generalization to the natural environment (Smith et al., 2007; Stokes & Baer, 1977). Teaching proceeds more effectively if instruction is conducted across environments; parents and peers are involved in training; and DTI is used in combination with other, more naturalistic approaches.

INCREASING GENERALIZATION: WHAT TO DO IN TEACHING SESSIONS

As the field of ABA has evolved, there has been an increased sensitivity to the need to program with generalization in mind—especially within the context of formalized instruction, where generalization may be most limited.

Promoting Setting/ Situation and Response Generality

To increase the likelihood of generalization during DTI, practitioners must account for both setting/situation generalization and response generalization. Setting/situation generalization occurs when the target behavior is emitted in the presence of stimulus conditions other than those in which it has been trained directly. In other words, a behavior (e.g., saying the word *dog*) that occurred in the presence of one stimulus (e.g., a picture of a Collie) also occurs in the presence of other stimuli (e.g., a picture of a German Shepherd). Setting/situation generalization has been used to refer to generality across settings and people.

Examples of generalization across settings may include being taught to count out money correctly in a school store and then being able to count out money in a store in the community. Another example would be correctly identifying a color (e.g., red) in the context of school instruction and subsequently being able to identify the color red in a tablecloth at home. Examples of generalization across people may include a learner correctly identifying the color blue with an instructor and then later with a parent. Another example would be if a student learned to tie shoes with his mother and is subsequently able to tie his shoes when prompted by his father.

Response generalization refers to the extent to which a learner performs a variety of similar, functionally equivalent responses—in addition to the trained response—under similar stimulus conditions. In other words, untrained responses begin to occur with no direct training, with these responses accomplishing the same thing that the original, trained response did. These generalized responses have no specific contingencies applied and acquire their effects because of the reinforcement of other similar (or functionally equivalent) responses. An example of response generalization is a student who says "How are you?" or "How's it going?" after being taught to say "Hello!" in response to a new individual entering a classroom. Another example is a student who was taught to identify a picture of a Collie and spontaneously says "dog" or "Lassie" when presented with the picture again.

Teaching Loosely

As mentioned by Stokes and Baer (1977), generalization should not be approached as a "train and hope" endeavor. Behavior analysts must plan for generalization in a systematic manner to ensure that the desired behavior occurs in similar settings and similar responses are reinforced as well. One such procedure for increasing the likelihood of generalization is what Stokes and Baer refer to as *training loosely.* Excessive standardization of instruction (i.e., having every component of the instructional settings the same every time) impedes both stimulus and response generalization. Training loosely refers to the process of varying as many noncritical dimensions of the antecedent stimuli as possible during instruction and accepting a wide range of correct responses to increase the likelihood that skills will generalize to the natural setting. It is important to note that training loosely is not the same as training sloppy.

When behavior analysts train loosely, they vary antecedent stimuli in a systematic manner. Baer (1981, 1999) suggested varying such stimuli as position (therapist or student), tone, words, how stimuli are presented (e.g., from different angles), settings in which instruction occurs, therapist clothing, reinforcers, time of day, and other environmental aspects such as individuals present, lighting, decorations, temperature, smells, and noise. To maximize the benefits of training loosely, these variations should occur as unpredictably as possible. For example, when teaching a student to make a peanut butter and jelly sandwich, the teacher may not only vary where he or she stands during instruction but may alternate between plastic or metal utensils, paper or ceramic plates, different brands of peanut butter and jelly, and wheat or white bread. Similarly, when a student is learning how to match pictures, the teacher may change the pictures, the area of the classroom or school in which the skill is practiced, and whether the task is done on a tabletop or blackboard. Each varied component does not significantly change the task itself but helps the learner to tolerate minor changes in the instructional context and prepares the learner for the wide variety of situations that he or she may encounter.

Training loosely is often a challenge for practitioners to implement because they often emphasize consistency in instruction and purposely try to avoid variability. Part of the art of ABA intervention involves understanding which instructional components must be consistently presented and which components can be varied. For example, in the previous example of sandwich making, varying the brand of peanut butter is appropriate for training loosely, but using ham to make the sandwich changes something fundamental about the process (i.e., different materials, type of sandwich, motor responses required) and may not be an appropriate way to train loosely in this situation.

Programming Common Stimuli

Another strategy that can be incorporated into instruction is programming common stimuli. Programming common stimuli involves incorporating stimuli and typical features of the generalization (natural) environment into the instructional setting to increase the likelihood of generalization. For instance, if a learner is being taught to purchase food in a grocery store, it may be appropriate to teach the skills necessary in a controlled setting with several actual stimuli the learner may encounter in a store (e.g., real food found on shelves in a supermarket, a counter, a cash register, a cashier). One of the benefits of programming common stimuli is that it allows for repeated practice in a controlled setting (i.e., instructors have more control of relevant contingencies, number of training trials, and unexpected events); also, it provides a safer environment for the learners to be instructed. To effectively program common stimuli, practitioners need to identify the critical components present in the natural environment that the learner would benefit from having in the instructional environment.

Training Sufficient Examples

Another instructional strategy for increasing the likelihood of generalization involves teaching a range of relevant stimulus conditions and acceptable responses, also known as *training sufficient exemplars* or *training diversely* (Stokes & Baer, 1977; Stokes & Osnes, 1989). These procedures include teaching multiple stimulus examples, teaching multiple response examples, general case analysis, and negative teaching examples. Teaching multiple stimulus examples involves instructing the learner to respond to more than one example of the antecedent stimulus conditions. Teaching multiple stimulus examples may involve teaching multiple variations of the specific item being taught (e.g., letters, numbers), varying the stimulus context (e.g., identifying the color red from a cue card, as well as the color of the instructor's shirt), the setting in which the instruction occurs (academic instruction in a one-to-one format and in a larger group setting), or the person doing the teaching (e.g., instruction by a teacher and a parent or peer).

Teaching sufficient response examples involves teaching a variety of acceptable, functionally equivalent response topographies. For example, a learner may be taught a variety of responses to greetings, such as "How are you today?"

"What's up?" or "How's it going?" to increase the likelihood that a nontrained variation occurs (e.g., "What's going on today?"). *General case analysis* (also known as *general case strategy)* involves teaching examples that represent a full range of stimulus situations and response requirements in the natural environment (Albin & Horner, 1988; Engelmann & Carnine, 1982). For instance, when training a learner to operate a cash register, a practitioner may teach the learner to operate a wide variety of cash registers (e.g., an old-fashioned push-button register, a digital cash register, a touch-screen register) to increase the likelihood that the learner will generalize to a novel register.

Teaching negative examples involves teaching the learner when *not* to use a newly learned behavior. In doing this, learners are taught to discriminate when they should do something and when they should not. For instance, Horner, Eberhard, and Sheehan (1986) conducted an investigation in which they taught learners with disabilities to clear tables in restaurants. Students were taught the necessary skills for cleaning off tables (e.g., removing dishes, wiping table and chairs, throwing away garbage) and were also taught when not to engage in table cleaning (e.g., when people were still seated at the table, if food remained on the dishes, no garbage on the table). From a social validity standpoint, understanding when not to engage in a particular behavior can be as important as knowing when a behavior should occur. It is often an overlooked step in the intervention process.

Attending to Fluency

Generalization can also be increased by ensuring that the behavior contacts reinforcement, thus helping to make the skill fluent. However, if a learner is unable to complete a behavior quickly enough after being presented with discriminative stimulus (i.e., latency) and at an appropriate duration or rate, it is unlikely that the behavior will contact reinforcement. For instance, a learner who has a latency deficit in social responding may not respond quickly enough to a greeting to contact reinforcement (e.g., social interaction, feedback). If it takes a preschooler 8–10 seconds to respond to a peer's greeting, the likelihood of the peer being reinforced is low. (Most preschoolers will not wait 10 seconds for a response.)

To address latency issues, practitioners need to instruct learners to respond to a stimulus within an appropriate period of time. In other words, short latencies should be reinforced to teach learners to respond more quickly to stimuli in the environment. Similarly, a learner who is unable to sustain a social interaction for longer than 10 seconds is not likely to contact reinforcement. To address this, practitioners need to teach learners to engage in the behavior (e.g., interaction) for increasingly longer periods of time to ensure that reinforcement is contacted. Duration is a critical dimension of behaviors such as conversation, play, and attending in a group. Finally, teachers need to broadly consider and examine the speed of responses. For instance, two learners may be able to complete math problems with 100% accuracy, but while one student can complete the worksheet in 5 minutes, the other student may only be able to complete a single problem during the same 5-minute period. To address concerns with the rate of responding, practitioners need to teach the learner to emit the response at a rate that is consistent with the rate required to contact reinforcement in the natural environment. Discrete trial sessions can be altered by adding a rate-based criterion during

Table 3.2.   How to enhance generalization within teaching sessions

Promote setting and situation generality

Promote response generality

Teach loosely

Program common stimuli

Teach sufficient examples

Attend to fluency

instruction. Table 3.2 provides a summary of suggestions for enhancing generalization within teaching sessions.

ENCOURAGING GENERALIZATION OF SKILLS OUTSIDE OF INSTRUCTIONAL SESSIONS

A number of things can also be done as extensions of instructional sessions to build the likelihood of generalization. Several of these strategies involve planning for the reinforcement of such responses.

Preparing the Learner for Reinforcement that Is Likely to Be Available

In general, the goal is for responses to be maintained by the reinforcement that is naturally available for those responses, which has several implications for teaching. First, practitioners should teach functionally relevant skills that will be needed frequently in the natural environment, ensuring many opportunities for natural reinforcement and maintenance of those skills. Secondly, teachers need to reduce the level of extrinsic rewards that are offered for the demonstration of skills and fade reinforcement to those rewards that are commonly available within the target environment. For example, if a child is reinforced with candy for sitting in circle time at preschool, it is important to fade out the use of the edible reward and replace it with rewards that teachers commonly use to reinforce on-task behavior and participation in this situation (e.g., positive teacher attention, nonverbal gestures of praise). The goal is to aim for natural contingencies of reinforcement to maintain the behavior. Similarly, learners should be accustomed to unpredictable and intermittent schedules of reinforcement; such schedules further mirror how reinforcement is typically distributed in the natural environment.

Increasing Available Reinforcement in the Natural Setting

Although it is essential to prepare the learner for the lean schedules of reinforcement likely to be encountered in the natural environment, it is also important to ensure that reinforcement for target behaviors is given to the student. In this regard, it can be helpful to instruct others to reinforce the behavior—sometimes referred to as *awakening the community of reinforcement*. As Baer (1999) said, "The problem may be simply that the natural community of reinforcement is asleep and needs to be awakened and turned on" (p. 16).

It therefore can be helpful to share information about behaviors in need of reinforcement with key people in the natural environment. If a student has been working on making requests in full sentences during speech therapy sessions, the speech therapist might alert both the student's classroom teacher and parents to reinforce all instances of full-sentence requesting. Similarly, if a special education teacher has been working on building hand-raising skills in small-group instructional situations, she might alert the general education teacher to reinforce instances of hand raising in the inclusive educational environment. Communicating these expectations can increase consistency between key educational team members and can provide many more opportunities for reinforcement of new and important behaviors.

This goal can be extended beyond those naturally thought of as partners in the educational process. Significant others who frequently interact with the student, even though they may not formally instruct him or her (e.g., cafeteria workers, bus aides, siblings, grandparents), should also be aware of key information. Such people are very important interaction partners in the student's daily life; their awareness of and reinforcement of critical behaviors can be tremendously important in strengthening skills.

Another way to increase reinforcement available in the natural setting is to contrive a mediating stimulus (Baer, 1999). At times, a mediating stimulus might be an existing cue in the environment. At other times, it may be possible to add a stimulus that promotes the behavior, such as a cue card or photo activity schedule (e.g., MacDuff, Krantz, & McClannahan, 1993).

Recruiting Reinforcement

Learners can also be taught to recruit reinforcement, which can be an extremely important skill in ensuring that learners derive reinforcement for appropriate behavior. It is often difficult for classroom teachers and parents to take time to reinforce behavior. As a result, attention frequently is given contingent on disruptive behaviors. By nature, adults have a tendency to take appropriate, on-task behavior for granted (e.g., Walker, 1997). Furthermore, students most in need of such feedback are frequently the least likely to ask for it (e.g., Newman & Golding, 1990).

Many learners have been successfully taught to recruit teacher attention. Preschoolers with developmental delays were able to recruit teacher attention for remaining on task and for completing their work (e.g., Connell, Carta, & Baer, 1993; Stokes, Fowler, & Baer, 1978). Students with intellectual disabilities also were taught to recruit reinforcement and to solicit feedback on their performance in general education environments (e.g., Craft, Alber, & Heward, 1998). In this study, using modeling and role playing, students were taught skills such as showing their work to the teacher and requesting information on performance with open-ended questions. Such skills ensure higher levels of interaction between student and teacher and set the occasion for the reinforcement of appropriate responses. Such strategies have been extended to improving work performance in vocational training settings (e.g., Mank & Horner, 1987).

Certain student characteristics increase the relevance of training recruitment skills (Alber & Heward, 1997). Students who are extremely quiet and withdrawn may be good candidates for such training because they may otherwise go unnoticed. In addition, students who impulsively rush through their work or who demand immediate feedback from the teacher can be helped to develop skills in self-assessment and in appropriate means of recruiting attention. Students who interrupt teachers excessively might also be exposed to such training, as the lessons involve understanding appropriate and excessive requests for feedback.

Teaching recruitment of reinforcement is a complex endeavor because students must be taught a variety of subtle social rules in this context (Alber & Heward, 1997, 2000). Intrinsic to the skill is the ability to determine if recruitment of reinforcement is appropriate. For example, learners must first be able to self-evaluate the quality and completeness of their work. In addition, learners must discriminate between circumstances in which interruption of the teacher is acceptable and circumstances in which interruption is ill-advised. For example, if a teacher is busy with another student or engaged in another task, the student should not interrupt at that moment. Students also need to learn unwritten rules for reinforcement recruitment, which are often very specific to a particular classroom or teacher. These rules include how to interrupt, which may be based on teacher preference (e.g., raising one's hand), and how often such attempts can be made, which varies with the nature of the task as well as with teacher preferences and the ages of the students. It may be that appropriate rates of requesting attention can be gleaned from direct observation in the environment. In this way, the student's rate can match that of peers in the setting (e.g., Cooper, Heron, & Heward, 2007). It is also important to prepare the learner for multiple possible responses, including being met with a request to come back later or even a negative response (Alber & Heward, 1997). Training needs to comprehensively address the array of possible experiences that may occur in the natural environment. The complexity of the behaviors involved supports the extensive use of modeling, role playing, and rehearsal with reinforcement and corrective feedback (Alber & Heward, 1997, 2000).

Self-Management Strategies

Another set of strategies that can tremendously help learners in generalizing responses in broad ways is to develop self-management skills. Like recruiting reinforcement, self-management skills are designed to help increase the amount of reinforcement available to the learner for appropriate behaviors. However, in the case of self-management, the agent of change is the individual. Self-management strategies involve making learners aware of and responsible for their own behaviors (e.g., Cooper et al., 2007). These strategies include skills in planning, such as making schedules and checklists; self-monitoring and self-recording, such as evaluating and recording the extent to which certain target behaviors were demonstrated; and self-reinforcement, such as providing oneself with rewards for meeting behavioral targets.

Self-management has a number of obvious advantages. Perhaps most importantly, it increases independence and decreases the need for an external agent of behavioral change. It also can build skills in corollary areas, such as self-awareness

Table 3.3.   How to enhance generalization outside of teaching sessions

Prepare the learner for reinforcement that is likely to be available

Increase available reinforcement

Teach the learner to recruit reinforcement

Teach the learner self-management strategies

of behavioral patterns and precursors. Table 3.3 provides a summary of suggestions for enhancing generalization outside of teaching sessions.

ASSESSMENT OF GENERALIZATION

It is important that generalization be assessed at multiple stages of instruction. Several clear goals of training for generalization can be readily assessed (Cooper et al., 2007). First, behaviors trained must be demonstrated in nontraining settings and situations—the essential and necessary outcome of all contrived or analog instruction. If this goal is not achieved, then the relevance of the instruction is questionable. Furthermore, functionally relevant behaviors should occur without direct training. Targets of instruction should be maintained by naturally occurring contingencies of reinforcement. Finally, undesirable generalization should not occur (e.g., the emergence of a functionally equivalent but undesirable response or the occurrence of overgeneralization of responses in nonfunctional ways).

When assessing for generalization, probes should be conducted without added reinforcement, in settings in which no training has occurred, and with novel stimuli. It is essential that the generalization probes be done in contexts that vary meaningfully from the training situation, which ensures that the probe is a relevant assessment of the likelihood of transfer into natural environments.

Before instruction, the generality of the skill can be assessed to guide teaching. During instruction, it can be helpful to assess for generalization as a measure of success (e.g., if generalization is occurring along with skill acquisition), as a measure of failure (i.e., the need to incorporate specific training for generalization), and as a tool for program planning (e.g., if formal training is still needed for all components of the skill). After instruction, generalization probes can be used to assess response maintenance and functional response variability.

LIMITATIONS AND SUGGESTIONS

As we have discussed, DTI is a teaching methodology that has limited generalization benefits. When skills are taught in an artificial context, the transfer of skills to the natural environment almost always requires additional training. It is therefore preferable to teach skills in natural situations, which increases the likelihood that skills will be demonstrated when needed in real life.

The variety of strategies discussed in this chapter can help to ameliorate the intrinsic disadvantages of teaching skills in formal ways. When formal DTI is used, it should be used in as naturalistic a manner as possible. The teacher's tone of voice should be conversational, new skills should be mixed with other known material, teaching should be conducted across environments, and teaching should be embedded into daily routines so that skills are practiced functionally. Peers and family members should be included in training to help increase the likelihood of transfer to the natural environments in which skills are needed.

ADDITIONAL THOUGHTS

It might also be helpful to think about generalization as a behavior, not just as an outcome of instruction (Cooper et al., 2007). Thinking about generalization in this way changes some of what we might do as instructors. First, it makes it more likely that we will reinforce response variability. Reinforcing response variability makes tremendous clinical sense because it prepares learners for more diverse circumstances and reinforces important classes of behavior with implications for successful coping, such as flexibility, problem solving, and adaptation. Individuals with the capacity for response variability have been shown to have greater problem-solving skills (e.g., Arnensen, 2000; Marckel, Neef, & Ferreri, 2006; Shahan & Chase, 2002). Instructors can be taught to use reinforcement differentially to increase response variability, offering more powerful rewards for novel and/or creative responses.

Finally, it is important to make generalization a priority in how we conceptualize skills, teach skills, and evaluate progress in learners. We need to program for, plan for, and assess for generalization at every stage of instruction. We need to equip significant others with tools to increase generalization, and we need to teach learners themselves skills which aid generalization. It is still the case that generalization does not occur without skillful planning, so we must incorporate that planning into all of our instructional efforts with students. As Baer (1999) said, "[N]o one learns a generalized lesson unless a generalized lesson is taught" (p. 1).

FUTURE DIRECTIONS

Generalization of skills remains an important outcome of instruction that clinicians seek in educating children with autism. Students need to be able to respond to a multiplicity of instructions and stimuli and need to demonstrate flexibility in their responses. Instruction in the absence of such generalization lacks functionality and fails to increase independence. Individuals who fail to generalize a skill may require translation from others in a way that seriously reduces their effective participation in the broader community. From a clinical perspective, generalization is critically important.

To enhance generalization, it is likely that clinicians will continue to pursue naturalistic forms of teaching in the development of skills. To the extent that skills can be taught in natural contexts, the efficiency and meaningfulness of instruction is increased.

Clinical guidelines for how to best teach naturalistically, however, are limited. Teachers and parents alike often struggle with how to best teach in a natural context. Suggestions for contriving such teaching opportunities are sorely needed. In addition, it is often more challenging to track progress in these instructional situations. How should data be collected? How should mastery be evaluated? A necessary clinical direction is the continued development of elaborate, clear, and specific guidelines for naturalistic teaching interactions. In addition, clinicians will likely need to continue to highlight the utility of instruction using discrete trials. There has been a trend toward devaluing the contribution of formal instruction, which is not warranted. Clinicians need to educate consumers about the need for and the role of DTI in building skills in youngsters with autism.

In a research context, there is still much to learn about how to best enhance generality. A greater understanding of how we can teach loosely is an area that would have great clinical and research relevance. While clinicians may understand the idea behind the clinical suggestions, more specific instructions on how to most efficiently and judiciously alter noncritical dimensions of instruction would be immensely helpful. It would also be helpful to get additional information on how response variability increases problem solving, especially for this population of learners. The application and utility of self-management and reinforcement–recruitment skills are other important areas of potential impact. These are especially compelling skills for individuals with autism, who often are passive regarding their need for attention and who may not possess skills in self-monitoring or self-reinforcement. Finally, information on how teaching skills to fluency may enhance generality and maintenance of skills would be very helpful to educators assessing how, when, and why to include rate building in their instructional efforts.

SUMMARY

DTI has been a critically important and effective technique for developing skills in learners with ASDs. A number of instructional changes have increased the natural quality of such instruction and helped to increase the transfer of skills taught via DTI into natural settings. These changes include the use of a more naturalistic tone of instruction, the use of task interspersal procedures, and the incorporation of variability into instructions.

Within instructional sessions, clinicians can enhance setting/situation and response generality by training loosely, programming common stimuli, using sufficiently diverse exemplars in training, and training to fluency. Outside of instructional sessions, generality may be increased by preparing the learner for the reinforcement likely to be available, increasing the reinforcement available for responses, teaching the learner to recruit reinforcement, and teaching self-management techniques.

Generalization should be assessed before, during, and after instruction. Educators and parents need to plan and program for generalization and assess for its presence at multiple stages of learning.

REFERENCES

Alber, S.R., & Heward, W.L. (1997). Recruit it or lose it! Training students to recruit contingent teacher attention. *Intervention in School and Clinic, 5*, 275–282.

Alber, S.R., & Heward, W.L. (2000). Teaching students to recruit positive attention: A review and recommendations. *Journal of Behavioral Education, 10*, 177–204.

Albin, R.W., & Horner, R.H. (1988). Generalization with precision. In R.H. Horner, G. Dunlap, & R.L. Koegel (Eds.), *Generalization and maintenance: Life-style changes in applied settings* (pp. 99–120). Baltimore: Paul H. Brookes Publishing Co.

American Psychiatric Association. (2000). *Diagnostic and statistical manual of mental disorders* (4th ed., text rev.). Washington, DC: Author.

Anderson, S.R., Taras, M., & O'Malley Cannon, B. (1996). Teaching new skills to children with autism. In C. Maurice, G. Green, & S.C. Luce (Eds.), *Behavioral interventions for young children with autism: A manual for parents and professionals*. Austin, TX: Pro-Ed.

Arnensen, E.M. (2000). *Reinforcement of object manipulation increases discovery.* Unpublished bachelor's thesis, Reed College, Portland, OR.

Baer, D.M. (1981). A hung jury and a Scottish verdict: Not proven. *Analysis and Intervention in Developmental Disabilities, 1,* 91–97.

Baer, D.M. (1999). *How to plan for generalization* (2nd ed.). Austin, TX: Pro-Ed.

Connell, M.C., Carta, J.J., & Baer, D.M. (1993). Programming generalization of in-class transition skills: Teaching preschoolers with developmental delays to self-assess and recruit contingent teacher praise. *Journal of Applied Behavior Analysis, 26,* 345–352.

Cooper, J.O., Heron, T.E., & Heward, W.L. (2007). *Applied behavior analysis* (2nd ed.). Upper Saddle River, NJ: Pearson.

Craft, M.A., Alber, S.R., & Heward, W.L. (1998). Teaching elementary students with developmental disabilities to recruit teacher attention in a general education classroom: Effects on teacher praise and academic productivity. *Journal of Applied Behavior Analysis, 31,* 399–415.

Dunlap, G. (1984). The influence of task variation and maintenance tasks on the learning of autistic children. *Journal of Experimental Child Psychology, 37,* 41–64.

Engelmann, S., & Carnine, D. (1982). *Theory of instruction: Principles and applications.* New York: Irvington.

Etzel, B.C., & LeBlanc, J.M. (1979). The simplest treatment alternative: The law of parsimony applied to choosing appropriate instructional control and errorless learning procedures for the difficult-to-teach child. *Journal of Autism and Developmental Disorders, 9,* 361–382.

Ferster, C.B., & DeMyer, M.K. (1962). The development of performances in autistic children in an automatically controlled environment. *Journal of Chronic Diseases, 13,* 312–345.

Green, G., Brennan, L.C., & Fein, D. (2002). Intensive behavioral treatment for a toddler at high risk for autism. *Behavior Modification, 26,* 69–192.

Horner, R.H., Eberhard, J.M., & Sheehan, M.R. (1986). Teaching generalized table bussing: The importance of negative teaching examples. *Behavior Modification, 10,* 457–471.

Lancioni, G.E., & Smeets, P.M. (1986). Procedures and parameters of errorless discrimination training with developmentally impaired individuals. In N.R. Ellis & N.W. Bray (Eds.), *International review of research in mental retardation, 14* (pp. 135–164). Orlando, FL: Academic Press.

Leaf, R., & McEachin, J. (1999). *A work in progress: Behavior management strategies and a curriculum for intensive behavioral treatment of autism.* New York: DRL Books.

Lovaas, O.I. (1981). *Teaching developmentally disabled children: The me book.* Austin, TX: PRO-ED.

Lovaas, O.I. (1987). Behavioral treatment and normal intellectual functioning in young autistic children. *Journal of Consulting and Clinical Psychology, 55,* 3–9.

Lovaas, O.I., Freitag, G., Gold, V.J., & Kassorla, I.C. (1965). Recording apparatus and procedure for observation of behaviors of children in free play settings. *Journal of Experimental Child Psychology, 2,* 108–120.

Lovaas, O.I., Koegel, R.L., Simmons, J.Q., & Long, J. (1973). Some generalization and follow up measures on autistic children in behavior therapy. *Journal of Applied Behavior Analysis, 6,* 131–166.

Lovaas, O.I., Schreibman, L., Koegel, R.L., & Rehm, R. (1971). Selective responding by autistic children to multiple sensory input. *Journal of Abnormal Psychology, 77,* 211–222.

MacDuff, G.S., Krantz, P.J., & McClannahan, L.E. (1993). Teaching children with autism to use photographic activity schedules: Maintenance and generalization of complex response chains. *Journal of Applied Behavior Analysis, 26,* 89–97.

Mace, F.C., Hock, M.L., Lalli, J.S., West, B.J., Belfiore, P., Pinter, E., et al. (1988). Behavioral momentum in the treatment of noncompliance. *Journal of Applied Behavior Analysis, 21,* 123–141.

Mank, D.M., & Horner, R.H. (1987). Self-recruited feedback: A cost-effective procedure for maintaining behavior. *Research in Developmental Disabilities, 8,* 91–112.

Marckel, J.M., Neef, N.A., & Ferreri, S.J. (2006). A preliminary analysis of teaching improvisation with the Picture Exchange Communication System to children with autism. *Journal of Applied Behavior Analysis, 39,* 109–115.

McEachin, J., Smith, T., & Lovaas, I. (1993). Long-term outcome for children with autism who received early intensive behavioral treatment. *American Journal of Mental Retardation, 97*, 359–372.

Newman, R.S., & Golding, L. (1990). Children's reluctance to seek help with school work. *Journal of Educational Psychology, 82*, 92–100.

Sallows, G.O., & Graupner, T.D. (2005). Intensive behavioral treatment for children with autism: Four-year outcome and predictors. *American Journal on Mental Retardation, 100*, 417–438.

Shahan, T.A., & Chase, P.N. (2002). Novelty, stimulus control, and operant variability. *The Behavior Analyst, 25*, 175–190.

Smith, T. (1993). Autism. In T.R. Giles (Ed.), *Effective psychotherapies* (pp. 107–113). New York: Plenum.

Smith, T. (1999). Outcome of early intervention for children with autism. *Clinical Psychology: Science and Practice, 6*, 33–49.

Smith, T., McAdam, D., & Napolitano, D. (2007). Autism and applied behavior analysis. In P. Sturmey & A. Fitzer (Eds.), *Autism spectrum disorders: Applied behavior analysis, evidence, and practice* (pp. 1–29). Austin, TX: Pro-Ed.

Stokes, T.F., & Baer, D.M. (1977). An implicit technology of generalization. *Journal of Applied Behavior Analysis, 10*, 349–367.

Stokes, T.F., Fowler, S.A., & Baer, D.M. (1978). Training preschool children to recruit natural communities of reinforcement. *Journal of Applied Behavior Analysis, 11*, 285–303.

Stokes, T.F., & Osnes, P.G. (1989). An operant pursuit of generalization. *Behavior Therapy, 20*, 337–355.

Sundberg, M.L., & Partington, J.W. (1998). *Teaching language to children with autism or other developmental disabilities.* Pleasant Hill, CA: Behavior Analysts.

Sundberg, M.L. & Partington, J.W. (1999). The need for both DT and NE training for children with autism. In P.M. Ghezzi, W.L. Williams, & J.E. Carr (Eds.), *Autism: Behavior analytic approaches.* Reno, NV: Context Press.

Terrace, H. (1963). Discrimination learning with and without errors. *Journal of the Experimental Analysis of Behavior, 6*, 1–27.

Touchette, P.E., & Howard, J. (1984). Errorless learning: Reinforcement contingencies and stimulus control transfer in delayed prompting. *Journal of Applied Behavior Analysis, 17*, 175–181.

Walker, H.M. (1997). *The acting out child: Coping with classroom disruption* (2nd ed.). Longmont, CO: Sopris West.

Wing, L. (1988). The continuum of autistic characteristics. In E. Schopler & G. Mesibov (Eds.), *Diagnosis and assessment in autism* (pp. 91–110). New York: Plenum.

Winterling, V., Dunlap, G., & O'Neill, R.E. (1987). The influence of task variation on the aberrant behaviors of autistic students. *Education and Treatment of Children, 10*, 105–119.

Wolf, M.M., Risley, T.R., & Mees, H. (1964). Application of operant conditioning procedures to the behaviour problems of an autistic child. *Behavior Research and Therapy, 1*, 305–312.

Zarcone, J.R., Iwata, B.A., Hughes, C.E., & Vollmer, T.R. (1993). Momentum versus extinction effects in the treatment of self-injurious escape behavior. *Journal of Applied Behavior Analysis, 26*, 135–136.

4

Generalization Issues Pertaining to the Picture Exchange Communication System (PECS)

Andy Bondy and Lori Frost

The Picture Exchange Communication System (PECS) was first described by Bondy and Frost in 1994. It has since become an effective and popular augmentative and alternative communication system that is used around the world (Mills & Wing, 2006; Stahmer, Collings, & Palinkas, 2005). Frost and Bondy (1994, 2002) developed a specific protocol, *The Picture Exchange Communication System Training Manual,* which describes a sequence of training that relies on the analysis of language and communication provided by Skinner (1957) and a host of teaching strategies guided by the principles of applied behavior analysis to promote functional communication. Each specific skill taught within the PECS protocol requires careful attention to a variety of generalization issues. Similarly, the specific teaching strategies also need to be implemented with generalization issues addressed from the onset. This chapter describes the sequence of skills taught within PECS, as well as an array of strategies that can be used to maximize generalization and decrease the chances of prompt dependency.

Some of the suggestions within this chapter have been supported by empirical evidence, whereas others are consistent with the principles of learning and clinical practice. Many of the issues related to generalization deal with specific PECS concerns; others may relate to broader issues associated with promoting functional communication. Clearly, any communication system must be in place at all times and in all environments and be effective with a large array of communicative partners. These issues are not related to PECS alone.

The first lesson in PECS involves establishing what Skinner (1957) defined as *verbal behavior*: a class of behaviors that are "reinforced through the mediation of other people" (p. 2) in which "the 'listener' must be responding in ways which have been conditioned *precisely in order to reinforce the behavior of the speaker* [by the verbal community]" (p. 225). In other words, a "speaker's" actions are under the stimulus control of a "listener" who then mediates provision of direct or social reinforcement. If someone acts in a manner that directly produces reinforcement without the intervention of others, then no verbal behavior has occurred. Skinner made it abundantly clear that the topography or form of the behavior has no impact on defining the functional act of verbal behavior: "In defining verbal behavior as behavior reinforced through the mediation of other persons, we do not, and cannot, specify any one form, mode, or medium. Any movement capable of affecting another organism may be verbal" (1957, p. 14). Thus, although vocalizations can involve verbal behavior, vocalizations are not necessarily verbal. A child can be engaging in verbal behavior even when there is no vocal behavior.

Skinner distinguished verbal operants by their controlling antecedents and consequences. For example, a *mand* differs from a *tact* with respect to both antecedents and consequences. That is, a mand is only under the stimulus control of the presence of a listener rather than any specific aspect of the environment (e.g., child asks a listener for a cookie), whereas a tact is under the specific stimulus control of some aspect of the environment (e.g., child sees a car). With regard to consequences, a mand is reinforced by specific outcomes related to states of deprivation or aversive stimulation (e.g., getting the cookie as requested), whereas the tact is reinforced by educational consequences—typically social in nature—supplied by the listener (e.g., receiving praise for pointing to the car). The first lesson in PECS aims at developing a manding repertoire because of the relative ease of finding concrete/direct reinforcers, especially for children with autism who, when young, are relatively insensitive to social reinforcers.

The only prerequisite for beginning Phase I of PECS is the identification of powerful reinforcers that can be offered and controlled by a communicative partner (CP). When such an item is presented to the learner by a CP (without any verbal statement or prompts of any kind), the learner is likely to reach for it. A second trainer then immediately physically prompts the child to pick up a picture, reach toward the CP, release the picture, and immediately receive the item. As rapidly as possible, the physical prompts are removed so that the PECS user solely interacts with the CP. This arrangement, however, is artificial with regard to the user's long-term typical environment. It is unlikely that someone will remain right in front of the user, displaying a powerful reinforcer, while a picture is directly in front of the user. Phase II therefore directs teachers to expand a number of critical variables, including the number of different reinforcers, the number of CPs, locations and time of day, the distance between the user and the CP, and the distance between the user and the pictures.

Up to this point in the PECS protocol, only one picture has been available to the user to be exchanged at any point in time. First, the child is taught the general benefit of using pictures to engage in verbal behavior; the child then must learn to choose between pictures. Phase III begins with simple discrimination between a highly preferred item versus one that is not reinforcing (i.e., nonpreferred or possibly mildly aversive). Once this simple discrimination is acquired, then the user is taught to discriminate between equally reinforcing items (i.e., conditional discrimination). Finally, the array of pictures is expanded from two to a virtually unlimited number of comparisons.

In Phase IV of the protocol, users are taught to construct simple sentences of the form "I want X" (where X corresponds to the specific reinforcer) placed on a removable sentence strip. In this manner, the "I want" icon specifies the function of the referent to the CP. Later in the protocol, the learner will learn to use other sentence starters (e.g., "I see," "I have," "It's a") to change the function of the referent picture on the sentence strip from a mand to a tact (or some other verbal function). At this point in the protocol, however, there are only two distinct expansions available: attributes and responsive requesting. The first expansion—broadly called *attributes*—includes pictures that specify distinct aspects of potential reinforcers (e.g., color, shape, size, position). Attributes are traditionally taught via listener or receptive skills (e.g., "Show me red," "Touch the little circle," "Give me the big spoon"). Within this type of lesson, the learner typically receives only social praise but no direct reinforcer; however, the manding function acquired via early PECS use allows these features to better specify reinforcers for the speaker rather than the CP.

Within the same time frame, although not within the same lesson, the protocol teaches users to respond to the simple question, "What do you want?" This Phase V lesson assures that the PECS user can engage in spontaneous requests (both the mand and the mand/tact) as well as requests in a responsive manner (intraverbal/mand). See Bondy, Tincani, and Frost (2004) for a full description of multiply controlled verbal operants.

The final phase of PECS attempts to teach both responsive comments (intraverbal/tact) and pure tacts. Phase VI begins by taking advantage of the previously acquired control of verbal response to questions but alters the function by modifying the consequences. Thus, when a child responds correctly to "What do you want?", he receives the requested item. However, if he responds correctly to "What do you see?", his response is followed by praise—an educational or social reinforcer.

BROAD ISSUES RELATED TO GENERALIZATION

This section describes an array of issues that relate to generalization and then applies them to the specific phases within the PECS protocol. Within behavior analysis, three key terms are required to identify the functional control of a behavior: *antecedent, behavior*, and *consequence* (i.e., the ABCs). Each of these terms can be viewed as related to a specific set of generalization factors.

In stimulus generalization, antecedent events establish functional control over a particular behavior. These stimuli include people, places, and things, as well as features of those people, places, and things. Stimulus generalization and stimulus discrimination are interrelated processes. For example, a very young child's vocalization of *doggie* may be reinforced in the presence of the family dog, as well as in the presence of dogs within the neighborhood; this is stimulus generalization (i.e., an expansion of the array of stimuli that control the response *doggie*). At some point, however, the child is likely to say *doggie* in the presence of a cat. In this case, no reinforcement should be provided; in fact, a new lesson may be arranged. Thus, the control over the vocalization of *doggie* would be narrowed through this type of discrimination training.

Another category of generalization pertains to response variation or modification of the response form itself. For example, the same child might say *doggie* with a lilting tone, which her parents understand implies that she sees (or hears) the dog. At other times, she says *doggie* in an emphatic manner, which her parents respond to as a request for her toy dog. Thus, the way in which she says the word alters its function. Other aspects of behavioral repertoires also are important, such as the rate, duration, intensity, accuracy, fluency, and complexity. Each of these variations may be under the same stimulus control, but other factors may lead to the types of response variations.

The third broad area of generalization is not well referenced in the literature but is supported by the symmetry suggested in the three-term contingency. That is, consequences that control an operant may also vary along particular dimensions; thus, we should plan for reinforcer generalization. At times, such variations may seem more akin to stimulus factors. For example, if a child learns to ask for apples when both apples and toys are shown, it is debatable whether that is more properly viewed as stimulus (two items) or reinforcer generalization (two motivational factors) because both have changed. However, Skinner also wrote about *free operants*, wherein the probability of an operant may vary but not under the specific control of environmental stimuli. Therefore, a child may learn to ask for items that are not in the immediate environment and thus not controlled by specific stimuli. Furthermore, children with autism are often relatively insensitive to social reinforcers, so making reinforcers effective is a generalization issue. Although it may appear reasonably simple to pair social events with currently effective reinforcers such that reinforcer generalization (or transfer of reinforcing properties) occurs, clinical experience suggests that such transfer is actually very difficult to arrange.

Finally, we will consider how generalization can best be promoted. Teachers are responsible for arranging lessons that promote generalization (see Appendices 4.1, 4.2, and 4.3 for sample instructional plans using PECS). Therefore, the learner does not fail to generalize. Rather, it is the teacher who has failed to teach generalization. One key strategy to promote generalization involves making changes in the critical variable—stimulus, behavior characteristic, or consequence factor—in very small steps. These changes should be large enough that the teacher recognizes a change has been made but small enough such that the change does not disrupt the performance.

PHASES I AND II

Generalization Issues

The simple goal of Phase I within PECS is to have a learner pick up a single picture, reach toward the CP, and release the picture into the CP's hand. Often, this lesson is accomplished within the first training session, especially when powerful reinforcers are used and the teachers are well trained. (The particular skills for both the CP and the physical prompter are detailed in Frost & Bondy, 2002, pp. 355–361.) Thus, there may be little time for generalization within this first lesson. However, steps should be taken to avoid conditions that may lead to resistance to generalization (see Table 4.1 for a summary of generalization issues). For example, trainers should avoid using a single reinforcer or a single CP for an extended period of time as these may undermine changes planned for Phase II. In fact, keeping environmental factors constant for an expanded first session can lead to unanticipated prompt dependency, even when the teacher is not aware that a stimulus may come to serve as a prompt. For example, if during the first session the child sat in a chair for 125 trials (assuming the reinforcer is exceptionally powerful and thus does not satiate), attempting to arrange for the child to get up from his chair on the second day of training may prove difficult. Thus, although a teacher may not put into place many variables that would constitute generalization training as planned in Phase II, care must be made during Phase I to avoid making these factors more difficult to introduce.

Table 4.1.   Generalization issues within each phase of the Picture Exchange Communication System (PECS)

Phase	Generalization issues		
	Stimulus	Response	Reinforcer
I: Initiation	Do not keep environmental variables static. Vary the people who serve as communicative partners (CPs). Change the location of the picture on the tabletop.	None	Use a variety of reinforcers.
II: Distance and persistence	Use school, home, and community settings. Use various adults and peers as CPs. Eliminate subtle CP cues.	Vary the distance from the PECS user to the CP. Vary the distance from the PECS user to the picture or book. Evaluate the speed of exchange. Encourage persistence in the PECS user.	Encourage a broad array of reinforcers. Encourage the development of a pure mand.
III: Discrimination	Vary the pictures' positions. Use different types of pictures. Change the organization of the pictures within the book.	Encourage an orienting response.	Compare the strength of reinforcers. Vary the timing of conditioned reinforcers.
IV: Sentence structure	Encourage proper picture order.	Encourage proper use of the sentence strip (speed, pattern). Teach "I want" equivalents. Use strategies to promote vocalizations.	Switch the timing of conditioned reinforcers. Provide differential reinforcement for vocalizations.
V: Respond to "What do you want?"	Ask a variety of questions. Vary the modality of questions.	Examine the time the PECS user takes to respond. Ensure that the proper sequence is used.	Maintain spontaneous and responsive requests.
VI: Commenting	Vary the type of object or event presented. Use surprise. Present responsive and spontaneous situations. Evaluate the source of stimulation (including private events).	Encourage use of all attributes. Teach a variety of sentence starters.	Use various social reinforcers.
Attributes	Present a variety of features of objects and events.	Encourage use of correct sentence order. Encourage use of current repertoire for new item.	Explain "need" versus "like."

Although mastery of Phase I can be accomplished within a single session, such is not the case with Phase II. In fact, it is often said that Phase II never ends; there are so many variables to introduce that they cannot all be provided within a set period of time. There always will be new situations in which to communicate, new people with whom to communicate, and new reinforcers about which one needs to communicate. A set of Phase II variables should be introduced prior to beginning Phase III, but one should continue to plan for and teach Phase II lessons throughout the expansion of PECS. As other skills become introduced via PECS, including using sentence structure, answering questions, using attributes, and commenting, all of the generalization issues related to Phase II must be introduced, as will be discussed in the following sections (see also Table 4.1).

Research

There are many stimulus variables to modify within Phase II, some of which are extremely important to promote functional communication. For example, a variety of CPs must be involved to expand the verbal community, including other teachers and adults (Carr & Felce, 2007b) and the use of peers and siblings (see Kravits, Kamps, & Kemmerer, 2002; Schwartz, Garfinkle, & Bauer, 1998). Environmental changes include areas within a school setting (Charlop-Christy, Carpenter, Le, LeBlanc, & Kelley, 2002; Heneker & Page, 2003; Kravits et al., 2002), community settings such as group homes and fast-food restaurants (Stoner et al., 2006), and the child's home (Koita & Sonoyama, 2004). Areas within a particular setting must also be incorporated into Phase II. That is, both rooms within a school setting and rooms within a home—including variations between floors—must be specifically taught.

Response characteristics of the CP must be planned. For example, the CP may use a wide-eyed, expectant look in Phase I, but such a facial expression may limit the occasions to communicate. Thus, in Phase II children are taught to approach and communicate with an adult who has his or her back turned to the child. Also during early training, the CP provides an open hand to the child for the picture to be placed. This open hand should never be presented prior to the child's initiation (either to the reinforcer or to the picture) or it may come to function as a prompt for communication. Rather, the open hand should be viewed as enhancing the qualities of the audience as described by Skinner (1957, Chapter 7). However, because other members of the verbal community may not know these particular audience features, these features need to be removed over time so that the PECS user learns to use the exchange with anyone available.

The physical location (and possibly the makeup) of the pictures must be varied within Phase II because the pictures (or binder) will not always be in the same location. Thus, children must be taught to take their system wherever they go, just as a child using glasses would be taught to wear them at all times. If the physical design of the picture does not promote easy handling, then modifications of the symbol design may be necessary, such as adding a wooden (or sponge) backing to the picture, using a round symbol so that corners do not promote actions that interfere with the exchange, or other adaptations.

A wide array of reinforcers have been overtly offered in the more than 30 articles published about PECS: food, drinks (including cappuccino vs. orange juice!), toys and games, access to the television, makeup and nail polish, going to the garden, going to bed, access to specific people, and going to the toilet. Obviously, the range of reinforcers must be individually assessed for each PECS user, and these assessments must be continuously updated.

Response generalization factors that are addressed within Phase II include distance to the CP, distance to the pictures (which are placed on or within a communication binder), and persistence with the CP. Most publications involving PECS to date have incorporated the issue of increasing the distance to the CP, typically within a set environment such as a classroom. If a child has ambulatory issues, then the use of a bell or other calling device is recommended, as empirically demonstrated by Almeida, Piza, and LaMonica (2005) with a child with cerebral palsy. Persistence is important because not every request will be reinforced immediately in the real world. Thus, although during the initial PECS sessions each exchange is ideally reinforced, within a reasonable time the schedule of reinforcement needs to be systematically thinned to build resistance to extinction for the exchange. Colloquially speaking, we may need to teach children to nag with PECS!

As noted previously, reinforcer generalization should involve more than just providing for an array of reinforcers. In Phase I, we take advantage of behaviors already in the repertoire associated with obtaining reinforcers: reaching for preferred items, taking them from the tabletop or out of someone's hand. These actions are not communicative nor are they verbal operants—even if the item is in the hand of another person. Within Phase I, the user learns to request a reinforcer by manipulating an available picture into the CP's hand. However, because these first requests are partially controlled by the presence of the reinforcer as well as the presence of the CP, these verbal operants are not pure mands; they may better be viewed as mand/tacts. To encourage the development of the pure mand, the CP must remove all stimuli directly associated with the reinforcer (e.g., its sight, sound, smell). If the PECS user requests a variety of items and events that are not present, then only the availability of an audience member and the current motivational factors control the occasion for the pure mand. The role of associated environmental stimuli in these mands is open to interpretation. For example, if I am in a bar, I have an increased probability of asking for a beer in that setting—even if I have no direct current experience with beer. Similarly, children are more likely to mand for food and drinks in the kitchen than in the laundry room. It is therefore the responsibility of the trainer to teach the PECS user to mand for items not in the immediate environment and to gradually expand the range and type of reinforcer requested.

Another aspect of reinforcer generalization is to work toward the development of new reinforcers. A child may enjoy playing with a marble but only in a highly repetitive and ritualistic fashion, such as bouncing it on a tabletop. Rather than control this response by attempting to limit or even eliminate access to the marble, a more effective strategy—and one consistent with the broad goal of education for all children—would be to expand the ways that the child might come to enjoy the marble. The child should be taught other ways to play with the marble, including using it in a variety of games. In this manner, the marble serves to reinforce a new set of behaviors associated with playing with it. This same approach is necessary for those using PECS to broaden their vocabulary via this expansion of effective reinforcers.

PHASE III

Phase III focuses on discrimination between pictures, but there are many generalization issues that arise within this area of training (see Table 4.1). For example, stimulus factors relate to the type of pictures used. Although discrimination between pictures is the goal of Phase III, the child should not be capable only of discriminating amongst the specific pictures in the binder. If the picture of a specific toy was lost, the child should be able to substitute a similar picture representing "toy."

The placement or position of a picture on the communication board should incorporate generalization from the start of Phase III. For example, if the first two pictures were initially moved back and forth between left and right sides, the user may resist new positions if the pictures were then arranged vertically or diagonally instead. Thus, from the beginning of Phase III, the pictures should show up in all possible positions on the binder during new trials. Similarly, some teachers carefully place the orientation of the individual pictures in perfect alignment with the edges of the binder. If the child responds to this ritualistic alignment issue, then he or she may not adequately respond to the contents of the picture. Thus, loose training (see Chapter 3 for more on this generalization training) should be followed with regard to this variable. To train loosely, one can move the relative position of the referent pictures in the communication binder rather than put them in fixed positions (such as typically occurs with an electronic system).

Some teachers are concerned that the type of picture must be held constant at all times (e.g., all black-and-white line drawings, all full-color photographs). However, children will have to come to discriminate between a wide array of picture types, including brand logos and other product features. Thus, a communication binder with some mixture between picture types is appropriate. For different settings (e.g., home vs. school), the same picture should be used to represent the same item. Also, it is not necessary to take a photograph of every single item of interest to the child. Rather, one should encourage the development of some generic pictures (e.g., cookie, toy, videotape). If these pictures have generalized relations to a class of objects, then further response elaboration will be possible when attributes are addressed. (We will return to this issue later.)

Response generalization issues within Phase III may involve eye orientation and hand actions. When a child is taught in Phase I to pick up a picture, teachers often assume that the eye orientation that preceded reaching for a reinforcer is also established when reaching for the picture. However, some learners do not show distinct orientation to the single picture; rather, they are able to pick it up with some degree of peripheral vision or by feeling for it on a table. If this pattern emerges in the early stages of PECS, the absence of eye orientation may undermine discrimination when two pictures are presented. In this case, several strategies can be used to promote generalized eye orientation to the pictures. For example, the pictures may be placed on a vertical board as opposed to flat on the tabletop. Alternatively, the CP can hold the binder just out of the child's reach; upon seeing the child's visual orientation to the pictures, the CP can then present the binder to the child. In this case, presentation of the binder acts as a reinforcer for eye orientation. Finally, the CP can slowly move the binder, thus encouraging the child to track the position of the binder before reaching for the picture.

Reinforcer generalization issues within Phase III relate to the type of reinforcer used for specific skills within this lesson. For example, in Phase I, placing the picture into the CP's hand is the specific behavior that must be immediately reinforced. Within Phase III, the new target skill is to choose the correct picture, not to give the correct picture. For effective learning to develop, immediate reinforcement for a new skill is necessary. By the time that the child chooses the correct picture, reaches over, and hands it to the CP, a substantial delay has occurred before the CP provides the reinforcer. Therefore, some type of reinforcer must be provided for the selection of the correct picture. It cannot be the item itself, which would erode the action of handing it over. Instead, use a conditioned reinforcer established during Phase I and II (or even before PECS training), such as a pleasant tone of voice (e.g., "Oooh!"), a visual sign (e.g., a thumbs-up), or something else that can be immediately given without interfering with the subsequent exchange. Therefore, upon the selection of the correct picture (as indicated by the child's fingers making contact with it), the CP would immediately provide the conditioned reinforcer; then, upon the placement of the picture into the CP's hand, the reinforcing item would be provided. Care should be taken to develop a range of conditioned reinforcers to prevent a ritualistic pattern from developing.

PHASE IV

The key to Phase IV is the establishment of simple sentence structure within the same requesting function taught in the initial phases. The sentence starter "I want" serves an autoclitic[1] function that specifies the use of the referent in the completed sentence. Because a simple sequential lesson is being developed, a backward chaining[2] strategy should be used to teach completion of the sentence. At this point, because no other sentence starters are being used yet, "I want" does not have meaning. Meaning can only be achieved later in PECS when discrimination between sentence starters is taught.

It is helpful to use a sentence strip (i.e., a removable strip that has room for placement, typically with Velcro, of both a sentence starter and the referent picture), which is placed on the communication book to encourage communicative interaction between the user and the CP. At first, the sentence starter is on the strip and the user is taught to place the reference picture (located on the front of the communication binder) on the strip (as opposed to handing it directly to the CP). Most young users quickly learn to hand over the sentence strip. However, for some this represents a deviation from what they had done in the earlier phases. These users may need to establish this skill as a separate lesson. In terms of generalization, if the user has too long a history of handing over just the referent picture (as in the first three phases), resistance to a change of placement of the referent picture may ensue.

Once the user learns to place the referent picture on the strip, the sentence starter is placed on the front of the communication binder, and the user is taught to place it on the sentence strip. The advantage of using backward chaining is that the

---

[1]Skinner defined *autoclitics* as verbal operants that depend on (or lean on) one's own verbal behavior. That is, the autoclitic is controlled by aspects of the speaker's behavior as opposed to aspects of the environment. For example, in "I want a red apple" *red* is controlled by an aspect of the apple. But in "I really want an apple" *really* is not controlled by the apple—rather it is controlled by properties of the speaker (including state of deprivation, etc.).

[2]*Backward chaining* is teaching a sequential lesson by helping (prompting) the initial steps and aiming to teach the last step first. Once the last step is acquired, the focus becomes the prior step, and so forth. A commonplace example is teaching a child to ride a bicycle. First, the child is helped on the bicycle. Then, he or she is shown how to pedal. Finally, the adult lets go of the bicycle to teach the child the last step—balancing the bicycle. The last step learned is how to get on the bicycle alone and make the bicycle move.

user will simply continue demonstrating the previous skill of putting the referent picture on the strip and handing that over to the CP. As before, physical prompts to put the pictures in their proper location on the strip are faded as quickly as possible.

Generalization Issues

An obvious stimulus generalization issue in Phase IV is the location of the pictures on the binder and strip (see Table 4.1). The CP is responsible for using a routine in which the pictures tend to go on the binder; the user is taught to place them in a proper left-to-right order (for English speakers) on the strip. To encourage the proper placement on the strip, the sentence starter should be placed on the left side of the front of the binder, with the referent(s) going on the right side. The sentence starter should not be moved all over the book; this helps with the speed of putting the sentence together. Once the user has learned to construct the sentence properly, referents can be expanded and all Phase II issues reintroduced.

The left-to-right sequencing presents several interesting issues. First, left/right discriminations are not easy for very young children to make, regardless of disability. Thus, adding visual prompts to help in the correct placement of the pictures may be appropriate for many users. These prompts may include aligning the physical placement and proximity of the pictures on the binder and the strip or using color to highlight type and location factors, either by color of the background of the pictures or color of the edge of the pictures. For example, sentence starters may have a thick blue rim, and referents may have a red rim, with corresponding blue and red squares on the sentence strip. This color coordination may be continued as other verbal functions are expanded and may relate more to stimulus generalization than response generalization.

Response generalization issues include the order of sentence construction, style issues, and speed of construction. For example, although the pictures need to end up in the correct placement on the sentence strip, one can arrange for that by first placing the sentence starter on the left side of the strip or by placing the referent picture on the right side of the strip and then filling in the remainder. A style issue may involve a user who uses both hands to simultaneously properly place both pictures. In either case, an error correction strategy is not necessary if the outcome is consistently correct. The speed issue may broadly relate to fluency issues: the more slowly a user manipulates any single picture, then the more slowly a sentence will be constructed. In such cases, isolating the movements associated with picking up and placing pictures on a target may improve the speed with which this sequence is accomplished.

Over time, users should be taught to expand upon the "I want" phrase and include other forms of request (e.g., "I'd like," "Pass the," "Give me"). These requests should conform not only to adult standards but should also capture the phrases that peers and siblings use within the community.

Reinforcer generalization issues may relate to the timing of the reinforcer from the CP during the construction of the sentence. That is, in the first lesson of this phase, if the user moves the referent onto the strip, the CP should provide some conditional reinforcer (e.g., tone of voice) for this new skill but await receipt of the strip before providing the requested item. Then, when the lesson shifts to placement of the sentence starter, the CP should switch the timing of the conditional reinforcer to the placement of that picture, but no longer for the referent.

Once the proper placement of the pictures is acquired, several steps are added to encourage the use of vocalization and speech. First, when the user hands over the strip, the user should be encouraged to point to the pictures while the teacher reads the sentence aloud. Once the child has learned to point while the teacher reads, a delayed prompting strategy is introduced (i.e., the teacher says, "I want," and then pauses for several seconds). If the child says nothing, the teacher completes the fixed-delay interval by saying the name of the referent and then providing the item. If the child says something during the pause, the teacher should immediately provide the item (in more generous proportions or durations) and provide substantial social reinforcement as well. In this manner, we hope to encourage and richly reinforce vocalization, but we do not view the user as having failed if no speech occurs.

Research

The general effectiveness of the aforementioned strategy for encouraging speech in Phase IV was observed by Bondy and Frost (1994) and then empirically supported by Ganz and Simpson (2004) and Carr and Felce (2007a). Further empirical support for the use of both the delay plus reinforcement during this phase to promote speech was demonstrated by Tincani, Crozier, and Alazetta (2006). Furthermore, Carr and Felce (2007a) also observed that 15% of PECS users increased their vocal production prior to Phase IV. In short, the strategies built into Phase IV promote generalization of functional communication from visual to oral modalities.

PHASE V

The first phases of PECS involved the development of spontaneous communication. Training does not begin with CP statements or questions (e.g., "What do you want?") in an attempt to avoid having such behavior become prompts that are difficult to remove. Of course, as a communicator's repertoire expands, a balance must be achieved between spontaneous and responsive communication. Thus, the goal of Phase V is to assure that a user can appropriately respond to the question of "What do you want?"

The recommended teaching strategy within this phase is to use a gestural prompt (pointing to the "I want" card) with the cue "What do you want?" A progressive time delay is used to transfer stimulus control from the prompt to the cue. Stimulus generalization issues during this aspect of training may involve the degree and type of gestural prompt. Because training is likely to occur across several CPs, a team needs to arrange for similar gestural prompts and good data collection; this assures that everyone is using the same gestural prompt and the same time delay. Once the prompt has been removed, then stimulus issues involve expanding the basic question to functionally equivalent forms, such as "What would you like?" "What'll you have?" and "May I take your order?" (see Table 4.1). It is important to assess the user's natural environment to determine what phrases that are equivalent to "What do you want?" are likely to occur, including assessing phrases used by peers and siblings.

Response generalization includes assuring that the user can respond to the question using proper sentence structure and all of the attributes previously acquired. The amount of time it takes for the user to begin responding to the question, as well as time to complete the response, may be issues in this phase. A very slow reaction to the question may undermine interactions, especially with peers.

Reinforcer generalization issues for this phase often involve ensuring that both spontaneous and responsive requests are maintained. In some settings, teachers rigorously avoid asking any questions in Phases I to IV. Within Phase V, because questions are now permitted to promote communication, some teachers respond as if release from inhibition was in effect—they suddenly ask, "What do you want?" all the time! If this pattern develops, there is a risk that all spontaneous requests may drastically dwindle. Therefore, it is imperative within this phase to ensure that a balance is struck between responsive and spontaneous requests. One way to achieve this goal is to create minimum levels of spontaneous requesting. Thus, a team may not keep precise data on how many times staff ask, "What do you want?" However, they do set a goal of at least 10 spontaneous requests before the end of the school day. Without an effort to keep track of spontaneous requests, their rate may be substantially reduced.

PHASE VI

The goal of the last phase of PECS is to promote commenting (tacting). The primary difference between a request and a comment is the source of reinforcement, from direct or concrete outcomes to social outcomes. Phase VI should begin by taking advantage of the strategies built into the previous phase—that is, responsive communication. Teachers can start by asking questions such as "What do you see?" or "What do you hear?" Once this skill is acquired, attempts can be made to promote spontaneous comments.

Many stimulus generalization issues are involved in this phase (see Table 4.1). One critical factor involves the materials used. Within Phase I, powerful reinforcers are used to elicit reactions that can be converted into communicative acts. If these same objects are used for the commenting lesson, several problems may arise. If a child is shown his or her favorite toy while being asked "What do you see?", the proper reaction to "I see toy" would be "Yes! I see the toy, too," without giving the toy to the child. That is, the provision of the item would shift the response from a tact (an intraverbal/tact, to be precise) to a mand/tact (or an intraverbal/mand/tact). Changing the reinforcer for a behavior may also change its function. Of course, upon seeing that favorite toy but only hearing "Yes, you're right," the child may not be convinced that this outcome is highly reinforcing. Therefore, powerful reinforcers cannot be used to help elicit a comment.

Items that are common to the user's environment should be used, especially at times when those items are not needed (e.g., using a spoon at a time when there are no contextual cues associated with eating or otherwise using a spoon). How the item is presented may relate to the rate of acquisition of commenting. The first comments by typically developing children tend not to be associated with boring events. Rather, children appear to comment about things that are interesting in some way—things that literally capture their attention. Therefore, teachers should present items in an interesting way as a strategy to enhance certain stimulus features that are likely to elicit orienting prior to commenting. Set patterns to the presentation of a series of items should be avoided. It is boring to lay out 10 items, point to them in a set order, and ask, "What do you see?" With a repeated presentation, children have been observed naming the items with their eyes shut! Such verbal behavior is not the tact.

Not only should items be varied, but locations of training should vary as well. Some children learn that it is "naming time" when a fixed location is used. As such, they appear to be commenting, but the primary motivation is to quickly end the lesson and get away from the CP. Commenting should be maintained by the social reinforcers involved. Obviously, it is important to vary the CPs so that commenting can occur with a variety of people in various settings.

Another stimulus factor relates to the type of comment. Essentially, the user should respond to a host of environmental stimuli associated with each sensory modality. Thus, children need to be taught to use a variety of comment starters, including "I hear," "I feel (i.e., touch)," "I smell," and "I taste." These sources of stimulation should be mixed from the start instead of focusing on and mastering one (e.g., seeing) before introducing another (e.g., hearing). Whenever any one modality is the focus of a lesson, teachers should ensure that no other modality is simultaneously provided. For example, teachers should not show a child a bell, ring the bell, and then ask, "What do you hear?" because the child has two sources of stimulation from the bell. With the introduction of a variety of stimulus modalities, the PECS user must learn to visually discriminate between various CP questions and sentence starters (e.g., between "I want" and "I see," between different comment starters).

Perhaps the most difficult stimulus factors involve teaching the child to respond to changes that are typically described as emotions. Statements such as "my knee hurts" are comments/tacts about what Skinner (1957) termed *private events* (i.e., changes that occur within the skin). The difficulty in teaching this skill is for the CP to know the current state of internal stimulation for the user. That is, a child can only be taught to communicate that his or her knee hurts while the knee actually hurts! As Skinner pointed out, the CP uses public information, such as observing a child fall and subsequently bleed from the knee, as well as collateral responses, such as crying. At that point, the CP must model the child's feeling, usually by saying (or using pictures to denote), "Oh, you poor kid! Your knee hurts!" The child can then respond, "My knee hurts." Stimulus and response generalization may occur later when the child falls again but lands on an elbow. The child approaches the CP and responds, "My elbow hurts"—in effect meaning that his elbow feels like his knee did when the CP told him that his knee hurts. This process must continue in similar fashion for other feelings, such as "I like," "I feel scared," and "I'm happy."

The final stimulus issue in this phase is to transfer stimulus control from the combination of the CP's question plus the item to the item itself—that is, to shift from an intraverbal/tact to a pure tact. A variety of strategies may be used to eliminate the question, including shortening the words (and sounds) associated with the question, gradually lowering the volume of the question, or using a time delay between the presentation of the item and the question. Once this shift is achieved, it is critical to ensure the transfer is observed in a variety of settings.

Response generalization issues include discriminating between pure mands and pure tacts, typically described as spontaneous communication. Another factor involves changing the use of attributes initially acquired within the request function into commenting (e.g., from "I want big ball" or "I want loud music" to "I see big ball" or "I hear loud music").

ATTRIBUTES

As noted previously, specifying a mand with an attribute (or tact) is possible without the user needing to acquire listener skills for the same attribute. Just as a child can learn to ask for a ball before he or she can successfully respond to "Give me the ball," so too can a child learn to ask for the red ball before he or she can successfully respond to "Give me the red ball." However, because these repertoires are acquired independently, teachers should not expect automatic generalization from speaker to listener. A child who can ask for a ball by various attributes still needs to be taught to respond to those same features as a listener.

Generalization Issues

One of the key stimulus generalization issues for attributes relates to the use of more than one attribute with a particular object as well as more than one object with a particular attribute. That is, if colors are being taught using crayons, teachers need to ensure that the child can use the same colors to specify other objects (e.g., toys, cups, clothing). Furthermore, other attributes need to be used to describe crayons (e.g., long/short, thick/thin, pointed/dull). If these multiple arrangements are not made, then an attribute can become narrowly associated with a particular object (or class of objects) and undermine long-term stimulus generalization.

The most commonly taught attributes relate to color, size, shape, and number, but it is important to expand such descriptors to location, relative position, speed, temperature, and even actions associated with items (e.g., "I want bounce ball" vs. "I want kick ball"). Here, too, it is important to teach "kick" and "bounce" with regard to other objects, not just balls.

Traditional reinforcer assessments create situations designed to determine what the learner likes by evaluating the learner's reactions to offered items. However, teachers should expand the items that a PECS user may request by creating opportunities in which various items are needed via strategies such as interrupted chains and blocked responses. For example, a child may display little interest in a box unless it contains a reinforcing item. If the child learns to open the container to obtain the item within, then various features of the container (e.g., color, shape, size) can be used within a requesting format.

Research

An important demonstration of response generalization comes from the work of Marckel, Neef, and Ferreri (2006). They taught two young boys with autism to improvise their PECS sentences using attributes such as color, shape, and function to request items for which they had no corresponding picture. These skills generalized to new items, CPs, and environments. This study therefore demonstrated that it is not necessary to have a one-to-one relationship between each picture and each item in the environment. In fact, it is the lack of such correspondence that promotes the novelty associated with improvisation.

REINFORCERS

One reinforcer generalization issue that relates to each phase of PECS concerns the schedule of reinforcement for requests as well as comments. As briefly noted in

Phase II, one aim is to teach users to be persistent with various CPs. In part, persistence is needed because in the real world not all potential CPs will be attentive to the communicative attempts of PECS users. Therefore, teachers need to systematically thin schedules of reinforcement (i.e., gradually reduce the ratio of reinforcement for the behavior) to promote resistance to extinction that could otherwise occur when schedules suddenly decrease in rate in certain situations.

Several strategies can be used to alter rates of reinforcement. For example, a CP can simply ignore the request initially for a short period of time and then gradually extend the delay between the request and the reinforcer. While ignoring the request, the CP can engage in various typical activities, such as working with another student, talking with someone else, or talking on the telephone. For some children, this is a perfect time to teach waiting, including the use of a specific "wait" visual cue. Another way of signaling that the reinforcer will be available later is to put the picture of the requested item on a visual schedule system. This strategy attempts to teach the child that the item is available after certain other activities are completed. Another way to thin the overall schedule is to withhold the reinforcer entirely. For example, a child may ask for something that is no longer available, either because all have been used or someone else is using the item. Finally, every child must learn at some point that at times the CP simply will not provide the reinforcer; instead, the CP may respond by saying "no."

The point of each of these strategies is to teach persistence—that is, to have the user maintain a high rate of communicative attempts under various local rates of reinforcement. With this training or without, some children engage in very high rates of requesting that some CPs view as nagging or generally bothersome. It is very tempting for the CP to consider removing access to the entire communication system or merely the picture of the requested item as a way to undermine the pestering requests. However, we must recognize the important ethical issue involved. The pictures belong to the user, not the CP. Children who speak also often nag us with their vocal requests; although some of us may think about taping the child's mouth shut, no one actually does it because it would be unethical. Similarly, we would not tie the hands of a signing nagger. The pictures belong to the user and should never be removed as a way to control the rate of requesting.

MAKING THE TRANSITION FROM THE PICTURE EXCHANGE COMMUNICATION SYSTEM TO OTHER MODALITIES

Although the primary goal of PECS is to teach functional communication skills, it is hoped, especially with younger children, that users will eventually acquire and solely use speech. However, for some children, the acquisition of speech will remain elusive at best. For these individuals, it may be helpful for someone who uses PECS to develop skills with another visual modality, such as an electronic voice output communication aid (VOCA).

Four standards should be observed to justify the complete transition from PECS to another modality.

1. *The repertoire size must match*—If a child begins to speak, he or she must continue to have access to PECS materials until vocal output matches the number of pictures in the repertoire.

2. *The rate of initiation for the new modality must be equivalent*—If a child can initiate 40 or more times a day with PECS but only signs in imitation or following a question from the CP, then removing access to PECS will undermine initiation.

3. *The complexity of the sentence structure must be the same*—If a child can reliably construct "I want two big red candies" using PECS but can only say the word *candy* (even if spontaneous), then removing access to PECS undermines the many communication skills that will not be immediately available.

4. *The communicator must be able to be understood by a large number of naïve CPs before limiting access to PECS*—If a child speaks (or signs) but is only understood by a limited number of CPs (e.g., mother and teacher), then removing access to PECS severely limits the size of the child's verbal community.

If these four guidelines are not followed, then the removal of access to PECS would essentially be taking skills away from the child; this too is highly unethical. Furthermore, it would be equally unethical to remove PECS in an attempt to force or promote the transition to another communication modality. If we want to alter the rate of PECS use, we must rely on contingencies of reinforcement. During a transition, no skills should be lost.

SUGGESTIONS AND LIMITATIONS

One broad issue relating to research about PECS involves how to separate factors that relate to the modality per se and the teaching strategies associated with particular skills. Poor teaching strategies can undermine any communication modality. Coupling poor picture-based teaching strategies with highly effective sign-based strategies (or vice versa) can readily bias the outcome of a study. However, trying to match teaching strategies across modalities can be very difficult. Instead, a two-person prompt strategy can be used to promote spontaneity in Phase I—a strategy that has been used with signing (Tincani, 2004) and a VOCA (Bock, Stoner, Beck, Hanley, & Prochnow, 2005) in studies comparing these modalities with PECS. Future research should determine whether this two-person strategy is effective at minimizing prompt dependency regardless of modality.

An important area for improved teaching strategies involves discrimination training. Within the PECS manual (Frost & Bondy, 2002), a number of alternative strategies are described because there are no perfect lessons. Improvements in discrimination training as well as in error correction strategies will need to be systematically incorporated into the basic protocol in order to increase the options that trainers have available.

Another critical generalization issue relates to strategies designed to promote and maximize speech production and development for those using PECS. Especially for the very young, it is not recommended to solely use an alternative modality; thus, the field must continue to expand on strategies that promote functional communication within any modality while also enhancing vocal expansion and hopefully replacement. Strategies that help promote vocal production may not be sufficient to promote full replacement of an alternative modality; thus, these two issues need to be researched as separate factors. Further research also is necessary to help in the early assessment of which modality may best fit the behavioral characteristics of individuals who display difficulty in acquiring speech. For example, although some suggest waiting a particular period of time before introducing PECS (or some other nonvocal modality), no research currently supports this practice.

SUMMARY

This chapter reviewed a wide array of issues pertaining to stimulus, response, and reinforcer generalization with regard to PECS use. Although some of these issues are unique to PECS and its medium, many issues relate to universal factors associated with effective teaching strategies to promote verbal behavior. Research should continue to focus attention on the design of teaching and generalization strategies that promote functional communication independent of modality, as well as issues pertaining to making the transition from any one modality to another.

REFERENCES

Almeida, M., Piza, M., & LaMonica, D. (2005). Adaptações do sistema de comunicação por troca de figuras no contexto escolar [Adaptation of the Picture Exchange Communication System in a school context]. *Pró-Fono Revista de Atualização Científica, 17*, 233–240.

Bock, S.J., Stoner, J.B., Beck, A.R., Hanley, L., & Prochnow, J. (2005). Increasing functional communication in non-speaking preschool children: Comparison of PECS and VOCA. *Education and Training in Developmental Disabilities, 40*, 264–278.

Bondy, A., & Frost, L. (1994). The Picture Exchange Communication System. *Focus on Autistic Behavior, 9*, 1–19.

Bondy, A., Tincani, M., & Frost, L. (2004). Multiply controlled verbal operants: An analysis and extension to the Picture Exchange Communication System. *The Behavior Analyst, 27*, 247–261.

Carr, D., & Felce, J. (2007a). Increase in production of spoken words in some children with autism after PECS teaching to Phase III. *Journal of Autism and Developmental Disabilities, 37*, 780–787.

Carr, D., & Felce, J. (2007b). The effects of PECS teaching to Phase III on the communicative interactions between children with autism and their teachers. *Journal of Autism and Developmental Disabilities, 37*, 724–737.

Charlop-Christy, M.H., Carpenter, M., Le, L., LeBlanc, L., & Kelley, K. (2002). Using the Picture Exchange Communication System (PECS) with children with autism: Assessment of PECS acquisition, speech, social-communicative behavior, and problem behaviors. *Journal of Applied Behavior Analysis, 35*, 213–231.

Frost, L., & Bondy, A. (1994). *The Picture Exchange Communication System training manual.* Cherry Hill, NJ: PECS.

Frost, L., & Bondy, A. (2002). *The Picture Exchange Communication System (PECS) training manual* (2nd ed.). Newark, DE: Pyramid Products.

Ganz, J., & Simpson, R. (2004). Effects on communicative requesting and speech development of the Picture Exchange Communication System in children with characteristics of autism. *Journal of Autism and Developmental Disabilities, 34*, 395–409.

Heneker, S., & Page, L.M. (2003). Functional communication: The impact of PECS. *Speech & Language Therapy in Practice*, 12–14.

Koita, H., & Sonoyama, S. (2004). Communication training using the Picture Exchange Communication System (PECS): Case study of a child with autistic disorder. *Japanese Journal of Behavior Analysis, 19*, 161–174.

Kravits, T.R., Kamps, D.M., & Kemmerer, K. (2002). Brief report: Increasing communication skills for an elementary-aged student with autism using the Picture Exchange Communication System. *Journal of Autism and Developmental Disorders, 32*, 225–230.

Marckel, J.M., Neef, N.A., & Ferreri, S.J. (2006). A preliminary analysis of teaching improvisation with the Picture Exchange Communication System to children with autism. *Journal of Applied Behavior Analysis, 39,* 109–115.

Mills, R., & Wing, L. (2006). *Researching interventions in autistic spectrum disorders and priorities for research.* Paper presented at the Second World Autism Congress, Cape Town, South Africa.

Schwartz, I.S., Garfinkle, A.N., & Bauer, J. (1998). Communicative outcomes for young children with disabilities. *Topics in Early Childhood Special Education, 18,* 144–159.

Skinner, B.F. (1957). *Verbal behavior.* Englewood Cliffs, NJ: Prentice-Hall.

Stahmer, A., Collings, N., & Palinkas, L. (2005). Early intervention practices for children with autism: Descriptions from community providers. *Focus on Autism and Other Developmental Disabilities, 20,* 66–79.

Stoner, J., Beck, A., Bock, S., Hickey, K., Kosuwan, K., & Thompson, J. (2006). The effectiveness of the Picture Exchange Communication System with nonspeaking adults. *Remedial and Special Education, 27,* 154–165.

Tincani, M. (2004). Comparing the Picture Exchange Communication System and sign language training for children with autism. *Focus on Autism and Other Developmental Studies, 19,* 152–163.

Tincani, M., Crozier, S., & Alazetta, L. (2006). The Picture Exchange Communication System: Effects on manding and speech development for school–aged children with autism. *Education and Training in Developmental Disabilities, 41,* 177–184.

Chapter 4
Appendices

Instructional Plan for PECS Staff Party

Goal domain:	Communication
Behavioral objective:	Upon seeing a desired item controlled by another person, the student will request that item using appropriate PECS skills.
Current lesson status:	☐ Acquisition ☑ Fluency ☐ Maintenance
Mastery criterion:	Independently request two items during a 10-minute activity using currently mastered PECS level

Reinforcement

Reinforcer (during task):	Social:	Natural:		Additional:	praise from staff
	Tangible:	Natural:		Additional:	
Reinforcer (end of task):	Social:	Natural:		Additional:	praise from staff
	Tangible:	Natural:	access to requested item	Additional:	

Current rate or ratio:	1 : 1
Goal rate or ratio:	1 : 2 (goal ratio reflects that not every request will result in reinforcement)

Generalization

Stimulus factors (e.g., people, place, materials, supervision):	New staff at school, people in the community, family members New activities: snack, play area, art, gym, playground with various items appropriate to activity.
Response factors (rate, accuracy, duration, etc):	Student will request within 20 seconds of seeing item being enjoyed by adults; student will request 5 times during a 15-minute activity.
Type of lesson:	☑ Sequential ☐ Discrete
Error correction:	☐ Backstep (if student approaches without picture or sentence strip, adult not holding the item takes student back to start level and physically prompts to PECS book) ☐ 4-Step
Current stimulus control:	All requests are to adults within structured activities
Long-term stimulus control (natural cue):	Requests from anyone who has a desired item
Teaching strategy:	Time delay, peer modeling, two-person prompting

Lesson details (include: activity, materials, teacher lead and/or student initiated):	One staff member boisterously walks into classroom, obviously enjoying items that are favorites of many of the students. The other staff members show exaggerated interest and approach her and begin eating/playing. All staff members "peripherally" ignore the students–turn their backs and so forth while still allowing students to see what they have. When students approach staff members, if they do not ask for the item via PECS, but instead revert to previously learned behaviors (e.g., pulling on arms, fussing, grabbing), continue to ignore the students or feign confusion ("I don't understand."). If a student gets his book and approaches and asks for the item, loudly praise him and make a big show of giving him the item. If students continue to not go get their PECS books, one staff member can casually walk toward the books with some of the toys/food. If students still do not get their PECS books, have the staff person near their books use one of the books to ask another staff person for some of her food/toys. If students still have difficulty and still show interest in the item, have one staff person give all of her "goods" to another and then go act as physical prompter for a student, helping a student to get his or her book and ask. If this level of prompting is necessary, after the student asks for something and gets it, put his or her book back in its original position and continue.		
Data:	1	times/week	Type:	Frequency count/level of independence

Instructional Plan for PECS Request to Peer

Goal domain:	Communication				
Behavioral objective:	When a peer has/controls a desired object/activity, the student will approach and request using PECS at an appropriate level.				
Current lesson status:	☑ Acquisition		☐ Fluency		☐ Maintenance

Reinforcement

Reinforcer (during task):	*Social:*	Natural:		Additional:	praise from staff
	Tangible:	Natural:		Additional:	
Reinforcer (end of task):	*Social:*	Natural:		Additional:	
	Tangible:	Natural:	access to requested item	Additional:	
Current rate or ratio:	1:1				
Goal rate or ratio:	1:3 (goal ratio reflects that not every request will result in reinforcement from a peer)				

Generalization

Stimulus factors (e.g., people, place, materials, supervision):	People: Peers at school, siblings and other children at home Activities: Snack, play area, art, gym, playground with various items appropriate to activity
Response factors (rate, accuracy, duration, etc.):	The student will request within 30 seconds of item being offered; student will request 5 times during a 15-minute activity
Type of lesson:	☑ Sequential ☐ Discrete
Error correction:	☑ Backstep (if the student requests from an adult, say "I don't have it" and guide back to starting point. If no correct response within 5 seconds, second trainer physically prompts to the peer.) ☐ 4-Step
Current stimulus control:	All requests are to adults within classroom
Long-term stimulus control (natural cue):	Makes requests to adults and peers at school; makes requests to parents and siblings at home.
Teaching strategy:	Two-person prompting toward peer as communicative partner

Lesson details (include: activity, materials, teacher lead and/or student initiated):	Peer/sibling may need encouragement to share items. Consider starting with items less preferred by peer. Arrange to reinforce peer for sharing.			
Data:	3	times/week	Type:	Frequency count/level of independence

Instructional Plan for Mr. Potato Head

Goal domain:	Communication: PECS Phase IV and beyond
Behavioral objective:	When given only the potato portion of any Mr. Potato Head toy, the student will request missing parts using a sentence strip
Current lesson status:	☑ Acquisition ☐ Fluency ☐ Maintenance
Mastery criterion:	90% accuracy in constructing sentence in correct order and in using correct body part picture

Reinforcement

Reinforcer (during task):	Social:	Natural:		Additional:	praise from staff
	Tangible:	Natural:		Additional:	
Reinforcer (end of task):	Social:	Natural:	access to requested item	Additional:	
	Tangible:	Natural:		Additional:	

Current rate or ratio:	1:1
Goal rate or ratio:	1:1

Generalization

Stimulus factors (e.g., people, place, materials, supervision):	New Potato Head toy
Response factors (rate, accuracy, duration, etc):	Add attributes such as color/size to requests
Type of lesson:	☑ Sequential (sentence structure ☑ Discrete (body part discrimination)
Error correction:	☑ Discrete ☑ 4-Step
Current stimulus control:	Can request desired items using "I want" and correct sentence strip length. Likes assembling Mr. Potato Head and can do so independently.
Long-term stimulus control (natural cue):	Has empty potato and no parts/accessories
Teaching strategy:	Discrimination training with correspondence checks

Lesson details (include: activity, materials, teacher lead and/or student initiated):	Present student with an empty potato from any Mr. or Mrs. Potato Head toy and withhold body parts and accessories. Present student with an activity board or PECS book with necessary pictures and wait for the student to construct and exchange a sentence strip. Conduct a correspondence check to determine correct body part/accessory picture use. Over subsequent opportunities for this lesson, reduce the frequency of correspondence checks. For response generalization, once the student has begun using attributes, add a variety of Mr. Potato Head toys to incorporate color, size, and other characteristics in requests.		
Data:	1	times/week	Type:	accuracy of body part/accessory picture use

5

Social Stories, Categorization, and Generalization in Autism Spectrum Disorders

Carol Gray

Parents and professionals use Social Stories™ at home, school, and in the community to help children with autism spectrum disorders (ASDs) understand and respond more effectively to people, situations, activities, and events. They equip themselves with pen, paper, and computer to become the authors of social understanding. Coupled with the urgency that parents and professionals often feel, Social Stories are placed in the role of ambassadors, negotiating the differences between two equally valid—but often different—perspectives. In this position, Social Stories have successfully addressed an extensive range of topics for many years.

Every author has an opportunity to paint pictures in the mind of another person, via words and illustrations that merge with the experience of the reader to create shared meaning. Authors of Social Stories have this same opportunity and a disarming responsibility. They write with an awareness of the need for accuracy, as well as a keen sense that the trust of this audience is to be continually earned and never assumed.

Children with autism are an interesting and challenging audience. They often have unique perspectives and interpretations of words and events that result in responses that take others by surprise. Children with autism also have difficulty with the development of concepts and the generalization of related skills. A child may successfully learn a skill in one setting and fail to demonstrate it in another.

This chapter discusses the challenge of categorization and generalization, focusing specifically on what authors of Social Stories can do to help children with ASDs learn accurate and meaningful concepts and categories and apply them effectively across time and place.

CATEGORIZATION, GENERALIZATION, AND AUTISM SPECTRUM DISORDERS

In this chapter, the terms *categorization* and *generalization* are used in reference to their role in social communication and behavior. Both require the perception of similar characteristics: the former to form a group, concept, or category; the latter to recognize and respond effectively to a similar stimulus across contexts. Categorization and generalization make it possible to note similarities among differences and support the filing and cross-referencing of information for future use. They are abilities rooted in cognitive processes that continually sort and re-sort our perceptions, experiences, and interactions—with everything inanimate, animate, or abstract—into a personalized, user-friendly system of identification, retrieval, and application across time and place. Simply stated, categorization and generalization are the ultimate in daily planners, continually building meaning into what we perceive while informing and guiding each of our responses—with cross-referencing and speed that would put any computer processor to shame.

Similar to the way plastic bins can be used to sort toys and bring order to a playroom, categorization organizes experience. Typically developing infants demonstrate an understanding of categories before their first birthday (Quinn & Oates, 2004). While there is relatively little research on categorization in children with ASDs, recognition of its importance is growing. Gastgeb, Strauss, and Minshew (2006) noted, "Categorization reduces demands on memory and allows individuals to focus on important aspects of objects and ignore irrelevant details" (p. 1717). They added that an inability to effectively organize experience could lead to overstimulation, withdrawal, and confusion. This may explain, at least in part, how impaired abilities "might become rapidly overtaxed by their failure to automatically categorize information" (p. 1717). An organized playroom is more conducive to play and learning than one that is in disarray.

Research to determine whether the categorization abilities of individuals with ASDs are impaired has been mixed and has varied according to the types of categories that are used. Some categories have boundaries that are clear, distinct, and more readily identified, as those defined by color or shape. Naturally occurring categories (Rosch, 1978), such as *birds,* follow classification rules that are not as readily apparent. If division lines between categories are not obvious, then the categorization task may be difficult. Typically, prototypes serve as models of the most average or best representative member of a category or concept. Evidence suggests that the formation of prototypes is impaired in individuals with ASDs (Gastgeb et al., 2006; Klinger & Dawson, 2001; Plaisted, 2000). Later in this chapter, we will look at the implications this may have on a child's understanding of a category like *apple* and discuss how carefully constructed Social Stories may address this concern.

Categorization supports generalization. For parents and professionals, the relative ease of generalization makes it hard to imagine navigating a day without it. Perhaps that is why—with all good intentions and near-heroic efforts—they sometimes fail to anticipate a child's difficulty with generalization and are surprised by his or her responses or distress. The key is to systematically expect and address generalization issues as a part of the educational process. According to the Committee on Educational Interventions for Children with Autism:

> The process of generalization of learning needs to be anticipated and supported, and so parents of children with autism need to be more closely involved in the educational process than do parents of children with many other childhood disorders. (2001, p. 35)

Speaking parent to parent in *The Oasis Guide to Asperger Syndrome,* Patricia Romanowski Bashe and Barbara L. Kirby provide a similar caution:

Your child may be learning a range of skills in different areas: how to greet friends in socialization, how to organize himself for work in school, how to tie his shoes in OT [occupational therapy]. Still, he needs you to help him learn to use them in the real world. (2001, p. 327)

These issues have implications for authors of Social Stories. Consideration of the perspective of the child with ASD has been important to Social Stories for many years. Now, it includes anticipation of the issues related to generalization as part of that process. This sets the direction for story research, development, and implementation, with planning throughout to support the generalization of concepts and skills.

SOCIAL STORIES

Social Stories (Gray & Garand, 1993) describe ideas, concepts, activities, events, skills, and interactions according to 10 criteria that define 1) their goal; 2) the process that develops and implements them; and 3) their individualized format, voice, and vocabulary. A Social Story may address any of the following topics (and beyond): demonstrating a concept; helping a child prepare for a future event; describing how to do something; explaining an anxiety-producing object or situation; providing reassurance; discussing a specific element of communication or interaction; sharing information about what others know, feel, or believe; or teaching a self-regulation strategy. In addition, half of all Social Stories describe, acknowledge, and/or praise what a child currently does well. For each story that introduces new information, another is developed that applauds positive understandings and skills that are already a part of a child's repertoire.

It is important to note that just as authors may fail to anticipate a child's challenges with generalization, so too are they at risk of missing the identification of many concepts and ideas that a Social Story can address. Authors easily and effortlessly form concepts; they have been doing so for years. Understandably, that which occurs outside of an author's awareness is likely to be missed as a potential Social Story topic. Interestingly, what does require a conscious effort is the identification of these concepts and their translation into practical topics and effective stories. It is these elusive, intuitive topics—which are so difficult for authors to conceptualize—that are likely to be among the most critical for them to address.

The term *Social Story* is most frequently used in reference to a physical document. By definition, a Social Story is both a product and the process that creates and implements it. Authors gather information, considering the perspective of their audience while at the same time filtering assumptions and attributions to ensure that a story is accurate. Text and accompanying illustrations are developed according to criteria that give a Social Story its characteristic patient and reassuring quality. Always introduced in a calm and comfortable context, every story is continually monitored and revised if needed. The process of gathering information and developing and implementing a story is critically important, although it is frequently overlooked in research and practice.

The definition of what is (and is not) a Social Story has varied little in terms of its basic features over time, with periodic revision to reflect current research and understanding. The first formal description of Social Stories was published by Gray and Garand (1993) and subsequently clarified as a list of 10 defining characteristics in Social Stories 10.0 (Gray, 2004). Research has since improved our understanding of the nature of ASDs, as well as the use of Social Stories as an educational tool, thus resulting in Social Stories 10.1 (Gray, 2008), the first major revision of its predecessor. (See Appendix 5.1 for a list of the defining criteria in Social Stories 10.1.)

Social Story Research

Developed in 1991, Social Stories gained widespread acceptance in a relatively short time, largely due to their often immediate and dramatic results. Educators were surprised. Considering the severity and complexity of autism, how could a simple document have such a big impact? In a field with more questions than answers, Social Stories spelled success for students with ASDs and educators alike, quickly earning the enthusiastic affection of their authors and "word-of-mouth" popularity. Their use in homes, schools, and clinics was soon widespread.

A paper by Carol Rowe (1999), a teacher, is representative of the case studies that initially fueled the popularity of Social Stories. Rowe's student, George, was a second-year pupil in a primary school. Daily preparations for lunch would initiate George's refusal to go to the cafeteria, with claims that the other children were "disgusting" and "noisy." George was interviewed, and his perspective of lunch in the cafeteria was considered. A Social Story titled *Lunch Time* was subsequently developed. The change in George's response was immediate and dramatic. George reviewed the story and said, "Now I'll know what to do!" He completed all aspects of the lunch routine and stated, "I've had a happy lunch time." Review of the story was gradually decreased from once each school day in the first 6 weeks to its discontinuation at 12 weeks. George's improved lunchtime behavior continued after review of the story ceased. Staff could support George in other school activities by cuing the story (i.e., repeating selected lines) to generalize story concepts to other school activities.

Successes similar to the one reported by Rowe fueled the grassroots acceptance and use of Social Stories in homes, schools, and clinics prior to any scientific scrutiny of their effectiveness. Several studies have since confirmed the benefit of using Social Stories with individuals with ASDs (Barry & Burlew, 2004; Dettmer, Simpson, Myles, & Ganz, 2000; Hagiwara & Myles, 1999; Kuoch & Mirenda, 2003; Kuttler, Myles, & Carlson, 1998; Lorimer, Simpson, Myles, & Ganz, 2002; Norris & Dattilo, 1999; Scattone, Wilczynski, Edwards, & Rabian, 2002; Swaggart et al., 1995), with evidence that Social Stories should be considered an established effective educational practice (Horner et al., 2005; Wright, 2007). Benefit is measured by decreases in negative behavior, increases in positive behavior, or both. If discussion of generalization of a target behavior is included, it is used in reference to the demonstration of a targeted behavior in other contexts.

Emphasis on evidence-based practice has increased the interest in Social Story research. However, there is variability in the quality of research and a need to improve evaluation of the approach. A research summary by Sansosti, Powell-Smith, and Kincaid (2004) concluded that many of the positive research outcomes that lend support to the use of Social Stories must be considered with caution. They noted several experimental flaws including "a lack of experimental control, weak treatment effects, or confounding treatment variables" (p. 200), factors that make it difficult to determine if Social Stories are responsible for the reported improvements in behavior. Their suggestions for future research include study of the generalization of acquired concepts and skills across contexts and over time.

Rust and Smith (2006) discussed similar concerns related to Social Story research, noting that "by their very nature Social Stories are *individualized* interventions that need to be appropriate to the specific levels of understanding and abilities of children. These factors make large-scale, systematic evaluation difficult" (p. 131). The authors detailed several suggestions for future testing and study, among them a concern related to the Social Story process: how each story is formulated and implemented.

The goal of a Social Story has always been to safely and meaningfully share accurate social information. It is an author-focused goal that does not include changes in the behavior of the person with ASD. To date, there has not been a study of how well this goal is being met. Although it is necessary to use a behavioral count to measure efficacy, authors are encouraged to focus on the experience of the person with ASD and the identification and sharing of information that he or she may be missing. Authors hold the responsibility for meeting the goal. Similar to tests that measure other quality factors in a study, any story can be compared against the 10 defining criteria to determine if it is (or is not) a Social Story. Although the topic and content of Social Stories will vary, adherence to the 10 criteria that define a Social Story should be consistent from one study to the next. This is central to ensuring that the object of study is similar across research efforts, results are comparable and cumulative, and perhaps most importantly, each story is safe for its audience.

Generalization in Social Stories Research

Very few studies have focused specifically on how well the ideas, concepts, and skills presented in a Social Story generalize to other settings. Kuttler et al. (1998) reported a decrease in precursors to tantrum behavior using two stories, one for each of two school contexts (morning class and lunch), whereas Hagiwara and Myles (1999) used one story (with slight revisions) across settings, reporting some generalization across two of them. In another study, Ivey, Heflin, and Alberto (2004) proposed that Social Stories may build flexibility for novel events within a familiar routine and context. Three children participated in the study, reviewing Social Stories describing unique activities that introduced changes in the typical routine. The authors concluded that the Social Stories were effective in introducing novel routines and may be helpful for a variety of purposes in other contexts.

In the discussion section of many Social Story research articles, generalization is often mentioned in terms of a story's effectiveness (i.e., behavioral changes were—or were not—observed in other contexts). However, examination of the stories used in these studies frequently reveals little evidence or description of efforts to gather information that would foster topic expansion. In addition, features that might support generalization are not a part of story development, nor are they evident in the stories themselves. Although Social Stories are good, they are not that good. Without attention to the Social Story process, specifically efforts to address the challenges related to generalization, an author relies on a wish and a hope that concepts and skills will transfer across time and context.

SOCIAL STORIES 10.1 AND THREE CRITERIA MOST RELEVANT TO GENERALIZATION

Research from a variety of sources continues to contribute to our understanding of the neurological basis of autism and the use of Social Stories as an educational intervention. As mentioned previously, Social Stories 10.1 reflects these new developments. Each criterion serves as a guide to story development and quality. The following section focuses on 3 of the 10 criteria that are most directly related to the organization and presentation of information and thus most likely to hold important links to categorization and generalization: the goal, the information, and the format. (See also Appendix 5.2.)

The Goal

The first criterion identifies the goal of every Social Story: *to share relevant and accurate information*, providing answers to questions that people typically take for granted. This has consistently been the goal since the introduction of the approach (Gray, 1998, 2004, 2008; Gray & Garand, 1993). Social Stories 10.1 formally reiterates this goal with inclusion of many of the current defining criteria.

The goal of a Social Story is to share relevant and accurate information that 1) has an overall patient and reassuring quality; 2) is presented via an audience-tailored content, format, voice, and vocabulary that supports meaning, understanding, and generalization; and 3) is socially and emotionally safe. Every aspect of story research, development, and implementation demonstrates consideration of this goal (Gray, 2008).

The goal of a Social Story has never included any reference to changes in behavior. Admittedly, behavior may be the impetus to develop and implement a story, a change in behavior may result, and behavior serves as the best empirical measure of a story's effectiveness. However, Social Stories are based on a goal that is broader than the behavioral focus of their research, with roots in the process that creates and implements them. Attention to behavior as a measure of effectiveness should not diminish the importance of the goal or the responsibility of authors to develop stories with this broader goal always in mind.

The goal includes audience-tailored content, voice, and vocabulary. Many authors readily tailor text and illustrations to the abilities of the audience, and these factors are important to generalization. If information is too difficult, it will not be understood, nor will it generalize. Similarly, if the text or illustrations are too easy, they will insult and lose their audience. This being said, practical experience suggests that the importance of tailoring to ability—although critical to comprehension and meaning—pales in comparison to the impact of incorporating a child's interest. Kluth and Schwarz (2008) have filled a book with ideas on how to use a child's fascinations, interests, or areas to build relationships, expand communication, and encourage risk taking, to name just a few. Informal experience suggests the same is true of Social Stories. When an author incorporates a child's interests into text, illustration, format, or delivery, he or she captivates the interest of the audience, fosters ownership of Social Story content, and creates an opportunity for generalization.

A case example from my previous position as a consultant in the school system provides a hallmark example of a parent's understanding of the Social Story goal and its important ties to generalization. Jacob was a wiry, intelligent 9-year-old boy who was fascinated by—and had a rather impressive command of details concerning—the U.S. Postal System. I was conducting several workshops during this period of time, which made it possible to send Jacob's stories to him via the U.S. mail in a variety of containers. Jacob was thrilled to receive these stories and delighted that they arrived from several different zip codes. Excited by his stories and their unique delivery, Jacob would create a postage stamp to represent the content of each. The stories were all stored in a file box that was decorated to look like a mailbox and were filed according to the postmark of the date they had been sent. This system of organization made sense to Jacob and was easy for him to use; he could recall in detail the content of any story by first thinking of its postmark.

Jacob's mother proved to be a central part of her son's opportunity to generalize the information in the stories and mix and match their topics as needed. Like her son, she memorized the postmark filing system, making flash cards for herself to painstakingly learn each postmark and its corresponding story topic and content. As Jacob would encounter a new situation, or when he was confused or concerned about what was occurring or what to do next, he would whisper to his mom, "Which postmarks do I need?" His mother would respond with, "Let's see. . . . You'll need April 1, 1998; August 7, 2000; and October 21, 2000." Jacob would nod and apply the associated, collective content of the stories accordingly.

There was an unanticipated benefit to their system. Because no one within earshot knew the meaning of their quick postmark exchanges, it provided Jacob with an opportunity to receive confidential, on-the-spot support. It also provided him with moments where he knew the meaning of what was being said and others did not, which was something he truly enjoyed!

The Information

The second criterion in Social Stories 10.1 guides how information for a story is collected and shared. A Social Story begins with an investigation that forms its foundation with identification of a specific topic and the type of information that will be included. The importance of this step is often acknowledged (Rust & Smith, 2006; Sansoti et al., 2004; Smith, 2001), although frequently overlooked in practice. In *Revealing the Hidden Social Code* (Howley & Arnold, 2005), a book about how to write and implement Social Stories, the authors devote an entire chapter to gathering information.

A Social Story has initial roots in a wide range of information, before information is subsequently shared with a child with ASD. A variety of information sources and perspectives are used (e.g., functional analysis, observation, insights from parents and professionals, child interview when possible). Authors look for the cues and concepts that define a targeted situation or skill, as well as those factors that may not be as readily apparent. For example, an author may observe an art class, noting that on this day class began at 9:00 a.m. The time of the class is evident; the fact that this is a factor that could potentially change is not as evident but nevertheless is relevant to story development. A broad base of data, insight, and perspective helps authors to 1) improve their understanding of the child with ASD and his or her relationship to a targeted situation, skill, or concept; 2) identify a specific topic; and 3) begin planning the story format and content. The greater the quality of gathered information, the more likely a suitable topic central to a child's confusion or current response will be identified—all of which contributes to generalization.

An author translates gathered information into a meaningful text and format. To structure and make this task easier, three types of information are considered. First, every story contains *The News,* basic descriptive information that answers relevant *wh-* questions (e.g., Where and when does this occur? Who is involved? What happens? What do the people do? Why and how does it happen?). In addition, *Ways to Think About the News* (which draws on a child's related past experiences and/or demonstrates problem solving to build meaningful connections) may also be included, along with *Connections and Implications of the News* (which ties new information to the current topic or future concepts, skills, or contexts or identifies general conclusions and new, more effective responses). In this way, a single Social Story may potentially include *three-dimensional information*—what is observed, its meaningful connection(s) to the past, and how it may be used now and in the future—to improve the likelihood of generalization.

The story in Figure 5.1, *An Invitation to Angela's Birthday Party,* was written for Stephanie, a 7-year-old girl with ASD, and includes all three types of Social Story information. It opens with news of an impending birthday party and the reason it will be held (i.e., Angela will be 6 years old). The story establishes a connection between the current invitation and relevant past experience, mentioning a birthday party held for Tracey last year. The story continues with guesses about what Stephanie might see and do at Angela's party, using fill-in-the-blank statements to structure the process. The story was illustrated with photos of the invitation, Tracey's party, and Angela's home. Despite its brief text, *An Invitation to Angela's Party* shares the news, makes connections to the past, and structures predictions regarding the food and events (i.e., what Stephanie might expect) at the party.

The Format

The third criterion from Social Stories 10.1—the format—guides the organization of information within each story. In any story, format determines the sequencing

---

An Invitation to Angela's Birthday Party

I have an invitation to Angela's birthday party. She is going to be 6 years old. (*The News: Basic information*)

To guess what we may eat and do at Angela's party, I may try to think of other birthday parties. Last year I went to Tracey's party. There was a cake. We played games. (*Ways to Think About the News: Related past experiences, information processing, problem solving*)

There is often a birthday cake at a birthday party. At Angela's party, there may be a _____. There are often games at a birthday party. At Angela's party, there may be _____. (*Connections and Implications: Suggested responses, current or future implications of the information, possible conclusions*)

Figure 5.1   A Social Story containing the three types of Social Story information.

of ideas and the arrangement of text and illustration, thus making information easy to follow and holding the attention of the reader. In a Social Story, format serves this role and more. Sometimes a traditional format is all that is needed to make a story reader friendly, with events presented in a time-ordered sequence coupled with appropriate text and illustration. Some topics, however, require a nontraditional format to underscore meaning and, in some cases, to tangibly demonstrate that which would be too cumbersome—or impossible—to describe or explain via text or standard types of illustration. Meaning contributes to generalization, and format contributes to meaning. With organization as its focus, it is likely that this criterion holds some of the most important opportunities for authors to support concept formation and the generalization of skills.

Format and Categorization

Typically developing children form categories long before they reach a preschool classroom. At 2 years of age, they can point at a Golden Retriever, Chihuahua, or Basset Hound and correctly identify each as a dog, despite the obvious differences among them. In many of her presentations, Dr. Temple Grandin, an adult with autism, often describes her struggle to identify *dog*. She finally determined that all dogs share a similarly shaped nose. In contrast, by the time a typically developing child reaches preschool, he or she is experienced at categorization without formal instruction.

A typically developing preschooler enters his or her first classroom with a mind that has already established countless prerequisite concepts. This makes the preschool curriculum—one that is traditionally organized around categories—a perfect fit for the learning of new skills. Preschoolers learn colors, shapes, foods, animals, and community helpers on a backdrop of themes that represent even larger categories (i.e., the colors of leaves in autumn). These themes build on an early understanding that every word titles a category of meaning.

Authors can use Social Stories to demonstrate that each word represents a category of similar, although not identical, meanings. Consider *apple*, for example. An apple is not always red. Rather, it may be green, pink, or yellow, or even a blending of these colors. The shape varies as well, as does the size and presence of a stem. For a child with ASD, the potential for confusion lies with every variation of color, size, or configuration.

The Social Story in Figure 5.2, *These Are Apples,* is an example of a story that teaches a concept—in this case, one with simple text and a format that demonstrates

Figure 5.2   *These Are Apples,* a concept Social Story demonstrating the varied meanings of the word *apple*. (Originally in color.)

the varied meanings of *apple*. The body of the story pairs *This is an apple* with a series of photos, each depicting a different apple. Due to the importance of literal accuracy in a Social Story, use of *This is an apple* in reference to a photo of an apple requires explanation. This problem is solved by opening with a brief description of what people mean when they look at a photo of an apple and say that it is an apple. This explanation in the introduction makes it possible to use the simpler wording, *This is an apple,* throughout the body of the story, and *These are apples* to conclude it. To encourage generalization further, the last page of the story may be repeated with a black-and-white version of the final photo.

Learning *apple* is just the beginning. For a child with ASD, the potential for confusion continues. Things happen, and the name that is assigned to an item can change in less than a minute. The apple is not an apple for long. A few bites and it *was* an apple; now it is an *apple core*. A second or two after that the teacher refers to it as *garbage*. The same thing happens with oranges, bananas, peaches, and cherries. Although they are all initially members of category *fruit*, ultimately they join several other items in the category *garbage*. One Social Story can 1) demonstrate how the name given to a single item can change, 2) introduce one or more new words, and 3) demonstrate their relationship to one another (see Figure 5.3).

Over time, several similar stories may help an author explain that change is continual and all around us. Continuing with the fruit-and-garbage example, a teacher may use the story *Apples to Garbage* as a template for several others, each depicting another fruit (e.g., bananas, oranges, peaches). Equipped with several stories and an empty (and clean!) garbage can, a teacher then reads the stories in sequence, placing each in the garbage can after it is read, to introduce the category *garbage*. A small revision to these stories and the teacher can introduce the category *fruit*, placing the stories in a large bowl (fruit salad) instead of a garbage can. In this way, an author extends the meaning of a carefully researched and developed story through creative and thoughtful implementation.

When an author writes with an awareness of categorization, he or she is likely to expand many topics by using a story as a template for others. Developing stories in this way helps an author depict the connections between the original topic and larger, more general, categories and concepts. Similar to how the *Apples to Garbage* story is easily transformed into a set of related stories about other types of fruit, almost any topic may be expanded in this manner to extend meaning and application, and support generalization.

Figure 5.3. *Apples to Garbage*, a Social Story to demonstrate how the name given to an item may change. (Originally in color.)

Format and Generalization

Many Social Story topics hold inherent challenges. The effort to keep text brief and explicit is complicated by the need to create a story that will support the generalization of concepts and skills to include the variations that daily life presents. For example, consider David, age 6 years, who was diagnosed with ASD. David becomes very upset whenever one of his toys is misplaced. How are his parents and teachers to effectively cover this topic when there are limitless individual toys that may be misplaced, several possible adults who may help, *and* a multitude of locations where lost items might be found? It is hard to be efficient with words when there are so many variations to consider. The solution lies in using a flexible format, keeping the text brief and to the point, and adequately covering the possibilities surrounding extraneous factors.

An effective format will demonstrate what text can only describe. In David's case, a comic-strip format, referred to as a *Story Strip,* may be helpful, as shown in Figure 5.4. Like comic strips, Story Strips use a series of small squares to tell a story one scene at a time. The squares are arranged from left to right in a time-ordered sequence. Words are used not only as narration but also as a part of the illustration to depict what the characters are thinking and/or saying. This format is conducive to expanding the meanings of words and/or generalizing concepts. It also simplifies an author's task, structuring the process and making it easy to use the original story as a template if needed. In addition, Story Strips are complete on one page, which will make it possible for David to see the entire process of finding a toy and the connections between the steps.

The Social Story *Finding a Toy* describes how David can work with adults to recover a missing toy. The text is brief and to the point, but through the eyes of a child with ASD its illustrations may be misleading: Will it always be a bear that is lost? What if I lose something somewhere else? Is Mom the only one who can help me find my bear? Will my bear always be found behind a red chair? The solution lies in creating several related stories that share the same text with slightly different illustrations. For example, changing the bear to a block (and replacing the word *bear* with *block* in the talk symbol) creates a second story that expands the meaning of *toy*. A computer game, ball, or skates may also be used to provide additional examples of *toy*. Similarly, changing the context from home to school or elsewhere; replacing Mom with Dad or a grandparent, aunt, or a teacher; or depicting other places where lost items might be found generalizes the meaning of the vocabulary across a variety of variables and contexts.

Figure 5.4.   Finding a Toy, a Story Strip describing the steps to retrieve a lost toy (illustrations by Nova Development Corporation, 1995–1998).

In a Social Story, a simple symbol can represent an important concept without additional text. A children's book, *Lost and Found* (Gellman & Hartman, 1999), provides sound advice about life's losses for children 8–12 years of age: keep moving through life's setbacks. In *Finding a Toy*, the arrow means *keep moving* through these steps toward a solution or resolution. For a population of children who are challenged in their abilities to problem-solve, the concept of movement through a problem is an important one; the use of an additional symbol to encourage movement (i.e., a truck in David's case) may encourage attention and add meaning. Anything that symbolizes movement (e.g., bird, plane, cheetah, train) may also be selected in line with a child's interests, as long as its use and meaning are clear.

By making alterations to selected parts of the illustrations, without any further revisions to the original text, the illustrations may depict a teacher placed in a classroom, cafeteria, or playground. In addition, the location of the lost toy may be altered. A series of Story Strips expand a child's understanding of applying a single concept to a variety of settings.

To write with the multifaceted goal of Social Stories in mind is to make every effort to use an audience-tailored format, voice, and vocabulary to meaningfully share information with the audience. The goal sets the stage for creative thinking, fostering many other ideas to support generalization. Although the focus in this chapter has been on 3 of the 10 criteria from Social Stories 10.1, a case could be made that each contributes to generalization. For example, a Social Story may describe the use of a visual support in the classroom. To help a child determine when to focus on the teacher's voice and when it is okay to ignore it to complete work, the teacher wears a card on a string around her neck. On one side of the card is an attentive stick figure face; on the other, a picture of a child working. A story describes the meaning of each picture, and the teacher flips the card accordingly. Another idea: After a story is introduced, a child may "take it on tour" to be read aloud by each member of the educational team in their offices to demonstrate that many people, in many places, all have the same information. This also provides an opportunity for each member of the team to comment on the story as it relates to his or her role and add related, context-specific details—perhaps in another story. Sending a story on tour not only applies content to other caregivers and contexts, but it also provides repeated review of the story early in its implementation.

The ideas are endless. Working in accordance with the Social Story goal, an author discovers new ways to build meaningful concepts and demonstrate the connections and relationships that may otherwise be missed by the audience, all of which work in support of generalization.

SUMMARY

Parents and professionals are the authors of social understanding. They write Social Stories with respect for a perspective that is often different from their own, negotiating the discrepancies to find common ground in accurate, assumption-free information. The goal of the approach focuses on the efforts of authors and the responsibility they assume throughout the entire process of developing and implementing a Social Story. In recent years, research has provided new insight into the cognitive roots of ASDs and the use of Social Stories as an educational tool. This has resulted in an updated definition of what is—and what is not—a Social Story. It has also provided authors with a more detailed background so that they are better equipped to address specific issues of ASDs—among them, the generalization of concepts and skills.

Anticipating that a child will have difficulty with applying learned concepts and skills to novel settings is the first step to developing stories with improved odds of generalization. Generalization is closely linked to the ability to form concepts and categories, or to organize and cross-reference experience. Three of the 10 Social Story criteria directly address the need for meaningful organization and careful presentation of information and thus are likely to be closely linked to generalization. Carefully crafted stories, with formats that merge with text and illustration to build concepts as well as address traditional topics, are likely to be better suited to support the challenges surrounding generalization in individuals with ASDs.

For many of the ideas presented in this chapter, this is their debut—the first time they have appeared in writing. Informal experience suggests that they have merit. Similar to the Social Stories that earned the enthusiastic affection of parents, professionals, and many children with ASDs prior to formal inquiry, it is hoped the ideas in this chapter may support children with ASDs—specifically the generalization of learned concepts and skills—and fuel future ideas, directions, and research.

REFERENCES

Barry, L. & Burlew, S. (2004). Using Social Stories to teach choice and play skills to children with autism. *Focus on Autism and Other Developmental Disabilities, 19,* 8–16.

Committee on Educational Interventions for Children with Autism. (2001). Family roles. In C. Lord & J.P. McGee (Eds.), *Educating children with autism*. Washington, DC: National Academies Press.

Dettmer, S., Simpson, R., Myles, B., & Ganz, J. (2000). The use of visual supports to facilitate transitions of students with autism. *Focus on Autism and Other Developmental Disabilities, 15,* 163–169.

Gastgeb, H.Z., Strauss, M.S., & Minshew, N.J. (2006). Do individuals with autism process categories differently? The effect of typicality and development. *Child Development, 77,* 1717–1729.

Gellman, M., & Hartman, T. (1999). *Lost and found*. New York: Morrow Junior Books.

Gray, C. (1998). The advanced Social Story workbook. *The Morning News, 10*(2), 1–21.

Gray, C. (2004). Social Stories 10.0: The new defining criteria and guidelines. *Jenison Autism Journal, 15,* 2–21.

Gray, C. (2008). *Social Stories 10.1*. Unpublished manuscript.

Gray, C.A. & Garand, J.D. (1993). Social Stories: Improving responses of students with autism with accurate social information. *Focus on Autistic Behavior, 8,* 1–10.

Hagiwara, T., & Myles, B. (1999). A multimedia Social Story intervention: Teaching skills to children with autism. *Focus on Autism and Other Developmental Disabilities, 14,* 82–95.

Horner, R.H., Carr, E.G., Halle, J., McGee, G., Odom, S., & Wolery, M. (2005). The use of single-subject research to identify evidence-based practice in special education. *Exceptional Children, 71,* 165–179.

Howley, M., & Arnold, E. (2005). *Revealing the hidden social code*. London: Jessica Kingsley.

Ivey, M.L., Heflin, L.J., & Alberto, P. (2004). The use of Social Stories to promote independent behaviors in novel events for children with PDD-NOS. *Focus on Autism and Other Developmental Disabilities, 19,* 164–176.

Klinger, L.G., & Dawson, G. (2001). Prototype formation in autism. *Development and Psychology, 13,* 111–124.

Kluth, P., & Schwarz, P. (2008). *"Just give him the whale!": 20 ways to use fascinations, areas of expertise, and strengths to support students with autism.* Baltimore: Paul H. Brookes Publishing Co.

Kuoch, H., & Mirenda, P. (2003). Social Story interventions for young children with autism spectrum disorders. *Focus on Autism and Other Developmental Disorders, 18,* 219–227.

Kuttler, S., Myles, B., & Carlson, J. (1998). The use of Social Stories to reduce precursors to tantrum behaviors in a student with autism. *Focus on Autism and Other Developmental Disabilities, 13,* 176–182.

Lorimer, P.A., Simpson, R.L., Myles, B.S., & Ganz, J.B. (2002). The use of Social Stories as a preventative behavioral intervention in a home setting with a child with autism. *Journal of Positive Behavior Interventions, 4,* 53–60.

Norris, C., & Dattilo, J. (1999). Evaluating effects of a Social Story intervention on a young girl with autism. *Focus on Autism and Other Developmental Disabilities, 14,* 180–186.

Nova Development Corporation. (1995–1998). *Art Explosion.* Calabasas, CA: Author.

Plaisted, K.C. (2000). Aspects of autism that theory of mind can't explain. In S. Baron-Cohen, H. Tager Flusberg, & D.J. Cohen (Eds.), *Understanding other minds: Perspectives from developmental cognitive neuroscience.* New York: Oxford University Press.

Quinn, P.C., & Oates, J.M. (2004). Early category representations and concepts. In J.M. Oates & A. Grayson (Eds.), *Cognitive and language development in children* (2nd ed.). Oxford, UK: Blackwell Publishers.

Romanowski Bashe, P., & Kirby, B.L. (2001). *The oasis guide to Asperger syndrome.* New York: Crown Publishers.

Rosch, E. (1978). Principles of categorization. In E. Rosch & B.B. Lloyd (Eds.), *Cognition and categorization* (pp. 27–48). Hillsdale, NJ: Lawrence Erlbaum Associates.

Rowe, C. (1999). Do Social Stories benefit children with autism in mainstream primary schools? *British Journal of Special Education, 26,* 12–14.

Rust, J., & Smith, A. (2006). How should the effectiveness of Social Stories to modify the behavior of children on the autism spectrum be tested? Lessons from the literature. *Autism: The International Journal of Research and Practice, 10,* 125–138.

Sansosti, F.J., Powell-Smith, K.A., & Kincaid, D. (2004). A research synthesis of Social Story interventions for children with autism spectrum disorders. *Focus on Autism and Other Developmental Disabilities, 19*(4), 194–204.

Scattone, D., Wilczynski, S.M., Edwards, R.P., & Rabian, B. (2002). Decreasing disruptive behaviors of children with autism using social stories. *Journal of Autism and Developmental Disorders, 32,* 535–543.

Smith, C. (2001). Using Social Stories to enhance behavior in children with autistic spectrum difficulties. *Educational Psychology in Practice, 17*(4), 337–345.

Swaggart, B.L., Ganon, E., Bock, S.J., Earles, T.L., Quinn, C., Myles, B.S., et al. (1995). Using Social Stories to teach social and behavioral skills to children with autism. *Focus on Autistic Behavior, 10*(1), 1–15.

Wright, L.A. (2007). *Utilizing Social Stories to reduce problem behavior and increase pro-social behavior in young children with autism.* Unpublished doctoral dissertation, University of Missouri, Columbia.

Chapter 5
Appendices

APPENDIX 5.1.

Social Stories 10.1

ONE GOAL

The goal of a Social Story is to share information using a format, voice, and content that is descriptive, meaningful, and socially and emotionally safe for its audience. Every Social Story has an overall patient and supportive quality.

TWO-STEP DISCOVERY

Keeping the goal in mind, educators gather information to 1) improve their understanding of a person with ASD in relation to a situation, skill, or concept and/or 2) identify the topic and type(s) of information to share in the story.

THREE PARTS AND A TITLE

A Social Story has a title, introduction, body, and conclusion.

FORMAT

A Social Story has a format that works to clarify content and enhance meaning for its audience.

FIVE FACTORS: VOICE AND VOCABULARY

A Social Story has five factors that determine its voice and vocabulary:

1. First- or third-person perspective
2. Positive and patient tone
3. Relevant positive past tense, past, present, or future tense
4. Literally accurate
5. Accurate meaning

SIX QUESTIONS

A Social Story answers relevant *wh-* questions, describing the context (where), time-related information (when), relevant people (who), important cues (what), basic activities, behaviors, or statements (how), and the reasons or rationale behind them (why).

SEVEN SENTENCE TYPES

A Social Story comprises descriptive sentences (objective, often observable, statements of fact), with an option to include any one or more of the following sentence types: perspective sentences (that describe the thoughts, feelings, and/or beliefs of other people); three sentences that coach (to identify suggested responses for the individual and/or his or her team of parents, professionals, and peers); affirmative sentences (that enhance the meaning of surrounding statements); and partial sentences.

A GR-EIGHT FORMULA!

A Social Story follows this formula to ensure that it describes more than directs:

$$\frac{\text{Descriptive} + \text{Perspective} + \text{Affirmative sentences (complete or partial)} = \text{Describe}}{\text{Sentences that coach (complete or partial)} = \text{Coach}} \geq 2$$

NINE MAKES IT MINE

A Social Story is tailored to the abilities, attention span, learning style, and interests of its audience.

TEN IMPLEMENTATION GUIDELINES

A Social Story is implemented with consideration of 10 guidelines:

1. Team review and revise.

2. Always share in a comfortable setting and casual manner.

3. Never present in a negative tone, force review of a story, or use as a consequence for misbehavior.

4. Introduce in a positive, matter-of-fact manner: "I have a Story for you!"

5. With a younger audience, introduce a story sitting at the child's side and slightly back, with attention focused on the story.

6. One at a time, team members read the story to the student.

7. Monitor the impact of the story.

8. Rewrite if necessary.

9. Save mastered stories in binders for easy reference and review.

10. Consider mixing and matching mastered stories from their original binders according to new topics.

Sample Social Stories

Three Social Story criteria are likely to be very important to categorization and generalization. The first is the goal, with an emphasis on sharing accurate information, using text and illustration that is tailored, and socially and emotionally safe, for the intended audience. The second criterion focuses on how information is gathered and the type of information that is shared. Here the emphasis is on not only describing a concept, situation, or skill but also creating ties between past experiences, the current context, and future implications. Finally, the story format organizes information, using the arrangement of text and illustration to support audience comprehension and practical application. This appendix includes stories that serve as examples of these three criteria at work.

THE GOAL

Social Stories address a limitless variety of topics; few are more challenging than those that address loss. Regardless of whether the topic is about misplacing a toy; the loss of health, information, or a loved one; or any one of life's many setbacks, Social Stories about loss require careful consideration as they are researched and developed. Understanding and relying upon the goal can provide an author with important direction. Thus, an author begins by identifying information that the audience may be missing and shares that information in a patient, respectful, and reassuring tone.

The following Social Stories are among several that were written to describe the many losses that surround a natural disaster—in this case, wildfires. Note that the stories include information that typically developing children may readily know but that children with autism spectrum disorders may not identify or apply independently. Personal information and illustration may also be included to enhance story content. With minor revision, these stories could be used as templates for other stories to address a variety of losses and/or natural disasters.

What Does Evacuate Mean?

Sometimes people are told to evacuate their house. Evacuate means "to empty and leave." Sometimes, though, evacuate means to take what is most important and leave the rest.

Usually, a family is asked to evacuate because their house may be in danger. Fire is dangerous to a house. The house may burn. It's very important to keep the family safe and away from the fire. For this reason families are asked to evacuate their house. They are asked to go to a safer place.

Most families never have to evacuate their house. Once in a very long while, though, some families do have to evacuate. When people are told to "evacuate" a house, it is very, very, very important to follow that direction.

Evacuation is one way that parents keep their children safe. I may be able to help if my family has to evacuate our house. I may be able to help to keep the people in my family safe. Mom or Dad will have ideas about how I may help.

Why Do We Have to Go?

Many children have questions about evacuation. Often they want to know why their family has to evacuate the house. Sometimes children will ask their mom or dad, "Why do we have to go?"

When firefighters tell a family to evacuate, it's very, very, very important for people to leave their house. Firefighters have studied fires for a long time. They are fire experts. Firefighters decide when a fire is too close and people have to evacuate their houses. It's intelligent to listen and follow their directions.

Sometimes, it may seem that a fire is not *that close*. It may *seem* like it would be okay to stay. The problem is, when a fire is out of control, it spreads quickly. That is why firefighters ask families to evacuate when it is still safe to go, *before* the fire is very close.

Firefighters decide when a fire is too close. They tell people when it is time to evacuate. If a firefighter says, "It's time to evacuate," then it's time to evacuate. Following the directions of firefighters helps people stay safe.

People Would Rather Stay in Their House

People evacuate a house because they *have* to leave. If they had a choice, they would choose to stay and do what they usually do. They wish the fire was out. They wish their home was farther away from the fire. They wish the fire was under control. Wishing doesn't put a fire out, though. If it did, the fire would be out by now.

By the time people grow to become adults, they have learned to do things they don't want to do without whining or having a tantrum. They may feel sad, nervous, or uncomfortable, but they know it's important to keep thinking and working to keep their family safe.

Sometimes adults help themselves feel better by remembering that life isn't always like this. They know that fires end and someday it will be possible to do the things that they usually do. That's when adults say things like, "It will be nice when life gets back to normal." That helps them to remember life without wildfires, and they feel better.

If my mom and dad say, "It's time to evacuate," it's important to follow their direction.

THE INFORMATION

After information is gathered, a topic is identified and a story developed. Three types of information may be shared in a Social Story. *The News* provides a basic description of a situation, concept, or skill, answering relevant *wh-* questions. *Ways to Think About the News* often draws from the reader's past experiences to demonstrate information processing and problem solving. Finally, *Implications of the News* creates ties to the future and often includes possible outcomes and/or suggestions for new, more effective responses. Despite its brevity, the following story serves as an example of a Social Story that includes all three types of information—with references not only to the past experience of the audience but Dad as well!

Learning to Use a Hammer

Dad knows how to do many things. He was a kid once, and he learned a lot as he grew. Grandpa taught Dad to use a hammer. Soon Dad will teach me to use a hammer.

Dad's words can help me learn to do things. Last week, Dad taught me to make a slip knot. I listened and learned.

This Saturday Dad will show me how to use a hammer. I will try to listen to Dad when he is showing me how to use a hammer. That way, I can begin to learn to use a hammer safely.

THE FORMAT

The organization and presentation of information, or format, provides an author with an additional opportunity to clarify story content and improve comprehension. A traditional format—with events presented in a time-ordered sequence—is often used to organize ideas within a Social Story. For many topics, it is the best choice for a story's format.

The following story was originally written for Fletcher, a young boy selected to serve as the ring bearer in a wedding. Fletcher's story served as a template for a similar story for Sophie, the flower girl at the same wedding. The story was illustrated with photographs, and supported Fletcher and Sophie—and reassured their parents, the bride, and the groom! Since then, the stories for Fletcher and Sophie have been used effectively as a template for many subsequent weddings—for ring bearers and flower girls with autism spectrum disorders, as well as typically developing children.

In this way, every story can serve as a template—or format—for others that follow. All that is needed is minor revisions to an original story, to personalize the context (e.g., synagogue) to make it relevant and interesting for the next audience.

Fletcher the Ring Bearer

My name is Fletcher. I am going to be in a wedding. A wedding is a special celebration of love and marriage. I have something special to do at the wedding. I am the ring bearer. I will try to carry the treasure box down the aisle of the church.

At a wedding, most people sit and watch the wedding. That's because weddings are very special.

At a wedding, some people are at the front of the church. Mr. Paul, Billy, and Pastor Simon will stand at the front of the church. They will stand quietly because they are in a church.

At a wedding, some people take turns walking down the aisle. At this wedding, Rachel is the first adult to walk down the aisle. Then, I will be the first child to walk down the aisle.

I will try to walk down the aisle with my treasure box. I will try to walk quietly because I am in a church. Adults will be happy to see me in the wedding. It's important to them.

When I get to the front of the church, I have a choice. I may stand quietly with Mr. Paul or sit in the front row with my mom.

This is a list of people who will come down the aisle after me:

Sophie will follow me. She's the flower girl.

Aunt Mary will walk down the aisle after Sophie.

The bride and Grandpa will be last. They will walk together.

Everyone will try to walk quietly because they are in a church.

When everyone is at the front of the church, it's okay for Sophie to leave with an adult to go to the nursery.

Sophie the Flower Girl

My name is Sophie. I am going to be in a wedding. A wedding is very special. I am the flower girl at the wedding.

At a wedding, most people sit and watch. Some people are at the front of the church. Mr. Paul, Billy, and Pastor Simon will stand at the front of the church.

At a wedding, some people take turns walking down the aisle.

First, Rachel walks.

Then Fletcher walks.

Then I walk.

Then Aunt Mary walks.

Then, the bride and Grandpa walk.

Everyone will try to walk slowly and quietly. That's because they are in a wedding. And they are all in a church.

When everyone is at the front of the church, it's my time to go with Candace to the nursery. There will be toys in the nursery. I may play with them.

6

Generalization in Computer-Assisted Intervention for Children with Autism Spectrum Disorders

Christina Whalen, Dominic W. Massaro, and Lauren Franke

The education industry has a lot of weight on its shoulders. With the ever-increasing number of students attending each year and the dwindling amount of funding and qualified teachers, the education industry is constantly on the lookout for ways to educate all types of children as efficiently as possible. Many researchers are thus searching for the most effective and efficient method for educators to treat students with autism spectrum disorders (ASDs). One popular method is the inclusion of computer-assisted intervention (CAI). Researchers believe CAI is able to meet many of the vast challenges facing students with ASDs in their learning.

CAI uses computer software to supplement a student's education and treatment goals. Primarily, CAI is used in drill-and-practice or tutorial settings. The major benefit of CAI is its ability to generalize concepts being taught by teachers in classroom environments. Using CAI is not only beneficial to students with ASDs or other special needs; all children can benefit from the creation of an environment that optimizes learning. For example, consider the importance of learning vocabulary for healthy perceptual and cognitive development (LaSasso & Davey, 1987; Massaro, 2006b). One might think that only students with language disabilities require direct instruction in vocabulary, whereas typically developing students will acquire vocabulary on their own. However, the accepted theory is that all students benefit from vocabulary instruction (Beck, McKeown, & Kucan, 2002). Similarly, children who use computers early in life have shown better school readiness and cognition compared with children who do not have computer exposure in the preschool years (Li & Atkins, 2006). Other benefits that have been reported include increased language and improved social interactions (e.g.,

Parts of this chapter, or the work discussed in this chapter, were contributed by the following individuals: Lars Liden, Eric Dashen, Brad McGuire, Kevin MacDonald, Jeanette Ryan, David Lockhart, Walter Schwartz, Aubyn Stahmer, Kelly Geddes, and Tom Thomas.

Haugland, 1999). Although these benefits hold true for typically developing children, the benefits for children with ASDs may be even greater.

Research on the use of CAI for children with ASDs is extremely promising. Children with autism do not tend to respond well to traditional teaching strategies (Schreibman, 1988), which is why approaches such as applied behavior analysis (ABA) are so frequently used with this population. However, due to the high costs of this and other treatments, as well as a shortage of qualified staff to implement them, more and more teachers are choosing new treatment choices for their classroom to accommodate children with ASDs (e.g., Schilling & Schwartz, 2004).

Although there is no conclusive evidence for any effective treatment for ASDs, research supports ABA techniques (e.g., Lovaas, 1987; Koegel et al., 1989) as effective methods for teaching these children. However, these services are often extremely time consuming, expensive, difficult to implement and maintain over time, and difficult to obtain. Visual teaching strategies such as video modeling, social skill programs, cognitive-behavioral therapy, and psychotherapy are also often used to treat children with ASDs. CAI has also emerged as an effective and motivating method for teaching this population.

Studies have demonstrated that children with autism may learn more quickly with a computer than with traditional teaching strategies. Bosseler and Massaro (2003) developed and assessed a computer-animated tutor to teach vocabulary and grammar to eight children with autism. Their program included receptive and expressive language activities. They were successful in teaching language to all participants, and generalization to the children's natural environment was reported.

Computerized techniques were also used to teach social understanding to children with autism via computerized Social Stories (Bernard-Opitz, Sriram, & Nakhoda-Sapuan, 2001). Children with autism did better with computerized visual Social Stories than without. In another computer-based intervention (Hetzroni & Tannous, 2004), children with autism were taught communicative functions using a specially designed software program that targeted form, use, and content of language. Children were able to learn the material and transfer skills to a natural classroom environment. This research offers promise of software-based interventions for children with autism and suggests that information learned on the computer may generalize to the classroom environment.

A CAI program for students with autism shares many principles of other ideal learning environments designed for all individuals across a variety of academic settings. Two of these shared principles are time on task and spaced practice. Given limited human resources, such as the dearth of qualified teachers and supportive staff, only technology can provide the needed pedagogy at any time. CAI grants children the opportunity to work on much-needed skills when it is most convenient for them. With CAI, there are no waitlists or cancellations of treatment sessions. Other benefits of CAI include increased motivation for using the computer (e.g., Moore & Calvert, 2000) and potentially faster acquisition of skills than with other types of learning (e.g., Williams, Wright, Callaghan, & Coughlan, 2002). There is also growing evidence that skills learned on the computer may generalize to the natural environment (e.g., Bosseler & Massaro, 2003; Hetzroni & Tannous, 2004). Key components for successful programs include the following:

- *Multiple exemplars*—Several different examples of concepts should be taught.

- *Variety in methods used to teach concepts*—Examples include receptive identification, matching, or sorting.

- *Nonrepetitive trials*—Repeating the same trial over and over again may result in memorized responding rather than a generalized response, which the child can use in different contexts.

- *Customization*—The user should be able to tailor the program to the child's individual needs.

In addition to choosing appropriate software, it is absolutely essential to work on the skills the child is learning on the computer in naturalistic or functional ways (i.e., off the computer). Some software programs offer suggestions for off-computer activities, but these may not be necessary if the child's team is able to come up with good activities that are specifically tailored to keep the child motivated. Off-computer activities may include play, chores, self-help tasks, and community skills.

Along with the potential benefits of using CAI for children with ASDs, there are some limitations to what it can provide. Some children with autism are known to have difficulty with generalization and may develop a therapy register, which is a response set that develops during learning sessions (Johnston, 1988). The child's responses are activated by characteristics of the learning sessions, and skills are not observed at expected levels away from the computer. Other limitations of CAI include the potential for children to get bored with programs that do not provide enough variety, frustration from children who think of the computer as a reward rather than a learning tool, obsessive or restricted interest in the computer or specific parts of a computer program, and the potential for not generalizing skills to the natural environment.

A variety of CAI programs are available in the market that target many of the skills needed to teach children with ASDs. The majority of the products in the market are not scientifically based and do not conduct quality research. Fortunately, however, some of these programs do focus on scientifically based instruction. Companies such as Fast ForWord and Laureate conduct ongoing research on the efficacy of their products. Two other companies, Animated Speech and TeachTown, have developed CAI programs that are based on scientifically validated treatment approaches. These programs are designed to address language, cognitive, and social impairments. The following sections will discuss these programs—TeachTown: Basics, TeachTown: Skill Builder, Team Up With Timo: Vocabulary (and Timo's Lesson Creator), and Team Up With Timo: Stories—in terms of their attention to generalization in their product development, research, and future directions.

TEACHTOWN

TeachTown is a company dedicated to software development and clinical research. The company creates research-based software programs designed specifically for children with ASDs. Each of TeachTown's products uses the scientific principles of ABA (i.e., applying the scientific principles of behavior analysis to issues that are socially important), developmental psychology, speech therapy, and special education to teach and generalize concepts.

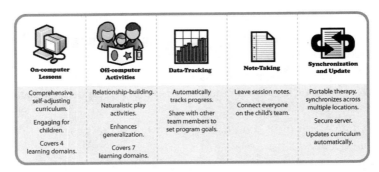

Figure 6.1.   Features of TeachTown software.

Children with ASDs commonly have trouble generalizing concepts and adapting the knowledge they have acquired to unfamiliar situations. To address this issue and increase generalization of the presented material, TeachTown's products are divided into two parts: on-computer lessons and off-computer activities (see Figure 6.1).

TeachTown: Basics, the company's first product, contains more than 500 on-computer lessons. The program was designed for children who are functioning in the 2- to 7-year developmental range and teaches language, social skills, academic/cognitive skills, play/imitation, motor skills, and life skills. Lessons within the program use discrete trial and ABA principles to teach everything from food and animal identification to early phonics and fractions.

On-Computer Lessons

A child's interaction with TeachTown: Basics during an on-computer session resembles the following example. The student's interface depicts a town scene, from which the student can choose which module he or she would like to study by selecting from one of the buildings (see Figure 6.2). Research has demonstrated that this child-choice technique keeps motivation high (Koegel, O'Dell, & Koegel, 1987). Although the student can select which module he or she would like to study, the software determines the list of modules that are available based on the current developmental needs of the student.

After selecting a module, the student begins a lesson. Depending on the student's previous history with this lesson, the lesson may be a pretest, a learning exercise, or a posttest. One fifth of the trials presented to the child will consist of maintenance tasks, during which material from previous modules that the student has already mastered are presented. Maintenance tasks help the student preserve previously learned skills and assist in keeping the student's motivation high (Koegel et al., 1989).

Reinforcement is presented intermittently throughout the trials. For testing purposes, the reinforcement is not contingent on the student responding correctly to the prompts. In a learning exercise, however, the reinforcement is dependent on a correct answer and will occur every three to five correct responses. Such reinforcement has been proven to be the most effective schedule for keeping responding high during a task (Neef & Lutz, 2001). When the child has earned a reward,

Figure 6.2. The town (child's home page) in TeachTown: Basics.

TeachTown: Basics again uses child choice and lets the student choose which reward he or she will receive. Once the child has completed all trials for the lesson, the program returns to the town map, where the student chooses another module. The process repeats until the learning session has expired.

Generalization in the on-computer lessons primarily occurs in the use of a variety of methods to teach targeted material. Lessons in the program take the form of one of three types: 1) receptive identification (e.g., "Can you find the blue bird?"), 2) matching (e.g., "Which face is the same?"), or 3) location identification (e.g., "Which way are the eyes looking?"). With these options available for lesson design, TeachTown: Basics is able to use different types of lessons to teach the same material. For example, when teaching early reading skills, the program introduces upper- and lowercase letters in receptive identification (i.e., comprehension) tasks and then asks the child to match an uppercase letter to its lowercase partner.

TeachTown varies the program's discriminative stimuli and exemplars during the discrete trials to help generalization. For example, one trial may ask, "Which one is an apple?" followed by the next trial asking, "Do you see an apple?" The same lesson would also contain multiple photographs, drawn images, and animations of apples. Use of multiple exemplars is extremely important for improving generalization, as has been demonstrated in many research studies (e.g. Jahr, 2001; Reeve, Reeve, Townsend, & Poulson, 2007). This variety ensures that children are not memorizing labels for individual images or cues but rather are learning the entire concept of the material being presented. Over time, the child will learn to cue in to the relevant information in a sentence or image and not focus on its specific structure. In fact, the program includes more than 15,000 sounds and images.

Furthermore, the exemplars and discriminative stimuli used in the testing portions of a lesson are different than the set of assets used in the learning-and-teaching portion. In other words, the images and cues that are used to teach the child the material are completely different from the images and cues used to test if the child learned what was taught. This process ensures that the child has learned the concepts and not simply memorized the images he or she learned during training in the lessons.

During a lesson, the child is also challenged to work on more than one concept at a time. For example, in the lesson Body Functions, the child is taught to receptively identify which body part is used for a particular function. In this lesson, the child simultaneously learns to identify eyes for seeing and ears for hearing. In other words, on one trial, the child may be asked, "Which one do you use for seeing?" while the next trial may ask, "Do you know which one we use for hearing?" This helps train the child to easily shift his or her attention from one target to another.

Once released, TeachTown's next product will target children with autism with a developmental age of 6–11 years. Tentatively called TeachTown: Skill Builder, the new product will follow the same methodologies as TeachTown: Basics. Specifically, the design of TeachTown: Skill Builder includes discriminative stimuli (i.e., instructions to the child), discrete trials (i.e., breaks skills down to basic components and rewards correct responses), intermittent schedules of reinforcement (i.e., the child gets a reward periodically for correct responding), contingent reinforcement (i.e., the child must get the trial correct or is prompted to get access to rewards), child choice, interspersed maintenance tasks (i.e., tasks the child has previously mastered), and multiple exemplars (i.e., several different examples).

Off-Computer Activities

In correlation to the on-computer lessons, the off-computer activities in TeachTown: Basics are designed specifically to generalize concepts (see Appendices 6.1–6.3). Every off-computer activity shares a learning subject with an on-computer lesson. The goal behind the activities is to further generalize what the child is learning on the software by bringing in real-world examples and applications. In addition, the activities improve skills that are not taught in the software program, including expressive language, social interaction, self-help skills, imitation, play, and motor skills.

The off-computer activities are based on naturalistic teaching approaches. They consist of a list of materials that should be readily available and a set of easy-to-follow instructions. An adult can use these instructions as a guide on how to teach the targeted concepts and interact with the child in an engaging and productive manner. The activities can be either viewed within the software or printed for later use.

Research Supporting TeachTown

Using the off-computer activities in conjunction with the software program is likely to result in the most successful use of the TeachTown: Basics program. However, some evidence suggests that using either of these elements alone may result in some success as well. In fact, as part of a U.S. Department of Education Small Business Innovation Research grant, TeachTown performed two studies examining the efficacy of the computer-assisted intervention for four preschool and kindergarten children with ASDs and four children with Down syndrome (Whalen, Liden, Ingersoll, Dallaire, & Liden, 2006). In the first study, parents, clinicians, and researchers were given a questionnaire that asked about their current therapy and their opinion of CAI for children with ASDs. Following the questionnaire, a TeachTown representative gave an extensive demonstration on a CAI program prototype. The participants were allowed to use the software, if they were inclined, under supervision. After being shown the software, participants were asked to fill out a longer questionnaire that polled their opinion about the interfaces, the modules, and other aspects of the software.

The data suggested that the perceived effectiveness of a software-based intervention for 3- to 6-year-old children increases after subjects have been shown how such an intervention might work. All participants felt that children would benefit from this type of software and from the parent–child supplementary activities. Teachers gave the highest ratings overall and felt that there was a great need for such a program in the schools. The information from this first study was used for the development of the TeachTown: Basics product.

In the second study, children were asked to use a prototype of TeachTown: Basics software and the off-computer activities for 2 months. Prior to using the program, the participating children were observed and videotaped in an interaction with a parent or other close adult. Communication, play, imitation, social skills, and challenging behaviors were coded by a trained research assistant, who was blinded to the purpose of the study.

Following pretreatment measures, each family was given a pilot version of the early intervention software and was asked to have their child play the game 3 days per week for a minimum of 15 minutes. Participating families were also asked to do the off-computer activities for an equal amount of time. The data from this study demonstrated early effectiveness of the TeachTown: Basics program for children with ASDs and Down syndrome. In addition, the research showed that for the four children with ASDs, dramatic increases in language and socialization occurred while using the software program compared with play interactions with their parents.

In addition to these early studies, TeachTown has upheld its dedication to clinical research with several other studies regarding TeachTown: Basics. In one study, 20 children with ASDs were observed using the TeachTown: Basics software to assess if the reinforcers (i.e., reward games) in the program were indeed reinforcing (Whalen & Cernich, in progress). In other words, did the rewards increase the child's attention and motivation to the computer? The data showed that children attended significantly more when the rewards were present versus when the lessons were present (see Figure 6.3). In addition, the children's overall attention was high when using the program, despite a lesson or reward being present. Disruptive behaviors, such as walking away or noncompliance, occurred less during the rewards than during the lessons. Increased spontaneous commenting, prompted speech, looking at the adult, positive affect, and pointing were also observed dur-

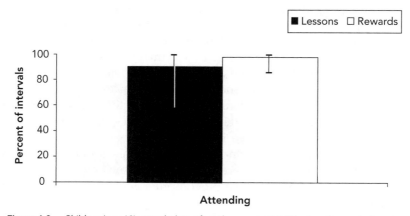

Figure 6.3. Children ($n = 10$) attended significantly more ($p < 0.05$) when the rewards were present than when the lessons were present. Overall, attendance to the computer was high in both conditions.

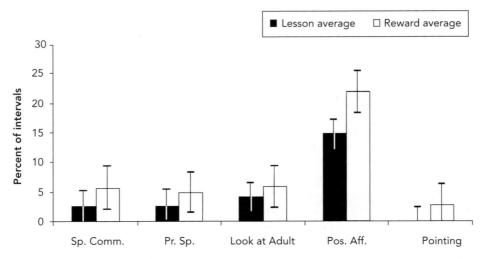

Figure 6.4. Children (*n* = 10) demonstrated more spontaneous commenting (Sp. Comm.), prompted speech (Pr. Sp.), looking at the adult, positive affect (Pos. Aff.), and pointing during the reward conditions than during the lessons.

ing the reward games for the children who had an adult sitting with them at the computer (see Figure 6.4). Ten children were also observed in a structured teaching session with school staff; it was demonstrated that the reinforcers used in the software program were more effective than those used in structured teaching sessions.

San Diego Children's Hospital recently implemented a clinical examination of generalization using TeachTown: Basics (Stahmer & Geddes, in progress). Two children with autism who were included in a typical preschool participated in this study. Both children had strong vocabularies, as measured by the Receptive One-Word Picture Vocabulary Test (Brownell, 2000), scoring in the low average range. In addition, they had developmental skills in the typical range as well. The children used the on-computer and off-computer tasks in TeachTown: Basics to learn new receptive labels. Using the TeachTown: Basics software, specific receptive labels that the children had not mastered were chosen: birds (e.g., pigeon, toucan, owl, pelican) for one child and bugs (e.g., ladybug, caterpillar, fly, cockroach) for the other. A pretest was conducted using built-in assessments in the TeachTown: Basics software. In addition, generalization to new pictures not used in the software was assessed by having the children identify four different examples of each target word, which was accomplished by placing pictures in groups of four on a table and asking the child to, for example, "Hand me the pelican." For each of the children, pretests had to indicate a correct rate of less than 60% for each label, both on the computer and off the computer, in order to use those labels for training.

All labels were taught using the TeachTown: Basics computer program during two 30-minute sessions per week until, according to the computer assessment, the child mastered the labels. Two of the labels from each group were also taught using off-computer tasks recommended in the TeachTown: Basics program during two 30-minute sessions per week. Once the labels were mastered on the computer, generalization was once again assessed using the novel pictures. It was hypothesized that for those labels in which off-computer activities were used, generalization would be increased and that time to mastery would be shorter.

The data, however, showed no differences between the time it took to master a lesson on the computer versus additional time spent off the computer (see

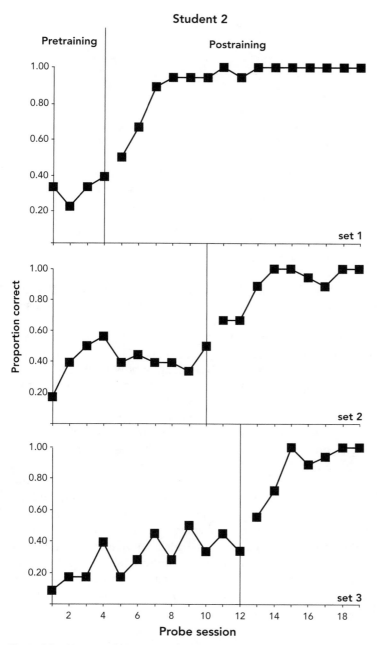

Figure 6.5. Mean proportion correct during pretraining and posttraining probes for each of the three-word sets for one of the six students. The vertical lines separate the pretraining and posttraining. Once training was implemented, identification performance increased dramatically.

Figure 6.5). In addition, the children were able to successfully identify the novel pictures with more than 80% accuracy in all cases. Although these data are only for two children and must be considered preliminary, it appears that for children with high-functioning autism, TeachTown: Basics may be used to increase vocabulary. It also appears that the children will generalize to new pictures using the

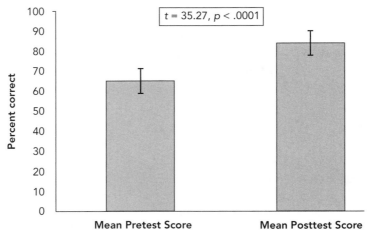

Figure 6.6.   Pre- and posttest scores for 851 students using TeachTown: Basics across four domains (Receptive Language, Academic-Cognitive, Social Skills, and Life Skills)

computer activities alone. Anecdotal data from teachers further indicated that the children were able to identify the new labels correctly when the items were used in play and during classroom activities such as circle time.

Most recently, TeachTown has compiled the data from all of the students currently using TeachTown: Basics (Whalen, Liden, MacDonald, Thomas, & Lockhart, in progress). The purpose of this analysis was to determine how well TeachTown: Basics achieved its goals of helping this population learn and master new information. The TeachTown database consisted of 851 students who have been using TeachTown: Basics, ranging in age from 3 to 22 years old. Using a crossed random effects model, 11,208 instances of pretests and posttests were analyzed, with a mean pretest score of 65% and mean posttest score of 84% (see Figure 6.6.). The 18.5% improvement was significant ($t = 35.27$, $p < 0.0001$). Significant changes from pretest to posttest scores in the software were shown in all four learning domains (Receptive Language, Academic-Cognitive, Social Skills, and Life Skills), with Social Skills taking the highest number of trials, on average, to reach mastery. Both sexes performed equally well on the software; younger children showed more improvement, but improvement was demonstrated for all ages. Because this data was collected automatically through the TeachTown: Basics program, only anecdotal information on the generalization of skills learned in the program for these children is available. In follow-up research, standardized measures will be implemented in a clinical trial, along with data on generalization.

Possible Limitations

In addition to the encouraging data these research studies have provided for TeachTown: Basics, limitations and attributes within the program that may affect generalization have been discovered. For example, the two-dimensional stimuli used in the on-computer lessons may or may not generalize to the child's natural environment. The basis of this theory is that, because the stimuli exist only in the limited space of a computer monitor, the learning encounter cannot be shaped by proximity or touch and is very different from encountering these stimuli in the natural environment. Another limitation of TeachTown: Basics is that all of the voices in the software are the same voice. This could limit the child's ability to respond to instructions in other voices. In addition, the software does not include all concepts and skills that children should learn in this age group. While TeachTown: Basics is a useful tool, other learning approaches must also be used for the child to reach full potential.

To increase generalization when using TeachTown: Basics, it is suggested that the off-computer activities included in the software be used just as often, if not more often, than the on-computer lessons for teaching children. If the off-computer activities are not appropriate for a particular child, it is suggested that the child's team adapt the off-computer activities to fit the child's needs. It is crucial that this be done for all concepts, especially those where the child may be experiencing difficulty. In addition, it is important to realize where there are holes in the curriculum and to spend time teaching the concepts that are not included. For example, TeachTown: Basics does not yet have a lesson for sequencing or sorting, which is an important skill for this age group. This type of lesson will be included in TeachTown: Skill Builder; however, until then it should be addressed independently of the program.

Generalization can also be enhanced by sitting with the child while he or she is using the software and working on expressive language skills, social interaction, and expanding what the child is learning. Using the expert-mode feature of the software may also allow opportunities for increasing generalization by choosing lessons that teach the same idea or concept but in different ways. For instance, there are lessons to teach letters and sounds through receptive identification and matching lessons. A reward can also be chosen for the child to have more exposure to letters. Although some research suggests that at least some generalization may occur without off-computer activities, incorporating these suggestions with regular use of the software is much more likely to result in overall success than using the software alone. See Appendix 6.1 for activities designed to supplement material that the child learns while using TeachTown: Basics.

ANIMATED SPEECH CORPORATION

Animated Speech Corporation develops educational software to improve the quality of life of children who are developmentally at prekindergarten through Grade 4. To achieve this goal, the company uses Timo (see Figure 6.7), a powerful animated tutor that is derived from 20 years of government-funded research. The Team Up With Timo product line consists of three products: Team Up With Timo: Vocabulary, Timo's Lesson Creator, and Team Up With Timo: Stories. Each of these products provides CAI for language acquisition skills and uses different methods to attain generalization.

Use of Timo, the animated tutor, in the Team Up With Timo products dramatically increases the rate of learning speech, reading, and other language skills. Research has shown that these programs increase vocabulary for children with autism (Bosseler & Massaro, 2003), English language learners (Massaro & Light, 2003), children with speech and language impairments, deaf students (Massaro & Light, 2004b), those with reading delays (Swanson, Fey, Mills, & Hood, 2005), and typically developing learners acquiring language and literacy skills. Baldi, Timo's hairless predecessor, was proven highly effective in numerous peer-reviewed studies (e.g., Massaro, Cohen, Tabain, Beskow, & Clark, 2005; Massaro & Light, 2004b).

Figure 6.7. Timo, the three-dimensional tutor who interacts with students and calls them by name.

For generalization to occur, it is critical to consider the learning environment. The learning environment for generalization is important for all children, but especially for children with autism. Because of challenging behaviors such as lack of cooperation and motivation observed in some children with autism, a motivating environment is essential for developing language skills. The Team Up With Timo products use Timo to create such an environment.

Timo is interactive, friendly, and patient and can work at the child's pace. He greets the child by name and provides feedback and reinforcement. There are numerous anecdotal reports that students enjoy working with Timo and appear to develop a relationship with him. Children have been heard to exclaim, "I want to work with Timo today" and "I love Timo." Because children are working with a tutor in the Timo programs, they are working with a face. Research has shown that some children with autism learn vocabulary and grammatical forms faster and show better retention working with a face than without a face (Massaro & Bosseler, 2006). Working with a face or a tutor also offers the child auditory and visual information. Using these two sources of information more closely replicates learning in the natural environment and is more informative than either alone.

Team Up With Timo: Vocabulary

Team Up With Timo: Vocabulary focuses on teaching both receptive and expressive vocabulary. The program includes a curriculum of 127 vocabulary-building lessons covering more than 650 words and images drawn from kindergarten through fourth-grade curricula. Timo's prompts, praise, and feedback teach children vocabulary words by identifying a picture, speaking, reading, or spelling. One of the core principles of Vocabulary is having multiple sources of information to teach vocabulary and increase perception, recognition, learning, and retention. By presenting the material in a variety of ways, Vocabulary increases generalization and decreases simple memorization. As in the previous implementations and tests of our pedagogy (Massaro, 2006b), in Vocabulary, students

1. Observe the words being spoken by a realistic talking interlocutor

2. Experience the word as spoken and written

3. See visual images of referents of the words

4. Click on or point to the referent or its spelling

5. Hear themselves say the word, followed by a correct pronunciation

6. Spell the word by typing

7. Observe and respond to the word used in context

Although half of the exercises involve multiple-choice testing, there is evidence that this experience boosts performance on later tests with other formats (Marsh, Roediger, Bjork, & Bjork, 2007). The other half of the tests involve either spoken or written generation of the students' answers, which facilitates learning (Metcalfe & Kornell, 2007). The test exercises can be viewed as learning exercises because testing has been demonstrated to increase learning and retention (McDaniel, Roediger, & McDermott, 2007).

Another feature of Vocabulary is that the tutoring can be individualized for each student. A profile is created for each student to specify which exercise should be included, the reward selection, and whether or not captioning should be on—an important concern for students with ASDs, deaf students, and hard-of-hearing students. This customizability allows the user to generate endless examples of concepts, change how the information is presented, and change what Timo says—all of which increase generalization possibilities.

Timo's Lesson Creator

Partnering with Vocabulary is Timo's Lesson Creator. Lesson Creator allows teachers or parents to produce completely new lessons for Vocabulary in minutes. Because vocabulary is essentially infinite in number, it is difficult to anticipate all of the vocabulary that a student will need. Teachers, parents, and even students can build original lessons that meet unique and specialized conditions. Users can incorporate new words illustrated by images from the Internet, from digital cameras, or from 3,500 supplied Mayer-Johnson Boardmaker pictures. The result is highly customized and personalized lessons on any topic that can be shared with any Vocabulary user.

Lesson Creator provides a realistic learning situation that should generalize effectively to the real world. Multiple prompts and feedback can be used, which are selected randomly during the learning session. In addition to using custom images, Lesson Creator allows users to further increase generalization by customizing anything Timo says. For example, if a teacher is composing vocabulary lessons, he or she can set up the greeting and instructions, the questions, and the feedback for one set of words to give an appropriate framework for the learning. Perhaps one of the most efficient features of Lesson Creator is that new lessons can be created easily as modifications of existing lessons. Once this is in place, a teacher can simply insert new vocabulary content into the same framework to make additional lessons.

One of the biggest benefits of Lesson Creator is to use the program to generalize material students are learning elsewhere. For example, if a teacher is taking the class on a field trip to the local aquarium, he or she is able to create lessons about the marine animals ahead of time. This way, the children will become familiar with the animals and then experience them in a real-world situation. Lesson Creator can also be used at home, where a parent can prepare lessons with words in the child's current reading and names of relatives, schoolmates, and teachers. Lessons can also be easily created for the child's current interests.

Team Up With Timo: Stories

Animated Speech Corporation's third product, Team Up With Timo: Stories, teaches children by having them read a story along with Timo. Timo asks questions for comprehension of content and concepts by engaging the student in story-based activities ranging from putting story events in sequence to simple problem solving. The broad goal of Stories is to improve expressive and receptive language skills and vocabulary through the process of retelling stories. Generalization is crucial because narrative skills lay the foundation for social and academic success. In Stories, six stories and correlated activities give children the opportunity to practice a range of skills including story comprehension, narrative skills such as retelling stories, speech-language skills, social thinking, and conversational modeling. For beginning readers, the pictures in each story closely match the action in the text to help the child understand the story.

Research has shown that being able to retell a story at age 4 years is predictive of later success in school. Storytelling also helps children participate in daily life with friends, family, and school. For these reasons, Stories follows the narrative-based language intervention approach of combining storytelling with skill-based activities. Children with ASDs and other communication disorders often cannot understand a story, speak in sentences, or organize information to retell others. Stories may help provide the communication skills that these children need.

When building language skills that generalize to other environments, Stories uses a few key ingredients to increase success. For example, an emphasis on engaging activities with multiple opportunities for mixed receptive and expressive tasks is necessary. Stories introduces 10 vocabulary words in each story. These vocabulary words are then practiced in six different language games that require differing levels of language processing of increasing complexity. The new vocabulary words are intermixed with words the child has already learned. To provide the expressive tasks in Stories, an adult can work with the child at the computer. During the story sequencing activity, the child tells the story to an adult while looking at the pictures and then retells the story when the pictures are turned over. In addition, to improve generalization, it is important to combine CAI with related activities in other settings. Stories has a list of extension activities for each story to be done away from the computer, such as reenacting the stories with toys and telling the story to an adult who is unfamiliar with the story. Strong reinforcement is also necessary, as well as visual support. For each game in the program, there is a visual reinforcement schedule that shows children how many trials they need to complete and a chart where children can see their progress; they also receive an animated sticker or puzzle piece for each correct response.

With Stories, generalization can be maximized for improved listening comprehension, vocabulary, and retelling skills by matching the child's background knowledge. This enables the child to expand on knowledge he or she already has and frees the child's processing resources to learn and practice linguistic forms and devote energy to retelling the story.

All of the stories use elaborated language. This means that all of the information presented is explicit and redundant. Writing the stories this way serves as a processing aid. Elaborated language reduces the need for inferencing and makes

Figure 6.8.   Home page for Team Up With Timo: Stories.

it easier for the child to understand the story. When the job of processing narrative discourse is made manageable for the child, he or she is more likely to learn and use skills away from the computer (see Figure 6.8).

Frequency of opportunities to tell and share stories with others is also important. *Stories* provides explicit instructions so that adults can support storytelling and retelling throughout the day by scaffolding opportunities to recount daily events and/or to retell the story from a lesson. This approach offers the child a blend of direct instruction and naturalistic teaching.

Research Supporting the Timo Programs

Stories and the other Timo programs are based on research and technology developed by Dr. Don Massaro. Massaro developed Baldi, Timo's bald-headed predecessor, primarily to research the value of visible speech in face-to-face communication (Massaro, 1998). Baldi provided realistic visible speech that was almost as accurate as a natural speaker (see http://mambo.ucsc.edu/psl/international.html). The tutor can be animated in real time and is able to say anything at any time in interactive applications (Massaro, 2004; Massaro, Ouni, Cohen, & Clark, 2005). One of the first applications of Baldi as an animated tutor was implemented for deaf and hard-of-hearing students at the Tucker-Maxon School of Oral Education. The school used Baldi in a variety of school exercises in mathematics, history, science, and social studies (Massaro, Cohen, & Beskow, 1999). Eventually, a lesson creator and tutor were developed for vocabulary learning, which evolved into Team Up With Timo: Vocabulary and Timo's Lesson Creator.

When Baldi was being developed, a great deal of research was completed to best understand the benefits of using a computer-animated tutor. Computer-animated tutors have the potential to provide students with autism with an effective learning environment because they can produce accurate visible speech, facilitate face-to-face oral communication, and serve people with language challenges. These embodied conversational characters can function effectively as language tutors, reading tutors, or science tutors. Animated tutors provide value because our perception and understanding are influenced by a speaker's face and accompanying gestures, as well as the actual sound of the speech (Massaro, 1998). Although the auditory signal alone is often adequate for communication, visual information from movements of the lips, tongue, and jaws enhance intelligibility of the acoustic stimulus (particularly in noisy environments that exist in many learning situations). Moreover, speech is enriched by the facial expressions, emotions, and gestures produced by a speaker. With these conclusions in mind, computer-animated tutors, such as Baldi and Timo, may have a significant benefit to learning.

Some individuals have raised concerns about whether an animated tutor's two-dimensionality hampers a child's learning process. Limiting the student's experience to the two-dimensional world of computer monitors may constrain learning relative to a live teacher. When addressing this concern, it is important to know if the visible speech from a three-dimensional face projected onto a two-dimensional surface is as informative as a live person seen in three dimensions. Surprisingly, research shows that there does not seem to be a direct comparison of these two conditions. In their study, Sumby and Pollack (1954) used a live talker, whereas Jesse, Vrignaud, and Massaro (2000–2001) used a video recording of the talker. The benefit that the participants received from visible speech appears to be roughly equivalent in the two cases. Finding conditions that matched as much as possible, the accuracy improved from about 30% with just auditory speech to about 58% when the three-dimensional visible speech was also present. This 28% improvement compares favorably with the 27% improvement using the two-dimensional presentation. Thus, it appears that the benefit of a visible tutor exists for two-dimensional viewing as well as for a live presentation.

The success of two-dimensional media such as the television and the Internet, however, is real-world experimental proof of the sufficiency of two dimensions for learning. Furthermore, the use of video-based sign language interpreting in the classroom does not seem to present more of a challenge for deaf students than live classroom presentations (Marschark et al., 2005). Thus, tutoring on two-dimensional surfaces appears to be as effective as live tutoring.

Researchers also studied the effectiveness of Baldi with children with special needs. For this study, researchers created 84 unique lessons with vocabulary items selected from the curriculum of two schools (Bosseler & Massaro, 2003). Eight children diagnosed with autism, 7–11 years of age, participated in the study. The results indicated that the children learned many new words, grammatical constructions, and concepts. In addition, a delayed test given more than 30 days after the learning sessions took place showed that the children retained more than 85% of the words that they had learned. This learning and retention of new vocabulary, grammar, and language use is a significant accomplishment for children with ASDs.

Although all children in this study demonstrated learning from initial assessment to final reassessment, it is possible that the children were learning the words outside of the program. For example, the students may have been learning words from speech therapists or in their school curriculum. Furthermore, it is important to know whether the vocabulary knowledge would generalize to new pictorial instances of the words. To address these questions, a second investigation was completed. Once a student achieved 100% correct, generalization tests and training were carried out with novel images. The placement of the images relative to one another was also random in each lesson. Assessment and training continued until the student was able to accurately identify at least five out of six vocabulary items across four unique sets of images.

Although performance varied dramatically across the children and across the word sets during the pretraining sessions, training was effective for all word sets for all children. Figure 6.9 displays the proportion of correct responses for

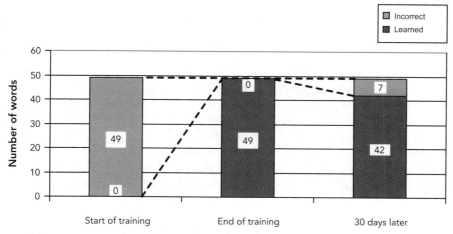

Figure 6.9. Vocabulary learned using Team Up With Timo: Vocabulary for one of the eight students with autism spectrum disorders.

one of the students during the test sessions conducted at pretraining and post-training for each of the three word sets. The vertical lines in each of the three panels indicate the last pretraining session before the onset of training for that word set. Some of the words were known prior to training and were even learned to some degree without training. Given training, however, all of the students attained our criterion for identification accuracy for each word set and were also able to generalize accurate identification to four instances of untrained images. The students identified significantly more words following implementation of training compared with pretraining performance, showing that the program was responsible for learning. Learning also generalized to new images in random locations and to interactions outside of the lesson environment. These results show that the learning program is effective for children with ASDs, as it was for children with hearing loss.

In another study, Massaro (2006a) evaluated Team Up With Timo: Vocabulary for teaching vocabulary to English language learners. This experiment was particularly significant because it was the first research study that used Timo as the animated tutor rather than Baldi. Children whose native language is Spanish were tutored and tested on English words they previously did not know. Using a multiple-baseline design, the children learned the words when they were tutored but not words that were simply tested. This result replicates the previous studies with children with autism and hard-of-hearing children that used Baldi as the animated conversational tutor. Other experiments have demonstrated that Baldi's unique characteristics allow a novel approach to training speech production to both children with hearing loss (Massaro & Light, 2004a) and adults learning a new language (Massaro & Light, 2003).

Possible Limitations

Although research suggests that Timo and Baldi are quite effective at teaching, several factors may limit the efficacy of learning. One potential limitation is that the visual input the student receives is necessarily on a two-dimensional screen rather than existing as an actual a three-dimensional person. Important pedagogical characteristics of the three-dimensional world might not be adequately represented in just two dimensions. A second possible limitation is that the lessons use synthetic speech and facial animation. Although these properties make our tutoring agent capable of saying anything at any time, they might compromise the instructional dialogue in the tutoring situation.

To better understand the effectiveness of the programs, more research is needed. Although research has examined the effectiveness of CAI for receptive language with regard to children with autism (Moore & Calvert, 2000), Team Up With Timo: Stories also seeks to do more. One of the goals with Stories is to study how effectively it can help a broader population of children to develop expressive language skills. In addition, more research is needed to study the efficiency of CAI with increasing a variety of language in adults and increasing narrative skills in typically developing children, at-risk children, and children with speech and/or language disabilities (Harkins, Koch, & Michel, 1994; Whitehurst et al., 1988; Yoder, Spruytenburg, Edwards, & Davies, 1995; Zevenbergen & Wilson, 1996). Currently, only studies involving interactive picture books have been conducted.

Along with additional research, improvements can be made to increase generalization in the Team Up With Timo products. One enhancement for Team Up With Timo: Vocabulary could be for the program to ask the child to use both the receptive and expressive language features of the software (i.e., have the child say the words, not just learn them receptively). In addition, working on vocabulary words outside of computer sessions will significantly enhance generalization. Currently, Timo's Lesson Creator can be used to increase the number of examples for each concept. The program allows the user to import as many images as he or she can find. To maximize generalization, it is suggested that a variety of drawings and photographs be used and that the customizable instructions offered by Timo vary throughout the trials. This will help the child to learn to respond to instructions in different ways.

SUMMARY

The use of computers to teach children with ASDs is growing in popularity and in necessity due to the increasing prevalence of the disorder and the expanding need for more accessible and affordable options for education and treatment. With the development tools that TeachTown and Animated Speech have created, new learning modules and features for existing products will be built with only modest development time and cost. Future products will address the needs of the ASD community, including products for all ages and programs and features to help parents, teachers, and service providers.

Despite the exciting advancements that have been made available in recent years, research is still needed to determine the efficacy of CAI, especially in terms of generalization. To date, most research has only looked at generalization in adult-presented tasks, which might be similar to the tasks on the computer. It will be important for researchers to set up generalization probes in unusual and less-structured situations to measure how well the child's skills generalize to the natural environment. Most studies have looked at generalization of language skills, but it is imperative that generalization of other skills also be studied, especially social skills. It is obvious that future research needs to study the effectiveness of CAI, but without generalization, it is questionable if the child has made any progress at all. Consequently, researchers must take a closer look at generalization of CAI; developers must also carefully consider how their programs address generalization issues and what tips they can provide to consumers to maximize generalization.

In sum, CAI promises to deliver more education and treatment options, effectiveness, increased accessibility, improved data collection, cost savings, greater motivation for the child, and—based on the research to date—at least some generalization off the computer.

REFERENCES

Beck, I.L., McKeown, M.G., & Kucan, L. (2002). *Bringing words to life: Robust vocabulary instruction.* New York: Guilford Press.

Bernard-Opitz, V., Sriram, N., & Nakhoda-Sapuan, S. (2001). Enhancing social problem solving in children with autism and normal children through computer-assisted instruction. *Journal of Autism and Developmental Disorders, 31*(4), 377–384.

Bosseler, A., & Massaro, D.W. (2003). Development and evaluation of a computer-animated tutor for vocabulary and language learning in children with autism. *Journal of Autism and Developmental Disorders, 33*(6), 653–672.

Brownell, R. (2000). *Receptive One-Word Picture Vocabulary Test.* Novato, CA: Academic Therapy Publications.

Harkins, D.A., Koch, P.E., Michel, G.F. (1994). Listening to maternal story telling affects narrative skills of 5-year-old children. *Journal of Genetic Psychology, 155,* 247–257.

Haugland, S.W. (1999). What role should technology play in young children's learning? *Young Children, 54*(6), 26–31.

Hetzroni, O.E., & Tannous, J. (2004). Effects of a computer-based intervention program on the communicative functions of children with autism. *Journal of Autism and Developmental Disorders, 34,* 95–113.

Jahr, E. (2001). Teaching children with autism to answer novel *wh*-questions by utilizing a multiple exemplar strategy. *Developmental Disabilities, 22*(5), 407–423.

Jesse, A., Vrignaud, N., & Massaro, D.W. (2000–2001). The processing of information from multiple sources in simultaneous interpreting. *Interpreting, 5,* 95–115.

Johnston, J.R. (1988). Generalization: The nature of change. *Language, Speech, and Hearing Services in Schools, 19,* 314–329.

Koegel, R.L., O'Dell, M.C., & Koegel, L.K. (1987). A natural language teaching paradigm for nonverbal autistic children. *Journal of Autism and Developmental Disorders, 17,* 187–200.

Koegel, R.L., Schreibman, L., Good, A., Cerniglia, L., Murphy, C., & Koegel, L. (1989). *How to teach pivotal behaviors to children with autism: A training manual.* Santa Barbara: University of California.

LaSasso, C., & Davey, B. (1987). The relationship between lexical knowledge and reading comprehension for prelingually, profoundly hearing-impaired students. *Volta Review, 89*(4), 211–220.

Li, X., & Atkins, M.S. (2006). Early childhood computer experience and cognitive and motor development. *Pediatrics, 113*(6), 1715–1722.

Lovaas, O.I. (1987). Behavioral treatment and normal educational and intellectual functioning in young autistic children. *Journal of Consulting and Clinical Psychology, 55,* 3–9.

Marschark, M., Pelz, J.B., Convertino, C., Sapere, P., Arndt, M.E., & Seewagen, R. (2005). Classroom interpreting and visual information processing in mainstream education for deaf students: Live or Memorex? *American Educational Research Journal, 42*(4), 727–761.

Marsh, E.J., Roediger, H.L., Bjork, R.A., & Bjork, E.L. (2007). The memorial consequences of multiple-choice testing. *Psychonomic Bulletin & Review, 14*(2), 194–199.

Massaro, D.W. (1998). *Perceiving talking faces: Insights into auditory attention.* Cambridge, MA: MIT Press.

Massaro, D.W. (2004). Symbiotic value of an embodied agent in language learning. In R.H. Sprague, Jr. (Ed.), *Proceedings of 37th Annual Hawaii International Conference on System Sciences.* Los Alamitos, CA: IEEE Computer Society Press.

Massaro, D.W. (2006a). Embodied agents in language learning for children with language challenges. In K. Miesenberger, J. Klaus, W. Zagler, & A. Karshmer (Eds.), *Proceedings of the 10th International Conference on Computers Helping People with Special Needs, ICCHP 2006* (pp. 809–816). Berlin: Springer.

Massaro, D.W. (2006b). The psychology and technology of talking heads: Applications in language learning. In O. Bernsen, L. Dybkjaer, & J. van Kuppevelt (Eds.), *Natural, intelligent and effective interaction in multimodal dialogue systems* (pp. 183–214). Dordrecht, The Netherlands: Kluwer Academic.

Massaro, D.W., & Bosseler, A. (2006). Read my lips: The importance of the face in a computer-animated tutor for autistic children learning language. *Autism: The International Journal of Research and Practice, 10*(5), 495–510.

Massaro, D.W., Cohen, M.M., & Beskow, J. (1999). From theory to practice: Rewards and challenges. In *Proceedings of the International Conference of Phonetic Sciences* (pp. 1289–1292). San Francisco: Regents of the University of California.

Massaro, D.W., Cohen, M.M., Tabain, M., Beskow, J., & Clark, R. (2005). Animated speech: Research progress and applications. In E. Vatiokis-Bateson, G. Bailly, & P. Perrier, (Eds.), *Audiovisual speech processing.* Cambridge, MA: MIT Press.

Massaro, D.W., & Light, J. (2003). *Read my tongue movements: Bimodal learning to perceive and produce non-native speech /r/ and /l/.* Presented at the Eurospeech, 8th European Conference on Speech Communication and Technology, Geneva, Switzerland.

Massaro, D.W., & Light, J. (2004a). Improving the vocabulary of children with hearing loss. *Volta Review, 104*(3), 141–174.

Massaro, D.W., & Light, J. (2004b). Using visible speech for training perception and production of speech for hard of hearing individuals. *Journal of Speech, Language, and Hearing Research, 47*(2), 304–320.

Massaro, D.W., Ouni, S., Cohen, M.M., & Clark, R. (2005). A multilingual embodied conversational agent. In R.H. Sprague (Ed.), *Proceedings of 38th Annual Hawaii International Conference on System Sciences.* Los Alamitos, CA: IEEE Computer Society Press.

McDaniel, M.A., Roediger, H.L., & McDermott, K.B. (2007). Generalizing test-enhanced learning from the laboratory to the classroom. *Psychonomic Bulletin & Review, 14,* 200–206.

Metcalfe, J., & Kornell, N. (2007). Principles of cognitive science in education: The effects of generation, errors, and feedback. *Psychonomic Bulletin & Review, 14*(2), 225–229.

Moore, M., & Calvert, S. (2000). Vocabulary acquisition for children with autism: Teacher or computer instruction. *Journal of Autism and Developmental Disorders, 30,* 359–362.

Neef, N.A., & Lutz, M.N. (2001). Assessment of variables affecting choice and application to classroom interventions. *School Psychology Quarterly, 16*(3), 239–252.

Reeve, S.A., Reeve, K.F., Townsend, D.B., & Poulson, C.L. (2007). Establishing a generalized repertoire of helping behavior in children with autism. *Journal of Applied Behavior Analysis, 40*(1), 123–136.

Schilling, D.L., & Schwartz, E. (2004). Alternative seating for young children with autism spectrum disorder: Effects on classroom behavior. *Journal of Autism and Developmental Disorders, 34*(4), 423–432.

Schreibman, L. (1988). *Autism.* Newbury Park, CA: Sage Publications.

Stahmer, A., & Geddes, K. (in progress). *Generalization to expressive language following receptive language training in TeachTown Basics computer-assisted software.*

Sumby, W.H., & Pollack, I. (1954). Visual contribution to speech intelligibility in noise. *Journal of the Acoustical Society of America, 26*(2), 212–215.

Swanson, L.A., Fey, M.E., Mills, C.E., & Hood, L.S. (2005). Use of narrative-based language intervention with children who have specific language impairment. *American Journal of Speech and Language Pathology, 14*(2), 131–143.

Whalen, C., & Cernich, S. (in progress). *Are the reinforcers reinforcing? Effectiveness of reinforcers embedded in TeachTown Basics for maintaining student attention.*

Whalen, C., Liden, L., Ingersoll, B., Dallaire, E., & Liden, S. (2006). Positive behavioral changes associated with the use of computer-assisted instruction for young children. *Journal of Speech and Language Pathology and Applied Behavior Analysis, 1*(1), 11–26.

Whalen, C., Liden, L., MacDonald, K., Thomas, T., & Lockhart, D. (in progress). *Effectiveness of TeachTown: Basics software for teaching language, cognitive, and social skills to children.*

Whitehurst, G.J., Falco, F.L., Lonigan, C.J., Fischel, J.E., Debaryshe, B.D., Valdez-Menchaca, M.C., et al. (1988). Accelerating language development through picture book reading. *Developmental Psychology, 24,* 552–559.

Williams, C., Wright, B., Callaghan, G., & Coughlan, B. (2002). Do children with autism learn to read more readily by computer assisted instruction or traditional book methods? A pilot study. *Autism, 6*(1), 71–91.

Yoder, P.J., Spruytenburg, H., Edwards, A., & Davies, B. (1995). Effect of verbal routine contexts and expansions on gains in the mean length of utterance in children with developmental delays. *Language, Speech, and Hearing Services in Schools, 26,* 21–32.

Zevenbergen, A., & Wilson, G. (1996). *Effects of an interactive reading program on the narrative skills of children in Head Start.* Paper presented at the Head Start's Third National Research Conference, Washington, DC.

Chapter 6
Appendices

126

TeachTown Generalization Activities

The following are just a few of the activities designed to supplement material that the child learns while using the TeachTown: Basics computer program (http://www.teachtown.com). The activities are deliberately written to be very simple so that someone with no training can implement them immediately. However, when implemented with a proven methodology, such as Pivotal Response Training (PRT; see Chapter 2), they can be a valuable part of a therapy program. They can be printed directly from the software and should be used to maximize generalization as the child moves through the curriculum. Other than generalization, the activities also have the advantage of producing collateral effects (i.e., changes that are not directly targeted by the activities but which are likely to improve by using them) such as improved play, imitation, motor, self-help, and social interaction. These activities, when implemented with no parent training, have also been shown to decrease inappropriate behaviors (e.g., tantrums, avoidance) and inappropriate language (i.e., saying things that are out of context or self-stimulatory).

The *primary benefits* specify the targets that the activities were designed to teach in the natural environment including receptive language, cognitive/academic, social skills, and adaptive life skills. The *secondary benefits* are skills that the activities also target and may include joint attention or other social interaction, play, imitation, motor, or self-help skills. The *materials required* lists what objects are needed to implement the activity. These materials are toys and objects that are typically found in the homes and schools of many children. There are some activities that may require special materials, but even these are materials that can easily be found in toy or educational learning stores. It is appropriate to replace materials as the facilitator sees fit either due to availability or due to increasing the child's motivation for the activity. The *instructions* tell the adult how to engage the child in the activity and how to teach the skills that are targeted. The *advanced instructions* instruct the adult how to move the activity on so that it is more advanced or more age-appropriate for older children.

ACTION FIGURES

Supplements TeachTown: Basics computer lessons: Actions

Primary benefits: Receptive vocabulary (verbs)

Secondary benefits: Expressive language, fine motor skill, object imitation, pretend play

Materials required: Action figures, dolls, or other toys that you can pretend to engage in movement

Instructions

Take a few dolls or action figures that the child enjoys and engage the child in play with the objects. On your turn, tell the child, "The doll is going swimming" and make the figure swim. On the child's turn, try to get the child to imitate your action or, if the child is catching on, ask the child to do something different with his or her character (e.g., "The doll is RUNNING home!"). You may need to model the new action if the child does not get it right away. Once the child is able to imitate several actions, ask the child to demonstrate actions on his or her own (e.g., "The doll needs to jump") and model when necessary to help the child understand.

ANIMAL STAMPS

Supplements TeachTown: Basics computer lessons: Multiple Cues—Color–Animals

Primary benefits: Identification of multiple cues (color and animals), responding to directions with multiple cues (following directions)

Secondary benefits: Expressive language, fine motor skills

Materials required: Rubber stamps of several types of target animals, at least two different target colors of ink pads, paper

Instructions

Say, "We are going to make a picture with lots of animals." Place three different stamps in front of the child. Then, show him or her two different colors of ink (you may need to show the tops of the containers as the ink may not appear to be the color that it is). If the child is unfamiliar with stamps, you may want to make a few practice runs before you start the activity. Prompt the child to choose a stamp and take his or her hand that is holding the stamp and guide it to the ink. Once there is ink on the stamp, guide the child toward the paper and press down on the child's hand to create the mark. Once he or she is capable of using the stamps correctly by him- or herself, start the activity. Say, "Let's make a blue cat." The child should pick the cat and the blue color. If the child needs help with this, verbally prompt him or her to first choose the animal and then give the child another prompt to choose the correct color. If verbal prompting does not work, use the hand-over-hand technique again but begin to fade your prompts until the child can do it independently. Once the child chooses the correct animal stamp and color, say, "Right! Make a blue cat on the paper." At this time, the child should press the stamp against the paper. On your turn, pick an animal and a color and say, "Look at mine; what is it?" Help the child to expressively identify the animal and the color. Show the child three other animals and have him or her pick one. Then, show two colors and have the child pick one.

Continue taking turns picking animals and different colors. You can use this time to ask questions about the animals and/or have the child use descriptive words about the animal or animal stamp.

BODY BATH

Supplements TeachTown: Basics computer lessons: Body parts, body functions

Primary benefits: Receptive vocabulary (body parts), self-help/independence

Secondary benefits: Expressive language, fine motor skills

Materials required: Bath (or shower), sponge or washcloth, soap, a doll that can get wet

Instructions

When it is time for the child's bath (or shower), instruct the child to wash his or her body parts one at a time. Tell the child, "Time to wash your foot," or you can make it a fun song and say, "This is the way we wash our foot, wash our foot, wash our foot. This is the way we wash our foot, so we can get all clean." For your turns, you can wash body parts on a doll to help the child with generalization (e.g., "Molly needs to get clean. I'll wash her elbow.") You can also have the child wash body parts on the doll. Ask the child to label body parts, too (e.g., "What is this?"), and point to your finger, the doll's finger, or the child's finger. Continue taking turns and have the child identify body parts on him- or herself, the doll, and/or you.

Advanced Instructions

To work on functions, ask the child to show you, "What do you hear with? What do you see with?" and so forth. You can also try this type of activity with birds to enhance your student's learning on the bird computer lessons. Create a bird bath and follow the steps described previously. This activity is also fun in a deep sea bath with sea life and aquatic animals to enhance your student's learning on the aquatic computer lessons.

BOOK SOUNDS

Supplements TeachTown: Basics computer lessons: Environmental sounds

Primary benefits: Auditory processing, identification of sounds in the environment, receptive vocabulary

Secondary benefits: Expressive language, pointing, prereading

Materials required: Children's books with pictures of things that make sounds in the environment (e.g., animals, vehicles). You can use flashcards or magazines or make your own book.

Instructions

Sitting with the child, say, "We are going to look at some pictures today!" Get the book and open it to the first page that has pictures of things that create sounds (e.g., a car would make a vroom, vroom sound; a turkey would make a gobble, gobble sound). Say to the child, "I will make a sound and see if it could be a noise that something in the book would make." Open the book to the first page (e.g., pictures of animals) and say, "Woof, woof." Pretend to search through the pictures on the page and say, "Where is the dog? A dog says, *woof, woof.*" Turn to the next page that you want to use and say, "It's your turn now! What do you see?" Let the child answer and then ask the child what sound the object makes. Have the child look at the pictures and encourage him or her to point to the correct object.

If the child has difficulty, repeat the sound and prompt him or her to identify the object. Say, "Look, a doorbell makes a ding-dong sound." Continue to take turns and make sounds for the pictures in the book. Allow the child to choose the page you will target some of the time.

CLOTHES SHOPPING

Supplements TeachTown: Basics computer lessons: Clothing; Multiple Cues–Clothing

Primary benefits: Receptive vocabulary (clothing)

Secondary benefits: Expressive language, fine motor skills

Materials required: Clothing catalogs (may also use clipart or coloring pages of clothes); scissors; glue; construction paper

Instructions

Before you do this activity with the child, find pictures of the target clothing in clothing catalogs. Using scissors, cut out the clothes and glue them to pieces of construction paper. (These pictures may also be laminated at a local office supply store in order to protect them.)

Draw a shopping cart, basket, or bag to paste the clothing items in. Arrange the pictures in groups of two or three different clothes per group on the floor or table. Say to the child, "We are going to shop for clothes." Bring the child over to the first group of clothes and say, "We need a hat. Put the hat in your cart/basket/bag." Take a turn and say, "I'm going to put a shirt into the basket." Next, bring the child over to the next group of clothes and ask him or her to find a different article of clothing. Combine the groups of clothing as the child shops in order to continue the game. Continue until all of the clothes have been purchased. Ask the child to label the different clothing items by asking, "What is this one?" to work on expressive language skills.

Advanced Instructions

When the child is ready to work on multiple cues, begin asking the child to discriminate between different colors and different items. For instance, say, "Put a red dress into the basket."

COLOR TRAIN

Supplements TeachTown: Basics computer lessons: Colors

Primary benefits: Color identification

Secondary benefits: Expressive language, fine motor skills, following directions, organizational skills

Materials required: Bin to keep materials in, construction paper of various colors, crayons, glue, yarn

Instructions

Before beginning the activity with the child, cut the yarn into 2-inch pieces. In addition, cut the construction paper into circles for the train wheels and rectangles for the train cars.

Tell the child, "It is time to make a train!" Present three rectangular pieces of construction paper to the child. Each piece should be a different color. Ask the child, "Can you find the red piece?"

If the child responds correctly, say, "That's right. That piece is the red one." If the child does not answer correctly, point to the correct piece and say, "This piece is the red one."

Say, "Now it's time to put some wheels on the train." Place three circular pieces of construction paper in front of the child. Each piece should be a different color. If the child struggled to answer the previous question, you should present only two choices instead of three.

Ask the child, "Can you find the yellow piece?" If the child responds correctly, say, "That's right. That piece is the yellow one." If the child does not answer correctly, point to the correct piece and say, "This piece is the yellow one." Help the child glue the wheel onto the train.

Say, "We need to add another wheel to the train." Repeat the last few steps with another circular piece of construction paper. Once both wheels are glued onto the train car, present the child with three crayons. Each crayon should be a different color. If the child has struggled with correctly identifying colors, reduce the number of crayons to make it easier to answer the question without prompting. Ask the child, "Which crayon is the black one?" If the child responds correctly, say, "That's right. That crayon is the black one." If the child does not respond correctly, point to the correct crayon and say, "This crayon is the black one."

Ask the child, "Do you want to draw people on the train?" It is acceptable if the child only scribbles with the crayon. Tell the child, "I love the people you are drawing. Can I draw a person?" Take a turn and draw your own person on the train. If the child seems to enjoy drawing people, ask, "Do you want to draw some more people?" Once the child is finished drawing people on that train car, help him or her glue a piece of yarn to the end of the train.

Continue to repeat these steps until you have three or four completed train cars. Glue the yarn from one train car to another to link the train cars together. When finished, hang the train on a wall to show the length of the train to the child.

Later, you can show the child the train again and ask him or her to show you the green train or the red wheel. This will further the child's understanding of color.

Advanced Instructions

If the child is verbal, ask the child to say the color of each piece of construction paper.

DRESS UP

Supplements TeachTown: Basics computer lessons: Occupations

Primary benefits: Pretend play skills, receptive vocabulary, social interaction

Secondary benefits: Expressive language, fine motor skills

Materials required: A variety of objects that could represent pretend things (e.g., hat or broom for witch, plastic teeth for vampire, red nose or wig for clown, wings or wand for fairy)

Instructions

Say to the child, "Let's dress up as pretend characters!" Show two types of accessories and say, "Here is a broom! I will pretend to be a witch." Take the object and use it/put it on and act as the character (e.g., cackle like a witch and ride the broom). After a few seconds, remove the accessory and set it aside. Show the child two other accessories and say, "Who do you want to pretend to be?" Encourage the child to choose an accessory and wear it or create an action.

If the child has difficulty, say, "Here is a clown nose. Let's put it on your nose!" Take the accessory and help the child use it. Continue to take turns pretending to be different characters.

Helpful Hint

The materials may be obtained cheaply after Halloween from discount stores.

FARM BOOKS

Supplements TeachTown: Basics computer lessons: Animals–Farm

Primary benefits: Receptive vocabulary

Secondary benefits: Expressive language, fine motor, following instructions, learning about books

Materials required: Photos, pictures, clipart, and so forth of farm animals; construction paper; scissors; glue; permanent marker; stapler with staples (or hole punch with paper fasteners)

Instructions

Gather the equipment and say to the child, "Let's make a book!" Show the child two pictures, each of a farm animal, and say, "I'll put the cow in the book." Take the picture, trim it if needed with the scissors, and glue it to a piece of construction paper. Label the picture with the permanent marker. Show the child two more pictures and ask, "Which animal do you want to put in the book?" When he or she identifies a picture, exclaim, "You want to put the chicken in the book!" If the child does not respond, help him or her pick out a picture to work on. Take turns making the pages.

Once the pages have been constructed, say, "Now it's time to put the book together." Stack the pages and place a blank piece of construction paper on top. Instruct the child on how to use the stapler or the hole punch and fasteners. The child may decorate the book cover. After you and the child complete the book, the book may be used to work on animal identification or naming the animals.

Helpful Hint

Remember that this can be done with all sorts of vocabulary words and categories (e.g., a food book, a vehicle book, things that are sweet book).

FIND THE TOYS

Supplements TeachTown: Basics computer lessons: Play

Primary benefits: Receptive vocabulary

Secondary benefits: Expressive language, gross motor skills, social interaction

Materials required: An assortment of the child's toys

Instructions

Bring the child into a room where his or her toys are typically kept. Say to the child, "Let's find your toys!" In a sing-song voice (or to the tune of "Where is Thumbkin?") sing, "Where are bubbles? Where are bubbles? I'll find them. I'll find them." Find the object and set it in front of you.

Now sing the same tune to the child, "Where is the ball? Where is the ball? You find it. You find it." Encourage the child to retrieve the object and set it on the floor. If the child does not respond, take his or her hand and retrieve the object together. Ask the child what else you can find together in order to increase expressive language: "What would you like to find next?" You can also ask the child, "What is this toy?" to work on expressive language skills. Continue taking turns to find different toys. At the end of the game, you can clean up the toys by singing, "Here's the doll. Here's the doll. I'll (You) put her back. I'll (You) put her back."

INSECT SEARCH

Supplements TeachTown: Basics computer lessons: Insects

Primary benefits: Receptive vocabulary

Secondary benefits: Expressive language, pretend play, social interaction

Materials required: An assortment of plastic insects, a container or box to hold the objects, a small butterfly/insect net (optional)

Instructions

Before beginning the activity, place the insects around the room so that they are easily seen from a central area in the room (if the plastic insects are very small, consider spreading them around a table). Say to the child, "We are going to catch some insects (bugs)!" Look around the room and say, "I see an ant! I will go catch it!" Take the net (or use your hands) and "capture" the insect. Place it into the container. Show the box to the child and say, "See, I caught an ant!" Take the insect out of the container. Hand the child the container and net and say, "What insect do you see? Catch it and bring it back to me!" When the child shows you the captured insect say, "Great job! You caught a ladybug! Now it's my turn again!" If the child has difficulty, use two insects at a time and present them within reach. Continue to take turns.

Helpful Hint

Plastic insects can be obtained inexpensively from dollar stores, discount stores, or party stores.

JOB PROPS

Supplements TeachTown: Basics computer lessons: Career Tools

Primary benefits: Functional relationships, pretend play

Secondary benefits: Expressive language, receptive vocabulary

Materials required: Assorted props for occupations (e.g., toy stethoscope for doctor, seed packet for farmer, book for teacher, bowl and spoon for cook, letter for mail carrier)

Instructions

After setting all of the props out, say to the child, "Look at all of these things that people use for their jobs!" Show two objects and say, "I'm going to find something cooks use." Look over the objects and say, "Here is a bowl and spoon. Cooks use these!" Using the objects, pretend to use them (e.g., make mixing motions using the spoon) and say, "See, I'm a cook!" Show two other objects and say, "Which would a doctor use? Can you pretend to be a doctor?" If the child does not respond, help him or her make the motions using the prop. Continue taking turns pretending with the props.

Advanced Instructions

Once the child masters the activity, offer him or her two props and ask the child to choose one. Have the child tell you what the prop is used for and who uses the prop. Then, have the child pretend to use it as that character.

MAKING MUSIC

Supplements TeachTown: Basics computer lessons: Musical Instruments

Primary benefits: Pretend play, receptive vocabulary

Secondary benefits: Expressive language, fine motor skills

Materials required: A set of toy musical instruments. Materials may be found at discount, department, or toy stores.

Instructions

Say to the child, "We are going to make some music!" Show two instruments and say, "I will play the drums." Pick the correct instrument and play it for a few seconds. Show two more instruments and say to the child, "Can you play the guitar for me?" Have the child pick the correct instrument and play it for a few seconds. When the child responds correctly say, "Very good! You are playing the guitar!" If the child has difficulty, take away the incorrect choice and say, "See. This is the guitar. Can you play it for me?" Take turns playing all of the instruments.

Helpful Hint

Remember that this can be done in imitation programs and other receptive identification programs. Since we are working off the computer in these activities, try adding an expressive component to your activities. You might also see what the child will initiate when given the chance. For example, say, "Do what I'm doing." Give the child a chance to imitate you, then prompt him or her with, "Your turn," to see if he or she will initiate a choice of an instrument.

NATURE HOP

Supplements TeachTown: Basics computer lessons: Nature

Primary benefits: Receptive vocabulary

Secondary benefits: Expressive language, gross motor skills

Materials required: A large, paved area (e.g., sidewalk, driveway)

Instructions

Before beginning the game, create a hopscotchlike grid on the pavement by drawing several rows of two squares next to each other. In each square, sketch a simple drawing of objects you find in nature (e.g., rainbow, tree, cloud, sun). Bring the child to the beginning of the grid and say, "We are going to play nature hopscotch!" Say, "Look, at these two squares. I will jump to the flower." Make the correct jump into one of the squares in the first row. Say to the child, "It's your turn; can you jump to the rainbow?" Take turns jumping to the correct squares. At the end of the row of squares, turn around and jump back to the beginning, mixing up the items that you ask the child to jump to.

Advanced Instructions

To work on expressive skills, ask the child, "Now where do you want me to jump?" or "Where do you want to jump?"

NEW HOUSE

Supplements TeachTown: Basics computer lessons: Household Objects

Primary benefits: Receptive vocabulary

Secondary benefits: Expressive language, fine motor skills

Materials required: Computer; printer; pictures, clipart, or photos of various objects that may be found in the house (furniture, appliances, household items); scissors; a large piece of poster board; markers; glue or tape

Instructions

Before beginning the activity with the child, draw an outline of a house on the piece of poster board. In the outline, divide the house into four or five rooms (bedroom, kitchen, living room, bathroom, dining room). Cut out the clipart (or pictures) of the objects and have them ready. Say to the child, "We are going to make a pretend house! Let's put your name at the top!" Using the marker, write the child's name at the top (e.g., Timmy's house). Show the child the rooms and tell him or her what they are (e.g., "Here is the bathroom"). Show two pictures and say, "Look, here is a sofa. I will put it in the living room." Take the adhesive and place the object in the correct room.

Present two pictures to the child and say, "Now, it is your turn! What do you want to put in the house?" Encourage the child to pick an item and glue or tape it into the correct room. When the child completes the task, say, "Great! The bed goes in the bedroom!" If the child has difficulty, show him or her one item and ask, "Where does the bed go?" Continue to take turns in order to finish decorating the house.

Advanced Instructions

To work on expressive language, ask the child, "What is this one?" and then let him or her put the household item in the house.

PAPER DOLLS

Supplements TeachTown: Basics computer lessons: People

Primary benefits: Fine motor skills, receptive vocabulary

Secondary benefits: Expressive language, pretend play skills

Materials required: Computer with printer (optional); paper, poster board, cardboard, or cardstock; scissors; glue; sticky tack (optional)

Instructions

Find a template of a paper doll that you can print out or draw one yourself. Create two paper dolls and several outfits that correspond with occupations (e.g., doctor/nurse, firefighter, farmer). Using the scissors, cut out the dolls and glue them onto the poster board in order to make them sturdier. Trim the dolls. Once the dolls are ready, assemble the outfits (more outfits may be clipped from magazines, old books, etc.). Say to the child, "Look at these paper dolls. Let's dress them!" Show two of the outfits and say, "My doll will be a doctor." Choose the outfit and put it on the doll. (Many paper doll cutouts have tabs to secure the clothing. However, using a little bit of sticky tack works well also.) Have the doll pretend to be the occupation that it is dressed to be (e.g., a doctor doll could pretend to examine the child). Show the child two other outfits and ask, "What is your doll going to be?" Have the child dress the doll. Exclaim, "Oh, your doll is a firefighter! Pretend to put out a fire!" Help the child act out the motions. Take turns dressing the paper dolls.

Advanced Instructions

You may also make a doll of each person in your family, the child's friends, and so forth. Create the body of the paper doll as you would in the previous instructions but instead of drawing a face, glue on a photo of an individual's head (make sure the head is proportional to the body). The paper dolls can also be used for other activities as well. You can ask the child to describe the different family members and name each person's likes and dislikes, or you can use the paper dolls as puppets when telling a story. You can also have the child dress the dolls according to the weather (e.g., What would you wear if it is sunny, rainy, snowy, windy, etc.)

Helpful Hint

Paper doll templates can be found in craft stores and on various web sites for purchase.

SHAPE BOX

Supplements TeachTown: Basics computer lessons: Shapes

Primary benefits: Receptive vocabulary

Secondary benefits: Expressive language, shape matching

Materials required: Toys and household objects of different shapes. You will also need a fun box to keep all the shapes in.

Instructions

Take all of the objects out of the shape box and put them out of reach of the child (e.g., in another box). Pull out a shape and hide it in your hand and say, "What do I have?" Then, show the child the shape and verbally label it (e.g., "Triangle!"). On the child's turn, present several choices of differently shaped objects and ask the child to find the square. When the child picks the correct shape, say, "That's right, the cracker is a square," and prompt the child to put it away in the shape box. Continue taking turns until you fill up the shape box.

Advanced Instructions

You can also "hide" objects around the room and find shapes to put in the shape box. Say, "Can you find something that is a circle? Great, let's put it in our shape box!" It's okay if the child chooses objects that are not the ones you hid.

Helpful Hint

You can use all sorts of objects to represent the different shapes. Examples for a circle: ball, coin (make sure child does not put coin in mouth), orange. Examples for a square: CD case, cracker (play food), photograph. Examples for a triangle: pizza (play food), triangle from puzzle, triangle from shape sorter. You may also choose to cut out shapes with construction paper or use foam shapes (found at many craft stores).

STICKER ZOO

Supplements TeachTown: Basics computer lessons: Animals–Zoo

Primary benefits: Receptive vocabulary

Secondary benefits: Expressive language, fine motor

Materials required: Stickers of animals, cardboard box (the zoo)

Instructions

Take out the zoo and show it to the child. Say, "Look, it's a zoo! Who belongs in the zoo?"

Take an animal sticker and show it to the child. Then say, "The zebra goes in the zoo," and put the sticker in the zoo. Present several stickers to the child and tell him or her, "Oh, you know what else goes in the zoo? The elephant!" Prompt the child to put the elephant in the zoo.

Continue taking turns putting animals in the zoo. Be sure to allow the child to remove the stickers and place the stickers on his or her own as much as the child is able, to help in the development of fine motor skills.

Advanced Instructions

You can expand this activity by using larger boxes with multiple habitats. The child can put like animals in their own habitats. Another way to expand this activity is by having multiple boxes, each with a different habitat. The child can put zebras with zebras, elephants with elephants, and so forth. You may even want to work on matching and have the child match toy animals to the correct animal stickers. If the child is verbal or able to make verbal approximations, have the child work on labeling the animals.

Helpful Hint

To make a zoo, draw black lines on a box like a cage at the zoo. If you have time and want to be more creative, create a natural habitat by drawing trees, water, and so forth on the box to create a modern-day zoo environment.

TOOL CARDS

Supplements TeachTown: Basics computer lessons: Tools

Primary benefits: Fine motor skills, following instructions, receptive vocabulary

Secondary benefits: Expressive language

Materials required: Hardware catalog or circular (e.g., Home Depot); scissors; construction paper, card stock, or cardboard; glue; permanent marker; envelope

Instructions

Collect the materials and say to the child, "We are going to make some tool cards." Show the child the hardware catalog and say, "I'll find a hammer." Look through the catalog and find the object. Using the scissors, cut out the object. Help or instruct the child to glue the picture to the construction paper. Label it with the marker. Now say, "What tool do you want to pick?"

Hand the child the catalog and ask him or her to point to a tool. If the child is verbal, encourage him or her to say the name of the tool. If the child seems unsure, ask him or her to find a specific tool. Once the tool has been identified, help the child cut out the picture. As before, help him or her glue the picture to the construction paper and label the item. Continue taking turns to create more tool cards. Once you have finished making the cards, put them in an envelope and label them with the child's name (e.g., Timmy's Tools). The child may also want to decorate the envelope.

Advanced Instructions

These cards can be used for future work (e.g., identifying the tools, naming the tools, matching with real or toy tools).

TRANSPORTATION WASH

Supplements TeachTown: Basics computer lessons: Transportation

Primary benefits: Receptive vocabulary

Secondary benefits: Expressive language, object imitation, pretend play, sensory development

Materials required: Bowl with soapy water, bowl with plain water, two washcloths, toothbrush, towel, transportation toys

Instructions

Tell the child it is time for the vehicle wash. Take one of the toys (e.g., a car) and say, "Clean the car." Put it in the soapy water. Take the toothbrush and say, "Scrub the car." The child may want to help at this point, and you should encourage it. Be sure to repeat *car* as much as possible. This is a good time to use the song: "This is the way we scrub the car, scrub the car, scrub the car. This is the way we scrub the car, so it can drive on home" (or something fun like that). Take the washcloth and say, "Wash the car." Rub the car with the washcloth. Again, let the child help if he or she wants. Put the car into the plain water and say, "Rinse the car." Then use the second washcloth and say, "Dry the car."

Advanced Instructions

Now you can work on other labels by asking the child to "Clean the airplane" or "Clean the truck." If the child is verbal, you can also ask the child to tell you the names of the vehicles and to tell you what he or she is going to do (e.g., "Scrub the train").

Helpful Hint

Use a towel to keep your floor clean and dry (or do the activity outside).

WHERE IS THE FAVORITE OBJECT?

Supplements TeachTown: Basics computer lessons: Eye Gaze

Primary benefits: Following eye gaze (joint attention)

Secondary benefits: Social interaction

Materials required: Miscellaneous toys, snacks, household objects

Instructions

Place favorite objects of the child around a room. Bring the child into the room and kneel or stand in front of him or her (depending on the child's height). Make sure you are in close proximity of the child's face (about a foot or so). Attempt to get the child to look at your face. In a playful way, say, "(Gasp.) Guess what I see? Elmo!" and look at the object you mentioned in a very obvious way. Make sure the child is attending and make sure the object is something that the child will find interesting. Allow the child to retrieve the desired item and engage him or her in a social interaction with that toy for a few minutes. During this time, try to get eye contact as often as possible by taking turns with the desired object and by making the desired object socially interesting (sound effects are great for this). Try to get the child's eye contact again and look to another desired object in the room. Repeat the interaction described previously.

Advanced Instructions

Cover desired objects by hiding them behind pillows, under a piece of furniture, under blankets, and so forth so the child is not distracted by the motivating objects in the room until you are ready to show him or her the objects with your eye gaze and social interaction.

Sample TeachTown Naturalistic Generalization Activity Data Sheet

To maximize generalization, have facilitators trade materials or work with the child in different settings when possible.

Identify at least two facilitators who will be working with the child on this activity:

1) _Shannon Rhodes (mother)_

2) _Dan Taylor (classroom aide)_

3) _Chris Dawson (behavior therapist)_

Identify at least two settings in which to practice this activity with the child:

1) _Home (playground)_

2) _School (classroom)_

3) _School (therapy room)_

Identify at least two different sets of materials you will use to work on this activity with the child:

1) _Star Wars figures with dollhouse accessories_

2) _Dollhouse with accessories and dolls_

3) _Royalty puppet set (king, queen, jester, knight, dragon, etc.) and portable puppet theater_

Identify at least three collateral skills you will work to increase while doing this activity (e.g., social initiations, positive affect, pretend play):

1) _Spontaneous imitation of nontarget expressive vocabulary (e.g., people, adjectives, prepositions)_

2) _Spontaneous imitation of pretend play acts with figures_

3) _Spontaneous expressive pointing (i.e., pointing to share experiences with adult)_

Session date: _March 6_

Date activity started: _Jan. 15_   Date activity mastered: _N/A_

Date lesson started: _March 2_

Date prerequisite lesson mastered: _Actions 1—Feb. 20_   Date lesson mastered: _N/A_

Child: _Simon Rhodes_

Facilitator: ①   2   3

Environment: ①   2   3

Materials: ①   2   3

TeachTown (or other) activity: _Action figures_

TeachTown lesson: _Actions 2_

TeachTown learning domain: (REC LANG)   COG/ACADEMIC   LIFE SKILLS   SOCIAL

(continued)

(continued)

Probe	Target 1	Target 2	Target 3	Target 4	Target 5	Target 6	Target 7	Target 8
Description	Sleeping	Standing	Going potty	Painting				
1 Notes:	Receptive C (NC) P / Expressive C (NC) P	Receptive (C) NC P / Expressive (C) NC P	Receptive C (NC) P / Expressive C (NC) P	Receptive C (NC) P / Expressive C NC P	Receptive C NC P / Expressive C NC P	Receptive C NC P / Expressive C NC P	Receptive C NC P / Expressive C NC P	Receptive C NC P / Expressive C NC P
2 Notes: Imitated "sleeping"; pointed to potty to get him to put Yoda on potty	Receptive C NC (P) / Expressive C NC (P)	Receptive (C) NC P / Expressive (C) NC P	Receptive C NC (P) / Expressive C (NC) P	Receptive C NC (P) / Expressive C NC P	Receptive C NC P / Expressive C NC P	Receptive C NC P / Expressive C NC P	Receptive C NC P / Expressive C NC P	Receptive C NC P / Expressive C NC P
3 Notes:	Receptive (C) NC P / Expressive C (NC) P	Receptive (C) NC P / Expressive (C) NC P	Receptive C NC P / Expressive C (NC) P	Receptive C (NC) P / Expressive C NC P	Receptive C NC P / Expressive C NC P	Receptive C NC P / Expressive C NC P	Receptive C NC P / Expressive C NC P	Receptive C NC P / Expressive C NC P
4 Notes: Imitated "sleeping"; imitated "go potty"	Receptive C NC (P) / Expressive C NC (P)	Receptive (C) NC P / Expressive (C) NC P	Receptive (C) NC P / Expressive C NC (P)	Receptive C NC (P) / Expressive C NC P	Receptive C NC P / Expressive C NC P	Receptive C NC P / Expressive C NC P	Receptive C NC P / Expressive C NC P	Receptive C NC P / Expressive C NC P
5 Notes: Imitated "sleeping"; no response with standing but got it when prompted "s" sound; attempt at "potty"—said "go pot"	Receptive C NC (P) / Expressive C NC (P)	Receptive (C) NC P / Expressive C NC (P)	Receptive (C) NC P / Expressive C NC (P)	Receptive C (NC) P / Expressive C NC P	Receptive C NC P / Expressive C NC P	Receptive C NC P / Expressive C NC P	Receptive C NC P / Expressive C NC P	Receptive C NC P / Expressive C NC P

(continued)

142   Appendix 6.2

(continued)

Receptive percent (80% or higher for mastery)	C: 20% P: 40% Mastery criteria: YES **(NO)**	C: 100% P: 0% Mastery criteria: **(YES)** NO	C: 60% P: 20% Mastery criteria: **(YES)** NO	C: 0% P: 60% Mastery criteria: YES **(NO)**	C: P: Mastery criteria: YES NO	C: P: Mastery criteria: YES NO	C: P: Mastery criteria: YES NO
Expressive percent (80% or higher for mastery)	C: 0% P: 60% Mastery criteria: YES **(NO)**	C: 80% P: 20% Mastery criteria: **(YES)** NO	C: 0% P: 40% Mastery criteria: YES **(NO)**	C: P: Mastery criteria: YES NO	C: P: Mastery criteria: YES NO	C: P: Mastery criteria: YES NO	C: P: Mastery criteria: YES NO

Percent calculations:

0/5 = 0%
1/5 = 20%
2/5 = 40%
3/5 = 60%
4/5 = 80%
5/5 = 100%

Collateral skills:

For each skill, rate how well the child did today:

1)   1   2   **(3)**   4   5
     Not observed   Done a few times   Done often/very well

2)   1   2   3   **(4)**   5
     Not observed   Done a few times   Done often/very well

3)   1   2   **(3)**   4   5
     Not observed   Done a few times   Done often/very well

TeachTown Naturalistic Generalization Activity Data Sheet

To maximize generalization, have facilitators trade materials or work with the child in different settings when possible.

Identify at least two facilitators who will be working with the child on this activity:

1) _____

2) _____

3) _____

Identify at least two settings in which to practice this activity with the child:

1) _____

2) _____

3) _____

Identify at least two different sets of materials you will use to work on this activity with the child:

1) _____

2) _____

3) _____

Identify at least three collateral skills you will work to increase while doing this activity (e.g., social initiations, positive affect, pretend play):

1) _____

2) _____

3) _____

Session date: _____

Date activity started: _____   Date activity mastered: _____

Date lesson started: _____

Date prerequisite lesson mastered: _____   Date lesson mastered: _____

Child: _____

Facilitator: 1   2   3

Environment: 1   2   3

Materials: 1   2   3

TeachTown (or other) activity: _____

TeachTown lesson: _____

TeachTown learning domain: REC LANG   COG/ACADEMIC   LIFE SKILLS   SOCIAL

(continued)

(continued)

Probe	Target 1	Target 2	Target 3	Target 4	Target 5	Target 6	Target 7	Target 8
Description								
1 Notes:	Receptive C NC P Expressive C NC P	Receptive C NC P Expressive C NC P	Receptive C NC P Expressive C NC P	Receptive C NC P Expressive C NC P	Receptive C NC P Expressive C NC P	Receptive C NC P Expressive C NC P	Receptive C NC P Expressive C NC P	Receptive C NC P Expressive C NC P
2 Notes:	Receptive C NC P Expressive C NC P	Receptive C NC P Expressive C NC P	Receptive C NC P Expressive C NC P	Receptive C NC P Expressive C NC P	Receptive C NC P Expressive C NC P	Receptive C NC P Expressive C NC P	Receptive C NC P Expressive C NC P	Receptive C NC P Expressive C NC P
3 Notes:	Receptive C NC P Expressive C NC P	Receptive C NC P Expressive C NC P	Receptive C NC P Expressive C NC P	Receptive C NC P Expressive C NC P	Receptive C NC P Expressive C NC P	Receptive C NC P Expressive C NC P	Receptive C NC P Expressive C NC P	Receptive C NC P Expressive C NC P
4 Notes:	Receptive C NC P Expressive C NC P	Receptive C NC P Expressive C NC P	Receptive C NC P Expressive C NC P	Receptive C NC P Expressive C NC P	Receptive C NC P Expressive C NC P	Receptive C NC P Expressive C NC P	Receptive C NC P Expressive C NC P	Receptive C NC P Expressive C NC P
5 Notes:	Receptive C NC P Expressive C NC P	Receptive C NC P Expressive C NC P	Receptive C NC P Expressive C NC P	Receptive C NC P Expressive C NC P	Receptive C NC P Expressive C NC P	Receptive C NC P Expressive C NC P	Receptive C NC P Expressive C NC P	Receptive C NC P Expressive C NC P

(continued)

(continued)

Receptive percent (80% or higher for mastery)	C: P: Mastery criteria: YES NO	C: P: Mastery criteria: YES NO	C: P: Mastery criteria: YES NO	C: P: Mastery criteria: YES NO	C: P: Mastery criteria: YES NO	C: P: Mastery criteria: YES NO
Expressive percent (80% or higher for mastery)	C: P: Mastery criteria: YES NO	C: P: Mastery criteria: YES NO	C: P: Mastery criteria: YES NO	C: P: Mastery criteria: YES NO	C: P: Mastery criteria: YES NO	C: P: Mastery criteria: YES NO

Percent calculations:

0/5 = 0%
1/5 = 20%
2/5 = 40%
3/5 = 60%
4/5 = 80%
5/5 = 100%

Collateral skills:

For each skill, rate how well the child did today:

1)

1	2	3	4	5
Not observed		Done a few times		Done often/very well

2)

1	2	3	4	5
Not observed		Done a few times		Done often/very well

3)

1	2	3	4	5
Not observed		Done a few times		Done often/very well

II

Generalization Applications to Parents, Schools, and Community

7

The JumpStart
Learning-to-Learn Model

Parent Training in Naturalistic Teaching
for Children with Autism Spectrum Disorders

Bryna Siegel and Anne Bernard

GENERALIZATION AND TEACHING MILIEU

Intensive approaches are widely accepted as being critical to early teaching for children with autism spectrum disorders (ASDs). Repeatedly, research has supported these strategies, with strong associations between intense intervention and positive child outcomes (Lord & McGee, 2001). Less well understood are the critical components of treatment intensity: number of hours per week of treatment, number of task demands or discrete trials given by a teacher, total number of responses provided by the child, and correct number of responses given by the child. Measures of acquisition of directly taught content include high mastery in response to specific discriminative stimuli, retention of content following curtailment of intensive teaching, spontaneous use of taught content, and generalization of taught content to new—but similar—situations.

One key variable that contributes to positive outcomes for early intensive behavioral intervention is parent training and participation (Koegel, Symon, & Koegel, 2002). Early research (Sheinkopf & Siegel, 1998) suggested that similarly positive outcomes for children receiving around 25 or 35 hours per week of early intensive behavioral intervention may be due to these programs having been home based, which enabled further incidental teaching by parents who may have used principles of the home program during nonprogram hours. Later work indicated that parent training alone is not as potent as early intensive behavioral intervention (Smith, Groen, & Wynn, 2000), but the synergistic effects of early intensive behavioral intervention plus parent training are only now being explored. Nevertheless, other work supports the efficacy of parent training when it is compared with a community-based "treatment-as-usual" condition (Drew et al., 2002).

Just as intensity relates to positive outcomes—although its active ingredients are not fully understood—the same can be said for parent training. Is there incremental benefit to the child when parents simply provide more hours of the same

149

treatment their children receive from therapists? Is there incremental benefit when parents consistently demand that children use their emergent skills in naturally arising and functional situations (e.g., asking for food at meal times)? Is there incremental benefit when parents create opportunities to use emergent skills (e.g., interject in the child's play)? The latter two questions refer to activities that serve to characterize parents as *generalizers*—agents of teaching who support broad and contextualized real-world applications for emerging attention, motivational, problem-solving, and language skills. One specific behavioral technology that has increased success in meeting these challenges has been Pivotal Response Training, or PRT (e.g., Koegel, 2001; Schreibman, 2000). PRT is predicated on instrumental teaching—creating presses for responses in situations that are pivotal for the child with respect to getting a need met. The learning milieu created by the pivotal press can either be contrived as part of a curriculum or recognized in more naturalistic and everyday situations. The use of PRT strategies can be deployed to facilitate motivation, self-management, and—more broadly—responsivity to multiple cues rather than just specifically, directly taught discriminative stimuli (Koegel, 2001).

The hallmark of autism is a lack of affiliative drive. The child with ASD is much less often motivated to practice new skills simply for the social gain of being noticed, included, or socially praised. Challenges to teaching a child with ASD therefore include the need to constantly create interesting situations in which the child will spontaneously employ emerging skills to make the world work in ways that he or she would like it to work. In this context, it has been possible to demonstrate increased self-initiation of social interactions (Koegel, 2001) and joint attention (Sullivan et al., 2007; Whalen & Schreibman, 2003).

With the key role of parents as teachers in mind (in particular, as behavioral PRT teachers), related instructional approaches were combined to form a teaching milieu replete with natural presses embedded in both social interaction and daily living. The goal was to exploit characteristics of engagement in preferred play, exploration, and daily routines and to generally meet the needs of the toddler with ASD within a naturalistic learning environment. This teaching program was to serve two purposes: 1) to create a wraparound environment in which parents could recognize natural opportunities to practice the directly taught skills from the child's intervention program(s) and 2) to train parents to recognize how and what their child was developmentally ready to learn so that they could dynamically modify the child's opportunities to generalize emerging skills as those skills developed. Furthermore, it was envisioned that parents would receive this sort of training as a first intervention (as distinct from early intervention)—an opportunity for the parents to learn how their child learns and for the child to learn how to learn.

Parent Training Research Foundational to the JumpStart Learning-to-Learn Model

The JumpStart Learning-to-Learn model was developed in response to a need recognized during clinical diagnosis and assessment of children with ASDs. In carrying out the recommended practice for diagnostic assessment (c.f., California Department of Education, 1997), the clinician is faced with a family in crisis, parents at a loss, and a child in need of intervention. The clinician's task of determining the diagnosis is possibly the easiest task in this situation. More difficult is the information the parents must assimilate about their child's current developmental status, learning potential, methods of possible intervention, the impact on the rest of their family, the effect on their marriage, and what to do next. In particular, support to the parents and their child should comprise a highly individualized treatment plan, as children with ASDs start with very different profiles of diagnostic signs, autism-specific learning differences, developmental levels, and behavioral profiles that may be incompatible with teaching. Early intervention for autism is not a one-size-fits-all proposition (Schreibman, 2000).

The use of PRT strategies is not synonymous with parent training, by any means, but PRT fits well into the purview of procedures that parents can use in a more naturalistic teaching milieu. Koegel, Carter, and Koegel (2003) showed how PRT procedures could be used to produce self-initiated use of questions and grammatical morphemes, including generalized use of verb forms. Related work uses PRT to develop the child's joint attention skills, a prerequisite to contextualized teaching of any sort (Siller & Sigman, 2002; Sullivan et al., 2007; Whalen & Schreibman, 2003).

The body of parent training research that has developed over the last 10 years provides a framework for involving parents in their child's treatment. This framework can be extrapolated to better facilitate coping with the diagnosis within the child's family. In addition, existing research provides specifications for creation of a naturalistic learning environment around the child.

What Is the JumpStart Learning-to-Learn Model?

JumpStart Learning-to-Learn approaches intervention with a focus on guiding the parent–child relationship for effective home learning. It is a week-long, intensive parent-and-child training program that supports parents as they are introduced to specific communication, play, and teaching practices. The goal is for JumpStart Learning-to-Learn to propagate a latticework of natural home activities that support and leverage the recommended interventions that the child receives in ongoing treatment (see Appendices 7.1–7.3). It consists of several specific components, each of which is aimed at making the child's home into a naturally effective learning environment. JumpStart Learning-to-Learn focuses on increasing the parents' awareness of opportunities to turn daily living and play activities into constructive learning. Ideally, these routine moments become mutually pleasurable activities in which the child learns about his or her world and parents learn about their child as his or her learning capacities expand.

In the context of this volume, the JumpStart Learning-to-Learn model provides an illustration of how behaviorally based practices for teaching the young child with ASD can be systematically reorganized so as to promote broad generalization of emergent skills. Specifically, parents are exposed to three strands of instruction:

1. Recognizing opportunities for pivotal direct teaching

2. Teaching paralinguistic and preverbal augmentative communication

3. Reinforcing play by following child-initiated, non–goal-directed activity

In each of these strands, parents are coached in the acquisition of skill sets that extend recommended principles of PRT, visual augmentative communication, and play-based interventions. These strategies build from those used by many treatment programs, individual therapists, and schools. The goal is to teach parents how to make interactions with their children more successful in three key ways. First, JumpStart Learning-to-Learn seeks to build a mutually gratifying parent–child relationship. This first component demonstrates how a parent can have fun with his or her child while still feeling that the time spent together is educational for both.

Second, JumpStart Learning-to-Learn aims to provide natural opportunities to practice emerging cognitive and communication skills. This is facilitated by teaching parents how to recognize and create more natural opportunities for the child to communicate his or her needs. Parents also learn ways to promote more spontaneous use of foundational nonverbal communication skills that developmentally precede the emergence of spoken language. This involves teaching parents naturalistic ways of using gaze, gesture, and facial expressions to signal needs and to get needs met.

Third, JumpStart Learning-to-Learn gives strategies for creating opportunities for the child to use emerging abilities as they are mastered in the context of direct teaching to promote generalization of emerging vocabulary, imitation skills, adaptive behavior, and play.

Parental Roles in the Development of the Young Child with Autism Spectrum Disorders

Parents are their children's first teachers. In the early years, they may be their children's main teachers. When parents are not available to care for their own children full time, they select proxies (e.g., extended family members, nannies, child care providers, preschool teachers) who provide socialization and teaching congruent with the parents' own values and goals for their children. When a child has been diagnosed with a developmental disability, the child is then referred to providers who can introduce him or her to special teaching methods designed to help overcome the disability. At this point, parents enter new terrain.

It is not uncommon for parents to feel a loss of efficacy or react to a loss of control over the child's development. One parent may spring into action, trying to reduce distress by proactively learning about the new situation. Another parent may feel weighed down, anxious, or even depressed by fear of the unknown. Parents may even experience both feelings simultaneously as they realize the new challenges they face in raising the child. JumpStart Learning-to-Learn aims to provide parents with supports for these situations and to deliver this support on an individualized basis. Individualization of direct work with parents is based on an open-ended parental interview about the child, preintervention measures of the parent's self-efficacy, dyadic adjustment, family functioning, and understanding of evidenced-based treatment standards in general and ASDs in particular.

Research supports the importance of parent training and shows that incorporation of parents into programs is a demonstrably effective approach to improving a child's outcomes. However, as discussed previously, there has been less focus on preconditions for successful parental involvement. Parents who do not yet understand the child's difficulties, parents who misunderstand the nature of the child's disabilities, or parents unsure of which resources are reliable or evidence based are at a disadvantage for successful intervention compared with those parents who have a better understanding.

Therefore, an early task in devising and executing effective early treatment is to work with parents so that they understand their agency with respect to their child's difficulties. In the context of the JumpStart Learning-to-Learn program, this approach consists of

- Using direct didactics about ASDs

- Understanding how to evaluate evidence for accepted and alternative treatment practices with respect to the child's specific difficulties

- Bringing the three strands of JumpStart Learning-to-Learn practices (i.e., natural environment teaching, early communication training, and socially reciprocal play teaching) into the home

JumpStart Learning-to-Learn is a manualized parent-training approach that teaches caregivers to understand how autism affects their child's learning, recognize their child's individual treatment needs, evaluate available services, and carry out key components of activities that promote behavioral, communicative, and play exploration. This approach creates a rich, wraparound environment for generalizing the skills acquired in the child's ongoing interventions.

The Concept of First Intervention

Often, studies of young children with ASDs focus on the primacy of early intervention and the thesis that the "window of opportunity" is open widest in the first 3 years of life. JumpStart Learning-to-Learn is based on the idea that if a parent can become an efficacious facilitator of meaningful engagement in learning from the time his or her child enters intervention, developmentally consequential early learning experiences are exponentially more beneficial. If a parent is taught to recognize and use opportunities for teaching the child whenever such opportunities arise, it can become an integral part of parenting. If the child has opportunities to consistently use skills and knowledge in both treatment settings and the home, the child will then have the highest intensity of services possible, with the greatest number of opportunities to have new knowledge reinforced through functional opportunities to use it.

In the sections that follow, the methodologies employed by the JumpStart Learning-to-Learn program will be described. The research on which the model is based incorporates outcomes from studies of family coping; parent training; early intensive behavioral interventions in general and PRT in particular; communication training based on promoting joint attention using a developmental, psycholinguistics-based curriculum; and play interaction based on promoting joint attention, pressing for pivotal responses, and dynamic parent–child reciprocal interaction models. As a whole, the JumpStart Learning-to-Learn approach is applied in a systematically individualized manner using the autistic learning disabilities (ALD)/autistic learning styles (ALS) approach (c.f., Siegel, 2003, 2008) following an integrated behavioral-developmental curriculum that is taught using behavioral principles that rely on developmentally organized curriculum content (Siegel, 2003).

JumpStart Learning-to-Learn is a manualized intervention carried out by a transdisciplinary team of interventionists, most often in the first weeks after diagnosis and with families in which early intervention specific to ASDs has not yet begun in earnest. Families (including both parents if possible) come to the JumpStart Center for 6 hours per day for 5 consecutive days. The team is headed by a Ph.D.-level special educator who is an early intervention specialist with expertise in family adjustment to ASDs. This specialist provides direct didactics on ASDs and treatments and works with the family to plan how they will incorporate the child's special needs into family life.

During each half day at JumpStart, the parents and child meet with one of three specialists. The first is an M.A.-level behavioral specialist experienced in a range of individual and group applied behavior analysis (ABA) teaching techniques, with a particular emphasis on PRT. The second specialist is an M.A.-level speech-language pathologist versed in early social-communicative milestones; a specially developed, visually augmentative curriculum called *visual interaction augmentation*; and PRT in the context of language development. The third specialist is an M.A.-level early childhood specialist with expertise in child-centric, play-based teaching approaches and social-communicative milestones. A junior interventionist assists all three specialists by repeating their direct teaching and curriculum content as parents and specialists watch, as well as discussing and analyzing the child's responses. This sets the stage for the parents to try modeling the techniques themselves, followed by more discussion, while the junior interventionist continues with related activities under the specialist's supervision. During snack times, lunch breaks, and naps, there is an opportunity for more informal discussion between parents, specialists, and the team leader.

On the fourth or fifth day at JumpStart, the parents may be joined for part of the day by a professional already serving the child, the team leader and parent may visit a proposed treatment placement, or the team may review videos of a child already in intervention with a particular service provider; this is in preparation for selecting services that will be initiated following the JumpStart Learning-to-Learn week. The goal of each component of the JumpStart Learning-to-Learn program is to prepare parents to work synergistically with ongoing service providers to generalize directly taught content so that it helps the child navigate his or her daily living in a way that is intrinsically reinforcing whenever newly emergent skills are applied. More detail on the activities carried out in each component is discussed later in the chapter.

Defining Parental Roles in Early Intervention

The concept of special education as a collection of methods and curricula geared to the individualized needs of a different learner has broad recognition. Teachers of children with learning differences who require special education need specialized training. Less well acknowledged, but logically just as true, is the idea that parents of a child with developmental disabilities will likely benefit from specialized training as well. JumpStart Learning-to-Learn facilitates this by 1) teaching parents to analyze their child's learning differences using the ALD/ALS model, 2) educating parents as consumers of special education services, and 3) modeling and directly teaching parents how to apply evidence-based learning principles in the context of parenting at home during nontreatment hours to wrap around formal service provisions.

Parents and the ALD/ALS Approach

The great heterogeneity of ASDs has stymied the progress of research on many aspects of treatment outcomes. Individuals with ASDs can present with few or many symptoms, mild or severe. ASDs can occur in the presence of expected rates of cognitive development, in the context of intellectual disability, and/or in association with maladaptive behaviors that need to be addressed to proceed with treatments. Each sign and symptom of ASDs can and should be scrutinized with respect to its meaning for learning (Siegel, 2003, 2008). In the JumpStart Learning-to-Learn model, parents are taught to link assessment results with an awareness of specific treatment needs. Table 7.1 summarizes the ALD approach.

By examining which diagnostic criteria for a specific child are met, parents and trainers work together to understand the child's ALD—the perceptual or cognitive inputs the child is either not perceiving (e.g., facial expressions), fully processing (e.g., auditory stimuli), storing (e.g., language that comes out echolalically), or able to express (e.g., representation in play of experienced events). Parents and trainers also work together to understand processing pathways that are functioning, even if in compensatory manners (i.e., ALS). Using this information, the team focuses on creating routines to increase predictability so that these strengths can form more efficient compensations for other areas (e.g., visual augmentation for linguistic inputs).

Table 7.1.   Criteria for diagnosing autism spectrum disorders and corresponding autistic learning disabilities (ALD)/autistic learning styles (ALS)

Criterion	ALD/ALS
Reciprocal social interaction	
1. Impairment in the use of nonverbal communication such as eye gaze, facial expression, and gestures for social interaction	Missing signals from faces and body language may result in the child receiving an incomplete message. Lack of pointing indicates lack of a theory of mind and the potential of others as a source of information.
2. Failure to develop peer relationships	Child has a lack of motivation from peer models. Child also lacks social imitation as an intuitive learning modality.
3. Lack of seeking to share enjoyment	
4. Lack of social-emotional reciprocity	Child has no social motivation. Activities are not done to please others, but rather to please the child him- or herself. Child has no motive to avoid censure in the presence of self-interest.
Communication	
5. Delay in spoken language not compensated for by other means of communication	Related to Criterion 1: Child is not able to express via nonlinguistic means other than physical enactment of desired ends (e.g., hand leading).
6. Marked inability to initiate or sustain conversation	Child has no drive for contact for its own sake. Social reciprocity is not reinforcing, verbally or nonverbally.
7. Stereotyped (e.g., echolalic) repetitive or idiosyncratic use of language	Child may have possible problems parsing language; his or her verbal memory may be more intact than comprehension. Child may have possible slow auditory intake with missed information.
8. Lack of make-believe play or of social imitation	Child has no drive to reenact/digest experience through his or her own activity. Child experiences reduced language practice.
Activities and interests	
9. Encompassing preoccupation patterns of interest, abnormal in intensity	Low curiosity and low novelty-seeking limits the child's variety of inputs/attentional foci.
10. Compulsive adherence to nonfunctional routines or rituals	Child may operate in a visual/procedural world where routines help make things predictable. This also may indicate overflow in the attempt to analyze certain kinds of social-communicative stimuli.
11. Stereotyped and repetitive motor movements	
12. Persistent preoccupation with parts (e.g., sensory aspects) of objects	This may indicate salient reinforcers that can become associated with more typical (social) ones.

Parents as Educated Consumers

By learning to understand and talk about their child's learning profile in terms of ALD and ALS, the parents become equipped to evaluate the suitability of available intervention approaches with respect to their child's specific learning profile. This ability is critical because most parents begin to learn about interventions on the Internet, even before they are certain of their child's diagnosis. The Internet offers parents incredibly valuable resources based on empirical evidence and solid theory, but it also offers false hope in the form of one-size-fits-all interventions that sound too good to be true—and, in fact, usually are.

JumpStart Learning-to-Learn includes a direct didactic training component to teach parents how to evaluate treatment outcome claims as they search the Internet, read books, network with parents, receive advice from family and friends, and attend lectures on autism. It is well understood among professionals that already-stressed parents are further strained by an overload of advice, especially early in the intervention when they have few criteria to winnow the many suggestions. This direct didactic component of JumpStart Learning-to-Learn includes helping parents develop guidelines for doing single-case experiments using strategies such as keeping one of the child's familiar caregivers blind to a new intervention, recording a priori expectations for the interventions, keeping baseline and progress data, learning to detect placebo effects, questioning mechanisms behind hypothesized efficacy of treatments, and using the ALD/ALS model to determine whether a particular treatment is a good fit for their child's learning profile at this time.

Once parents come to see the autism spectrum as something that affects individual children quite differently, they more readily understand and accept that many non–evidence-based interventions such as dietary manipulations, so-called biomedical treatments (e.g., the Defeat Autism Now! [DAN!] protocol), and homunculus-based theories (e.g., facilitated communication, rapid prompting) lack face validity. Parents are supported in seeing the child as a developing child first and the signs and symptoms of ASDs overlaid on the typical developmental trajectory. More explicitly, JumpStart adds the notion of each child's unique ALD/ALS profile—the specific ways in which this child perceives, processes, and responds to stimuli—and the fact that interventions need to directly address these learning differences, rather than spray bullets at this heterogeneous collection of things called the autism spectrum and hope that some targets are hit.

Parent Trainer as Docent

In addition to providing direct didactics about autism-specific learning differences and how to weigh the validity of potential treatments, JumpStart Learning-to-Learn educates parents as consumers of autism services by visiting, observing, and reviewing potential or ongoing interventions with JumpStart Learning-to-Learn staff. This component of JumpStart Learning-to-Learn has two aims: 1) to teach parents how to evaluate services and providers using the criteria they have developed based on their child's specific developmental level and learning profile and 2) to show parents how to interact with professionals who will help their child.

The docent component of JumpStart Learning-to-Learn most often consists of visits to early intervention programs, either school- or home-based. Just like a docent in an art museum, the JumpStart interventionist explains to the parents what they are seeing and why practices are as they are. The docent may point out how the children being observed are similar to or different from the parent's own child, the range of functioning served in a class setting, the developmental levels and language levels of other children, examples of effective practice, examples of when one-to-one versus shared instruction is used, how the availability of visual supports (e.g., picture schedules, visual schedules, activity schedules) comports with their child's needs, or how much opportunity for teacher-led versus child-initiated activity there is.

The additional focus of these visits is to emphasize to parents that just as JumpStart Learning-to-Learn has been a parent–professional collaboration, their future interactions with teachers and therapists will require similar working relationships. Many parents have been primed to expect the worst, to be defensive, to believe that the best defense is a good offense, and to contact educational professionals with guns blazing, insistent on what their child must have. JumpStart Learning-to-Learn prepares parents to approach the situation with less hostility, with the knowledge that parents and providers can work together to figure out how to give the child what he or she needs. This approach is founded on the principle that parents are wraparounds or generalizers of what the child receives in his or her formal treatment hours. The chances of this happening—and of the child's needs being met—are diminished if parents and providers cannot communicate with a shared vocabulary enabling them to work together.

On this account, as in all aspects of the JumpStart Learning-to-Learn program, parent education proceeds from the perspective of the typically developing child. Parents of typically developing children generally recognize that starting with hostile feelings or low expectations about a nanny, a child care provider, or a preschool teacher will not help them or their child in any way. Importantly, parents of typically developing children approach the parent–provider relationship with a shared vocabulary of developmental expectations and approaches for how they hope their child will learn. Thus, JumpStart Learning-to-Learn encourages parents of a child with ASD to see how the same will be true for their child. JumpStart Learning-to-Learn prepares parents for a collaborative relationship with special educational providers through hands-on modeling opportunities and teaching of key intervention techniques to develop understanding of their child's learning so that it can be discussed with treatment providers on a level playing field.

Parents as Wraparound Service Providers

The JumpStart Learning-to-Learn program grew out of our own personal experience, our earlier research, and the research of many others who demonstrated the efficacy of intensive programs, as reviewed previously. Parents are in a unique position to work on generalization of the direct teaching that occurs during formal treatment hours. Again, our model for supporting parents in this role is to relate it to what happens in high-quality parenting of typically developing children. Nonschool hours are filled with formally and informally constructed learning experiences that involve both direct parent teaching and self-guided learning. Parents may directly teach their child in a very individualized manner when they oversee homework. However, parents seldom view this as the most stress-free (or even educational) way of interacting with their child, nor is it an appropriate model of early childhood education. Instead, education-oriented parents of typically developing children create natural presses for learning, much as organized PRT can be used for the child with ASD. A mother of a typically developing child may read and discuss a pop-up book of barnyard animals with her 2-year-old son, who simply enjoys being told that he is very good at naming the animals. A father of a 3-year-old daughter with autism may set up a similar opportunity but instead allow the child to choose a tummy tickle or a cheek raspberry each time an animal is correctly touched after its name is read. The critical difference here is the set of special skills that the parent of the child with ASD must have to tweak the book-reading activity so that it leads to the same desirable outcome as that for the typically developing child (i.e., knowing the animals).

Wraparound special parenting is predicated by good communicative conduits between parents and treatment providers. Assigning parents homework—such as specific books, play materials, and places to go that create natural opportunities to practice emerging skills—is critical. Parent–provider brainstorming, which stems from and reinforces a good working relationship between parent and provider, is necessary. By educating the parent about what the provider can and should do, JumpStart Learning-to-Learn provides the parent with the vocabulary necessary to not just participate in, but contribute to, the dialogue.

Generalization and Natural Environment Teaching

The concept of generalization of directly taught concepts has some specific considerations for the child with ASD. In typical development, children have an internal, intrinsic drive to experiment and to expand their means of doing things by associating the results of one experiment with another. Without direct teaching, a baby can be expected to intuit similarities among situations and thereby understand how previously learned schema can be applied in new ways. For children with ASDs, this process does not always work so automatically. Lovaas (1981) argued that the child with autism needs to be explicitly taught each behavior he or she is to master. This logic remains a foundation of the field of ABA, in which oral language development is construed as verbal behavior consisting not so much of a qualitative continuum of social-pragmatic functions (as it is in the developmental literature), but rather as behavior acquired through operant conditioning of mands (requests) and tacts (labels) (Partington, Sundberg, Iwata, & Mountjoy, 1979). Enumeration of explicitly taught mands and tacts serves as a good operational framework for direct teaching procedures such as discrete trial training (DTT) but is less useful when working with parents to encourage use of verbal (or even preverbal) communicative strategies in nondirect teaching situations at home.

Similarly, the child with ASD often does not acquire nonlanguage skills automatically. The child may fail to associate key features of similar situations to facilitate problem solving; therefore, a teaching strategy for these children is to set up the situation so that there is a natural opportunity to request (mand) in a context where the successful operation is in itself rewarding. Schreibman (1988) showed that language skills can indeed be improved through a natural language paradigm (NLP), a child-initiated teaching strategy that involves repeated trials using toys or other objects of interest and value to the child. Similarly, natural environment teaching (Sundberg & Partington, 1996) and naturalistic teaching approaches (LeBlanc, Esch, Sidener, & Firth, 2006) take advantage of the child's interests to create natural teaching and language opportunities during everyday experiences. As opposed to NLP, however, natural environment teaching does not just concentrate on acquiring language but facilitates development and generalization of all functional skills.

The need to learn through generalization of similar stimuli is intrinsic to parent training in JumpStart Learning-to-Learn. The program models natural environment teaching strategies during meal and snack times, pleasurable daily activities like bath time or a trip to the playground, and choice making during daily routines like dressing and getting ready to leave the house.

INTEGRATING DEVELOPMENTAL AND BEHAVIORAL PERSPECTIVES

Fundamental to the JumpStart Learning-to-Learn approach is the use of a developmental perspective to move beyond these evidence-based aspects of ABA. The tenants of ABA are seen as specifying a series of methodologies for teaching that are, in fact, agnostic as to curriculum content. The earliest developed ABA/DTT programs (e.g., Leaf & McEachin, 1999; Maurice, Green, & Luce, 1996) inserted content based on vocabulary and activities that could be useful in a typical preschool setting (e.g., names of body parts and animals; following directions; discrimination of size, shape, and color).

Verbal Behavior versus Developmental Psycholinguistics

The traditional ABA/DTT curriculum was often chronologically age appropriate for children with ASDs who were beginning treatment at 2½–3½ years old. This timing neglected the developmental sequence of receptive and expressive communication skills: a baby's first words can actually be seen as a primer to a natural environment teaching curriculum, with frequent use of mands such as *up*, *mine*, *more*, and *gimme*, as well as *mama* and *dada*, which serve as universal requests. With this in mind, JumpStart Learning-to-Learn relies on developmental psycholinguistics research (Wetherby & Prutting, 1984) as the source of curriculum content for promoting early spontaneous communication.

This psycholinguistics framework is also useful in guiding how communicative behavior is taught. The first goal is for the child's communicative attempts to be successful and thereby reinforced so that he or she makes more rather than fewer of them in the future. ABA principles used on their own have led to a practice of prompting the child with autism to "say it better" to get the understood need met. Interestingly, principles of typical child psycholinguistic development and natural environment teaching support a different approach—reinforce the child by responding to any utterance as soon as what is requested is clear to the listener. For example, a baby boy who says "buh" while looking at a bottle is given the bottle, but if he says "buh" in the presence of his binky (pacifier), he is given the pacifier. Parents of these typically developing infants do not ask the infant to say it better before reinforcing the spontaneous communicative attempt; they are essentially differentially reinforcing spontaneity and communicative effort (two very hard things to promote in a toddler with ASD) over linguistic content. The parent of a typically developing child may repeat "bottle" as the bottle is handed to the baby but will not frustrate the child further once it is clear that parent and child are jointly attending to the same thing. The JumpStart Learning-to-Learn model teaches parents this technique as part of natural environment teaching, so as to highlight opportunities to promote spontaneity of responding and self-initiated communication.

Spontaneous Communication and Joint Attention

Deficient joint parent–child attention is a hallmark for early identification of autism (Robins, Fein, Barton, & Green, 2001; Siegel, 2004). Deficient joint attention has been characterized as the first manifestation of theory-of-mind defects, posited as the primary deficit defining the autism spectrum (Baron-Cohen, Leslie, & Frith, 1985). Importantly, shared attention and awareness of that shared attention allow the infant to essentially see the parent as the ancillary hard drive to his or her own computer (i.e., brain) and to call for downloads of files whenever the infant surmises the parent has a file on a topic of current interest. This understanding is lacking in the toddler with ASD who displays deficits in theory of mind.

A goal of the parent training in JumpStart Learning-to-Learn is to encourage a quick response to the child as soon as his or her communicative attempt conveys the content of his or her request. Parents are trained in this manner because it lets the child know that the parent understands what the child has in mind, thereby laying down a foundational experience upon which to build the child's implicit theory of mind. This procedure varies considerably from the PRT technique, which essentially misses an opportunity to reinforce spontaneity and nurture theory of mind.

Operationalizing the Strands of JumpStart Learning-to-Learn

In the sections that follow, the three key parent training components of JumpStart Learning-to-Learn are operationally described. Each comports with the principles of developmental psychology and ABA and uses the same developmental-behavioral approach. The first component introduces parents to fundamental concepts of PRT and natural environment teaching in the context of daily living tasks and preferred activities. The second component focuses on early, often preverbal, communication skills. The final component focuses on development of play reciprocity and expansion of the child's interests and play repertoire. Prior to beginning the JumpStart week, the child undergoes a brief assessment to collect baseline data and gauge the developmental level of his or her social and communicative skills. At this point, the program director works with parents to refine their goals for the JumpStart week with respect to the relative emphasis they want on communication, play, and/or overall learning readiness.

Naturalistic Home Learning Opportunities

The behaviorally trained early interventionist, who coaches parents during 3 or 4 half days of the JumpStart Learning-to-Learn program week, begins by identifying reinforcing foods, activities, toys, and other objects that can be used to constitute focused teaching goals (e.g., asking for a preferred toy). The interventionist may begin by having parents demonstrate how they get their child to do or ask for this object, which provides a window into the parents' current approach and reveals differences in how each parent may understand or work with the child. These interactions form the basis for initial discussions and formation of a plan to redo the activity using DTT or PRT behavioral shaping strategies, which either the interventionist or the parent then initiates.

Over the course of each session, activities shift according to the child's interests and the parents' goals. Demonstrations by the interventionist (or the parent modeling the interventionist) may be videotaped for later critique and revision of strategies. The sessions are not focused like a DTT session but rather constructed in a way that is mindful of the parents' experience at home: looking at books on a favorite topic is interspersed with trips to the toilet (which are also training times) or snack times (during which choice making or visual schedules are introduced). Parents may be given homework for the next day; they have as much time as needed to fully discuss all their concerns about how to shape behavior, determine prompt levels, and use verbal or visual cues to practice assigned tasks. This approach serves as practice for future brainstorming with professionals. The discussions demonstrate to parents their critical role in identifying individual differences in their child's learning style that can be leveraged. In addition, these discussions move parents toward a more individualized understanding of intervention methods and curricula that fit with the child's current developmental level and profile.

Social Communication and Visual Interaction Augmentation

Depending on a child's current level of communicative competence, the family will have two to four half-day sessions with a speech-language pathologist working within the JumpStart Learning-to-Learn developmental-behavioral framework. Children who are already using spoken words to communicate (but usually have little or no nonverbal pragmatics) may receive fewer speech and language sessions than preverbal children. In both groups, but especially in the preverbal group, emphasis is on use of visual interaction augmentation (Siegel, 2004, 2005), an errorless learning, visually augmentative communication system that, like the Picture Exchange Communication System (Bondy & Frost, 2001), relies on exchange of icons or three-dimensional objects. The critical differences include

1. Use of only photographic icons of exact objects (of what the child has in mind) to promote development of theory of mind

2. Shaping of concomitant nonverbal communication (e.g., gaze at listener, exposure to listener's facial affect congruent to child's request)

3. Use of only high-value (i.e., reinforcing) mands as icons

4. Use of motherese voice and gesture by the adult communicative partner

5. Differential reinforcement of spontaneity of communicative initiative over completeness of mand

6. Placement of icons where specific communicative opportunities for use arise rather than in a binder

As with typical language development, parents are coached to expect and accept many "baby-talk" efforts at picture exchange, as well as word approximations and a prolonged period of single-word utterances before phrases. The progression from single- to multiword utterances is modeled psycholinguistically (e.g., from "juice" to "more juice" or "all gone juice" rather than from "juice" to "I want juice"). The goal is for longer utterances to have more meaning, rather than just complicating the communication (i.e., because "I want juice" has the same functional significance as "juice" alone).

Both for verbal and preverbal children, parents are coached to use motherese, including repetitions and recasts both vocally and gesturally. Parents are taught how to use natural grammar, modified with emphasis on operational parts of the utterance (e.g., "Yes, you showed me the *giraffe!*"). This method is in contrast with the agrammatical models often associated with DTT (e.g., "Good touching giraffe!") because children acquire grammar from grammatical models (Karmiloff & Karmiloff-Smith, 2001).

As a final aspect of the social communication coaching, parents are helped to plan how a visual interaction augmentation system or other use of icons for natural environment teaching can be set up around their home, in places where communicative opportunities for foods, preferred activities, or specific toys might occur.

Teaching Play While Keeping It Playful

The final component of the JumpStart Learning-to-Learn program is play teaching. Because this program is a parent training program, its goal is to support development of parent–child interaction in all the ways parents and children typically interact. The first component emphasizes how the parent can come to see daily routines as a natural teaching milieu. The second component gives parents specific skills for facilitating their child's ability to communicate. This third component acknowledges that parents typically teach their child cognitively, as well as imbue social values and understanding, through the more informal and playful interactions they have with their children. Parents of children with ASDs are often so worried about intensity and associating that with direct teaching by professional interventionists that they fail to appreciate the loading that play carries for their child's learning.

Two approaches to child-centric or child-led play that have influenced therapeutic work with young children with ASDs are the Floortime approach (Greenspan, Wieder, & Simons, 1998) and the similar but more manualized Relationship Development Intervention (Gutstein & Sheely, 2002). In Floortime, reciprocal circles of interaction are built with a stagewise developmental model of social skills development in mind. In a Relationship Development Intervention, the emphasis is also on increasing social interaction using strategies that place emphasis on playful interaction rather than drills and following the child's interests rather than prescribing a fixed curriculum designed with specific cognitive objectives in mind.

Some parents coming to JumpStart already have the idea that these approaches are anti-ABA or the ABA antidote. Rather than encourage this thinking, the JumpStart play interventionist borrows heavily from these frameworks while supporting parents to see opportunities to select activities that comport both with their child's developmental level, natural interests, and principles of natural environment teaching and PRT. The ultimate goal of this component is to promote parents' recognition of the educational and adaptive benefits to their children when they are "just having fun" with the children in ways guided by learning objectives. Aspects of play that may be encouraged include introducing slightly more challenge in a reciprocal interaction; inventing a new twist on a reciprocal game; or showing the perseverative, nonexploratory child with autism that a slight variation of a narrow theme can be rewarding, too.

Floortime embraces a conceptualization of many ASD symptoms as a result of sensory dysregulation and/or an expression of sensory cravings. The JumpStart approach uses a more empirical conceptualization that highly sensory stimuli may be highly reinforcing and builds them into situations with pivotal presses that can become the basis of the play activity. Parents are taught to reply to sensory overresponding by using playful desensitization/habituation strategies, rather than relying on the nonempirical sensory integration techniques (e.g., brushing, joint compression).

An interesting aspect of the JumpStart Learning-to-Learn play component is that it is often particularly successful with fathers. Daily living tasks in most of the participating families have fallen much more often to mothers, and communication training is embedded in daily living skills, at least initially, more than it is embedded in play situations. Most of the JumpStart children are boys, so the play component has proven to be the area where fathers are most enthused to "do their homework." Coincidentally, JumpStart was piloted with two male play interventionists, both of whom take up more stereotypical boy play (e.g., races, calamities, physicality) rather than girl play (e.g., dollhouses, feedings); this approach often interfaces well with the rudimentary play interests of the children in intervention.

Measuring Expected Progress from JumpStart Learning-to-Learn

The JumpStart Learning-to-Learn protocol is currently under study with respect to child and parent outcomes. Over the last few years, the parent training protocol has been standardized and manualized. Pre- and posttest measures of parent and child outcomes have been selected and piloted. Parent measures focus on self-efficacy, parenting efficacy, family and marriage functioning, and understanding of ASDs. Child measures focus on social and communicative milestones, as well as adaptive behavior measures with an emphasis on functional communication benchmarks.

In the next few years, we hope to collect enough data to complete analyses of how JumpStart families compare at program onset, program exit, and at 6 and 12 months after parent training. We hypothesize that they will be functioning better as families, report better dyadic relations in the marriage, have more understanding of ASDs, feel more successful in their ability to choose services, and access systems of care for their children confidently. We expect that the children will show greater gains in social and communicative behaviors controlled for actual levels of receptive and expressive language, as well as lower levels of maladaptive behavior.

In preliminary analysis of data to date, parents have endorsed their participation in JumpStart as a positive experience in 96% of cases. Only one case in the last 3 years has filed for an educational due process hearing. A number of parents have reported that at JumpStart, they experienced their first moment when their child "really noticed it was me," "listened to me," or "cared I was there," or reported that "we were really having a lot of fun together." We have observed children begin to grasp the educational contract (i.e., that they must do something to get something) for the first time. We feel this is infinitely different from the parent being told what is possible, or even seeing an experienced interventionist get their child to behave or communicate in an expected manner. Parents seem more confident and less anxious; they enjoy parenting more. We believe these differences will transfer to the child in both measurable and immeasurable ways. As Lao Tzu, the founder of Taoism, taught: "Give a man a fish and you feed him for a day. Teach him how to fish and you feed him for a lifetime."

REFERENCES

Baron-Cohen, S., Leslie, A.M., & Frith, U. (1985). Does the autistic child have a"theory of mind"? *Cognition, 21*(1), 37–46.

Bondy, A., & Frost, L. (2001). *A picture's worth: PECS and other communication strategies in autism.* Bethesda, MD: Woodbine House.

California Department of Education. (1997). *Best practices for designing and delivering effective programs for individuals with autistic spectrum disorders.* Sacramento, CA: Author.

Drew, A., Baird, G., Baron-Cohen, S., Cox, A., Slonims, V., Wheelwright, S., et al. (2002). A pilot randomized control trial of a parent training intervention for pre-school children with autism: Preliminary findings and methodological challenges. *European Child & Adolescent Psychiatry, 11*(6), 266–272.

Greenspan, S., Wieder, S., & Simons, R. (1998). *The child with special needs: Encouraging intellectual and emotional growth.* Reading, MA: Addison-Wesley.

Gutstein, S.E., & Sheely, R.K. (2002). *Relationship Development Intervention with young children: Social and emotional development activities for Asperger syndrome, autism, PPD and NLD.* London: Jessica Kingsley Publishers.

Karmiloff, K., & Karmiloff-Smith, A. (2001). *Pathways to language.* Cambridge, MA: Harvard University Press.

Koegel, L.K., Carter, C.M., & Koegel, R.L. (2003). Teaching children with autism self-initiations as a pivotal response. *Topics in Language Disorders, 23*(2), 134–145.

Koegel, R.L. (2001). Pivotal areas in intervention for autism. *Journal of Clinical Child Psychology, 30*(1), 19–32.

Koegel, R.L., Symon, J.B., & Koegel, L.K. (2002). Parent education for families of children with autism living in geographically distant areas. *Journal of Positive Behavior Interventions, 4*(2), 88–103.

Leaf, R., & McEachin, J. (1999). *A work in progress: Behavior management strategies and a curriculum for intensive behavioral treatment of autism.* New York: DRL Books.

LeBlanc, L.E., Esch, J.W., Sidener, T.M., & Firth, A.E. (2006). Behavioral language interventions for children with autism: Comparing applied verbal behavior and naturalistic teaching approaches. *Analysis of Verbal Behavior, 22,* 49–60.

Lord, C., & McGee, J.P. (Eds.). (2001). *Educating children with autism.* Washington, DC: National Academies Press.

Lovaas, O.I. (1981). *Teaching developmentally disabled children: The me book.* Austin, TX: Pro-Ed.

Maurice, C., Green, G., & Luce, S.C. (1996). *Behavioral intervention for young children with autism: A manual for parents and professionals.* Austin, TX: Pro-Ed.

Partington, J.W., Sundberg, M.L., Iwata, B.A., & Mountjoy, P.T. (1979). A task-analysis approach to time telling instruction for normal and educably mentally impaired children. *Education and Treatment of Children, 2,* 17–29.

Robins, D., Fein, D., Barton, M., & Green, J. (2001). The Modified Checklist for Autism in Toddlers: An initial study investigating the early detection of autism and pervasive developmental disorders. *Journal of Autism & Developmental Disorders, 31*(2), 131–144.

Schreibman, L. (1988). Training parents to use the natural language paradigm to increase their autistic children's speech. *Journal of Applied Behavior Analysis, 21*(4), 391–400.

Schreibman, L. (2000). Intensive behavioral/psychoeducational treatments for autism: Research needs and future directions. *Journal of Autism and Developmental Disorders, 30*(5), 373–378.

Sheinkopf, S.J., & Siegel, B. (1998). Home based behavioral treatment of young children with autism. *Journal of Autism and Developmental Disorders, 28*(1), 15–23.

Siegel, B. (2003). *Helping children with autism learn: Treatment approaches for parents and professionals.* New York: Oxford University Press.

Siegel, B. (2004). *Pervasive Developmental Disorder Screening Test II (PDDST-II).* San Antonio, TX: Harcourt Assessment.

Siegel, B. (2005). VIA: Visual interaction augmentation. *Autism News, 2–3,* 2–6.

Siegel, B. (2008). *Getting the best for your child with autism: An expert's guide to treatment.* New York: Guilford Press.

Siller, M., & Sigman, M. (2002). The behaviors of parents of children with autism predict the subsequent development of their children's communication. *Journal of Autism and Developmental Disorders, 32*(2), 77–89.

Smith, T., Groen, A.D., & Wynn, J.W. (2000). Randomized trial of intensive early intervention for children with pervasive developmental disorder. *American Journal of Mental Retardation, 105*(4), 269–285.

Sullivan, M., Finelli, J., Marvin, A., Garrett-Mayer, E., Bauman, M., & Landa, R. (2007). Response to joint attention in toddlers at risk for autism spectrum disorder: A prospective study. *Journal of Autism and Developmental Disorders, 37*(1), 37–48.

Sundberg, M.L., & Partington, J.W. (1996). *Teaching language to children with autism and other developmental disabilities.* Pleasant Hill, CA: Behavior Analysts.

Wetherby, A.M., & Prutting, C.A. (1984). Profiles of communicative and cognitive-social abilities in autistic children. *Journal of Speech and Hearing Research, 27,* 364–377.

Whalen, C., & Schreibman, L. (2003). Joint attention training for children with autism using behavior modification procedures. *Journal of Child Psychology and Psychiatry, 44*(3), 456–468.

Chapter 7
Appendices

APPENDIX 7.1.

Home Activity Planning Form Instructions

JumpStart Learning-to-Learn aims to help parents translate recommended practice therapeutic and educational techniques into culturally and ecologically valid parenting skills that will support the child's learning and development. With an eye toward broad-based generalization of skills, JumpStart Learning-to-Learn helps parents identify ways in which to continue their child's learning outside of traditional therapy time.

Because we understand that the demands on a parent's time are already enormous, we encourage parents to embed learning within naturally occurring daily activities in ways that are similar to the interactions that occur with typically developing children. This teaching strategy provides consistent opportunities for children to practice emergent skills and generalize them to the real-world environments where they will be needed.

The Home Activity Planning Form is used by families who attend a JumpStart Learning-to-Learn program as a basis of discussion about how to contrive daily activities to include presses for skill development and generalization. We encourage service providers and parents to work collaboratively, using the Home Activity Planning Form as a basis for discussion regarding parent involvement in the child's education, generalization, and parent training needs.

The Home Activity Planning Form is designed to help families structure opportunities to allow their child to generalize newly learned skills during everyday activities. Using the strategies included on the form should add no more than a few minutes to any given routine but will have an enormous payoff. Embedding learning in these everyday activities can be an enjoyable way to help your child generalize skills from school and therapy and acquire new skills more rapidly.

INSTRUCTIONS FOR PARENTS

The following instructions explain to parents how to complete the Home Activities Planning Form.

Routines/Activities

Fill out the Home Activities Planning Form with activities you and your child must do every day. The form contains suggested activities that many families do each day, but there may be some additional activities you want to add. You can do this in the last two rows on the form.

Goals

Use the goals from your child's applied behavior analysis program, individualized family service plan, or individualized education program or use your own goals for your child to decide which skills you will work on during each activity. Try to limit yourself to one to two goals per activity. You can make goals as specific (e.g., child will make a choice using a 1- to 2-word sentence) or as general (e.g., expressive language) as you are comfortable with. The key is to make sure that you know what response you are looking for from your child.

Strategies

With the input of all of your child's therapists and teachers and your own creativity, develop two to three strategies you will use during each activity to help you reach a goal. Silly and fun strategies are encouraged. Strategies should be specific and brief so that incorporating these activities in your routine is easy! Make sure that the strategies are clear enough that a babysitter or grandparent can also follow them. This will ensure that your child not only generalizes skills across new settings and activities but also across caregivers.

APPENDIX 7.2.

Home Activity Planning Form Example

Routines/ activities	Goal	Strategy
Dressing	Verbal and gestural communication Language understanding Compliance	Encourage the child to respond to simple commands and questions with words and gestures. Encourage the child to identify body parts and clothing by pointing or reaching.
	Self-help Joint attention	Help the child to dress. Be silly: Put clothes on the wrong body part (or on your own body) and let the child correct you or ask for help.
Changing/ bathroom	Verbal/picture communication	Help the child follow a picture schedule indicating the steps for toileting and washing hands.
	Social	Play social games (e.g., Peekaboo, How Big?) with the child.
Mealtime/ snack	Expressive communication Making choices Initiating requests	Put food in a closed container to provide a reason for the child to make a request, then play dumb. Let the child ask for help opening the container. Offer a choice between two foods using photo icons.
	Fine motor Self-help	Encourage the child to feed him- or herself with a spoon or fork.
	Vocalizations	Use a spoon and cup as tools for engaging in vocal play.
Cleanup/ transitions	Compliance Understanding	Help the child clean up by giving simple commands. Use a photo-based transition schedule to help the child anticipate what is next.
	Joint attention	Take turns putting individual toys (e.g., cars, trains) away.

(continued)

(continued)

Routines/ activities	Goal	Strategy
Car travel	Expressive language Reciprocity Vocalizations	Sing songs and ask the child to fill in words. Encourage the child to engage in vocal imitation.
Bath time	Receptive language	Identify body parts using songs (e.g., "This is the way we wash our _____ " or "Head, shoulders, knees, and toes").
	Social/play	Encourage imaginary play with bath toys, bubbles, and so forth.
	Oral motor skills	Practice blowing bubbles in the bath with the child.
Bedtime	Language understanding Joint attention Reciprocity	Read books and sing songs. Ask the child to identify pictures by pointing. Snuggle and be close to the child.
	Verbal and picture communication	Give the child a choice of which book to read or which song to sing. Give the child a massage and let him or her tell you where to massage next.

Home Activity Planning Form

Routines/activities	Goal	Strategy
Dressing		
Changing/bathroom		
Mealtime/snack		
Cleanup/transitions		

(continued)

(continued)

Routines/ activities	Goal	Strategy
Car travel		
Bath time		
Bedtime		

8

Increasing Generalization by Training Teachers to Provide Parent Training for Young Children with Autism Spectrum Disorders

Brooke Ingersoll and Anna Dvortcsak

Children with autism spectrum disorders (ASDs) have pervasive deficits in social and communication skills, as well as restricted interests and attention, which interfere with learning and disrupt family life (American Psychiatric Association, 2000). The educational needs of children with ASDs are significant, with most children requiring many hours of intensive intervention provided by highly trained staff. Interventions that are applied early and intensively have been found to lead to significant improvements in child outcome (Dawson & Osterling, 1997; National Research Council [NRC], 2001). In fact, after a comprehensive review of the scientific, theoretical, and policy literature surrounding the education of young children with ASDs, the NRC (2001) recommended that "educational services should include a minimum of 25 hours a week, 12 months a year, in which the child is engaged in systematically planned, developmentally appropriate educational activity aimed toward identified objectives" (p. 220). The educational requirements make providing effective intervention for children with ASDs within a cost-effective, public program a challenge for school districts throughout the nation. With the growing number of children qualifying for special education services under the ASD eligibility guidelines, school districts are hard pressed to provide the level of intensity required to educate their toddler and preschool-age students with ASDs. Many publicly funded early intervention (EI) and early childhood special education (ECSE) programs have difficulty meeting the recommended number of hours (Hume, Bellini, & Pratt, 2005).

Even when provided with the recommended number of hours, many children with ASDs still struggle to generalize gains shown in treatment to meaningful life activities (Schreibman, 1988). This lack of generalization is an issue for all interventions; however, children with ASDs seem to have more pronounced generalization deficits than children with developmental delays (Schreibman, 1988). Thus, it is necessary to develop intervention models for young children with ASDs that maximize opportunities for generalization and maintenance of skills.

173

One effective strategy for promoting generalization is to provide instruction in the natural environment (Sandall, Hemmeter, Smith, & McLean, 2005). The *natural environment* has been defined as routines, materials, and people familiar to the child and family (Dunst, Hamby, Trivette, Raab, & Bruder, 2000). This approach has been adopted by the Individuals with Disabilities Education Act of 1990 (PL 101-476) for the education of young children with special needs (Walsh, Rous, & Lutzer, 2000); it requires that services provided by the public sector use more naturalistic approaches to intervention (Wetherby & Woods, 2006). There is still debate as to which settings constitute the natural environment for young children with ASDs in relation to service provision (e.g., center vs. home, group vs. one-to-one). However, interventions that teach families how to use intervention strategies are an excellent option since the family is the most "natural environment" for young children. A further benefit of teaching parents is that it can lead to increased hours of intervention, making it more likely that families can achieve the recommended intensity of intervention for their children with ASDs.

BENEFITS OF PARENT TRAINING

A significant body of research demonstrates the benefit of teaching parents of children with disabilities to implement the intervention themselves (Shearer & Shearer, 1977). Although less research exists for children with ASDs, parent training has also been shown to be effective for this population (see McConachie & Diggle, 2007, for a review). A variety of intervention methods have been taught to parents of young children with ASDs, including discrete trial training (e.g., Smith, Groen, & Wynn, 2000) and structured teaching (Ozonoff & Cathcart, 1998). Most parent-implemented approaches are naturalistic, meaning that instruction occurs around the child's focus of interest and during meaningful routines and activities. For this reason, only naturalistic parent training approaches are reviewed herein.

Several reasons exist for using a naturalistic approach with parents of young children with ASDs. First, naturalistic intervention strategies have been shown to be effective for teaching a variety of social-communicative skills, including language (see Kaiser, Yoder, & Keetz, 1992, for review), gestures (Ingersoll, Lewis, & Kroman, 2007; Warren, Yoder, Gazdag, & Kim, 1993), play skills (Stahmer, 1995; Thorp, Stahmer, & Schreibman, 1995), peer interaction (Pierce & Schreibman, 1995), and joint attention skills (Pierce & Schreibman, 1995; Whalen & Schreibman, 2003) in children with ASDs and developmental delays. Second, research indicates that naturalistic strategies lead to better generalization and maintenance (Charlop-Christy & Carpenter, 2000; Delprato, 2001; McGee, Krantz, & McClannahan, 1985; Miranda-Linne & Melin, 1992), as well as more spontaneous use of skills (Schwartz, Anderson, & Halle, 1989) than more structured teaching approaches. Finally, these approaches are more similar to natural adult–child interactions (Schreibman, Kaneko, & Koegel, 1991); this fact makes them more acceptable to parents and easier to implement in the course of daily routines. Indeed, research has shown that parents who were taught to use Pivotal Response Training (PRT), a naturalistic intervention, used more positive affect while teaching their children (Schreibman et al., 1991), and both the parents and children exhibited more happiness and interest and less stress during family interactions than families in which the parents were trained to implement highly structured behavioral techniques (Koegel, Bimbela, & Schreibman, 1996).

NATURALISTIC PARENT TRAINING APPROACHES

Two general naturalistic intervention approaches have been used with parents: one approach based on the developmental, social-pragmatic (DSP) literature and one based on the naturalistic behavioral literature.

Developmental, Social-Pragmatic Approaches

DSP interventions are derived from research on typical parent–child interactions, which suggests a relationship between a parent's responsiveness to a child's behavior and the child's level of social-communicative development (Bornstein, Tamis-LeMonda, & Haynes, 1999; Hoff-Ginsberg & Shatz, 1982; Mahoney & Perales, 2003; Prizant, Wetherby, & Rydell, 2000). Thus, the goal of developmentally based, parent-implemented interventions is to teach parents strategies to increase their responsiveness to the child's behavior. These interventions share several common characteristics (Prizant et al., 2000):

1. Teaching follows the child's lead or interest.

2. The adult arranges the environment to encourage initiations from the child.

3. All communicative attempts including unconventional (e.g., jargon, echolalia, hand leading, nonverbal protests) and preintentional communication (e.g., reaching and grabbing, eye gaze, crying, facial expressions, body postures) are responded to as if they are purposeful.

4. Emotional expressions and affect sharing are emphasized by the adult.

5. The adult uses simplified language around the child's attentional focus.

Several studies have examined the effectiveness of teaching parents to use DSP interventions with their children with ASDs. For example, Mahoney and Perales (2003) examined the efficacy of responsive teaching for promoting social-emotional functioning in young children with ASDs using a single-group, pre-/posttest design. In their study, 20 young children with ASDs and their mothers participated in an 8- to 14-month intervention in which the mothers were taught a variety of strategies that increased their responsiveness to their children's behavior. At pre- and posttreatment (approximately 1 year later), the children and their mothers were videotaped while playing with a set of developmentally appropriate toys, and mothers were asked to complete the Infant Toddler Social Emotional Assessment (Carter & Briggs-Gowan, 2000) and the Temperament and Atypical Behavior Scale (Bagnato, Neisworth, Salvia, & Hunt, 1999). Mothers exhibited significant improvements in their responsiveness, and the children exhibited significantly higher ratings on social interactive behavior during the videotaped interactions from pre- to posttreatment. The children were also rated as showing significant improvements in social-emotional functioning on the two standardized rating scales at posttreatment. This study did not include a control group of children whose mothers did not receive training, so it is difficult to conclude that the positive gains seen in the children were due to responsive teaching. However, there was a positive correlation between changes in the mothers' level of responsiveness and changes in the children's social interactive behavior on the videotaped observations. In addition, changes in maternal level of responsiveness were predictive of a child's improvements on the standardized assessments of social-emotional functioning. These findings are consistent with the authors' hypothesis that maternal responsiveness promotes developmental gains in children with ASDs and other developmental disorders.

Wetherby and Woods (2006) used a quasi-experimental design to examine the effectiveness of the early social interaction project, a developmentally based, parent-implemented intervention designed for very young children with ASDs. Seventeen at-risk children younger than 2 years and their families were selected to participate. Children were identified as at risk for ASDs based on the presence of a significant number of indicators from the Communication and Symbolic Behavior Scales Developmental Profile behavior sample (Wetherby & Prizant, 2002). Parents received individualized coaching twice per week in the home for a minimum of 12 months. These coaching sessions were focused on teaching the parents to use a variety of developmentally based intervention strategies during daily routines with their child. Participating children were assessed at pre- and posttreatment on the Communication and Symbolic Behavior Scales (Wetherby & Prizant, 2003). An independent comparison group of 18 children who were referred for concerns of ASDs were also examined at age 3 years to determine developmental trajectories of children with ASDs who did not receive the parental intervention. The results suggested that the children whose parents were trained in early social interaction made statistically significant gains in a variety of social-communicative skills from pre- to posttreatment. In addition, the early social interaction participants scored significantly better than the comparison group at age 3 years on measures of social signals, rate of communicating, communicative functions, and understanding.

These findings suggest that the children whose parents received training made improvements over the course of a year on their social-communicative development and outperformed a group of children who did not receive treatment at age 3 years. Although this study offers some preliminary evidence for the effectiveness of a developmental, parent-implemented approach, because the participants were not randomly assigned, it is possible that the groups were not similar at intake.

Interestingly, the early social interaction participants' pretreatment profiles resembled the comparison group's profiles, although the comparison group was an average of 1 year older. This finding could be interpreted to indicate that the treatment group would have continued to look similar to the control group at age 3 years had they not received treatment. However, additional research using a randomized or single-subject design is needed to conclude that the children's changes were due to the intervention.

In a randomized trial, Aldred, Green, and Adams (2004) examined the efficacy of a developmentally based, parent-implemented intervention on social-communicative development in young children with autism. Twenty-eight children with autism and their parents were randomly assigned to a treatment or a control group. Parents of the children in the treatment group participated in workshops, followed by individual coaching sessions that focused on teaching the parents to use a number of developmentally based intervention strategies with their child. After 1 year, the parents of the children in the treatment group showed improvements in their responsiveness towards their children on an observational measure of parent–child interaction compared with parents in the control group.

In addition, the children in the treatment group showed more improvement (reduced symptomology) on the Reciprocal Social Interaction subdomain of the Autism Diagnostic Observation Schedule (Lord et al., 2000), greater gains in expressive language as measured by the MacArthur Communicative Development Inventory (Fenson et al., 1993), and a greater increase in number of communication acts on an observational measure of parent–child interaction than the children in the control group.

These studies offer preliminary evidence for the effectiveness of developmentally based, parent-implemented approaches for promoting social-communicative development in young children with ASDs. The studies found general improvements in social engagement (Mahoney & Perales, 2003) and general communicative behavior (Aldred et al., 2004; Wetherby & Woods, 2006). However, they did not examine whether the children also experienced increases in specific language behaviors, such as acquisition of language targets or mean length of utterance. Thus, the effect of this approach on the development of more specific language skills is unknown. In addition, in each of these studies, parent training was conducted individually over an extended period of time. Therefore, it is unclear whether children with ASDs and their parents would benefit from a shorter or less intense parent training format. This issue is particularly important because many publicly funded programs may not be able to offer such extensive parent education services.

Naturalistic Behavioral Approaches

Naturalistic behavioral approaches focus on teaching parents to use prompting, shaping, and reinforcement strategies to increase specific social-communicative skills in their child with ASD. In keeping with the naturalistic emphasis, parents are taught to use these teaching strategies around their child's focus of interest and within daily routines and activities (Kaiser et al., 1992). Parent-implemented interventions using a naturalistic behavioral approach share the following characteristics (Delprato, 2001; Kaiser et al., 1992):

1. The learning environment is loosely structured.

2. Teaching occurs within ongoing interactions between the child and the adult.

3. Teaching materials are selected by the child and varied often.

4. The child initiates the teaching episode by indicating interest in an item or activity.

5. The child's production of the target behavior is explicitly prompted.

6. A direct relationship exists between the child's response and the reinforcer.

7. The child is reinforced for attempts to respond.

A large body of work has examined the effectiveness of naturalistic behavioral interventions for teaching language skills to children with ASDs and other developmental disorders (see Kaiser et al., 1992, for review). Among this literature, several studies have trained parents to be the intervention providers. For example, Laski, Charlop, and Schreibman (1988) used a multiple-baseline design to examine the effect of teaching eight parents to use the natural language paradigm, now referred to as PRT, with their children with ASDs. The results suggested that parents increased the frequency with which they required their children to speak. In addition, all children increased their frequency of speech with their parents. These increases generalized to three nontraining settings, suggesting that once the parents learned the intervention techniques, they were able to elicit their child's language in a variety of environments.

In addition, research has shown that parents can also learn naturalistic behavioral intervention strategies for increasing other social-communicative skills, including imitation, joint attention, and play. For example, Ingersoll and Gergans (2007) taught three parents naturalistic intervention strategies to increase their children's object and gesture imitation during play. All parents improved their abilities to use the intervention techniques, and their children showed concomitant improvements in their imitation skills. Rocha, Schreibman, and Stahmer (2007) taught three parents to teach their children with autism to respond to joint attention bids. Children improved their abilities to respond as well as to initiate joint attention, despite the fact that the intervention did not directly target joint attention initiations. Gillett and LeBlanc (2007) taught three parents to use the natural language paradigm with their children with autism; they found that, in addition to improvements in spontaneous and prompted language, two of the children also showed improvements in their use of appropriate play.

These studies have mainly used single-subject designs with a small number of participants, which limits the generalizability of the results to a wide range of children with ASDs and their parents. However, the use of an experimental design allows for the determination that changes in the parents' behavior directly affect their children's behavior.

Combined Approaches

One additional naturalistic intervention approach has been to combine intervention strategies from both the DSP and naturalistic behavioral models with the hope of developing even more powerful interventions. For example, Kaiser, Hancock, and Niefeld (2000) used a multiple-baseline design to examine the efficacy of parent-implemented enhanced milieu teaching with six mother–child dyads. This intervention included both naturalistic behavioral strategies designed to teach specific language targets and DSP strategies to increase parent responsiveness. Parents learned a variety of naturalistic behavioral strategies to use with their children with ASDs via 24 weekly coaching sessions. Although coaching was conducted in a clinic, all parents generalized their use of the strategies to the home and maintained their use of the strategies (although at a lower rate than posttreatment) at a 6-month follow-up.

All children in this study showed an increase in their use of language targets (e.g., two-word requests, action verbs, attribute object combinations), and most children also increased the complexity and diversity of their language. Not surprisingly, those children who exhibited less significant communication delays made the most gains in productive language. This study indicates that a parent-implemented naturalistic behavioral approach combined with responsiveness strategies can be effective for increasing specific social-communicative skills. However, additional research is needed to determine whether the combined approach is more effective than either component implemented in isolation.

ADDITIONAL BENEFITS OF PARENT TRAINING

Parent training appears to confer a number of other benefits when compared with therapist-implemented interventions. For example, one early study compared the effects of teaching parents to implement behavior therapy with their child to clinician-implemented intervention (Koegel, Schreibman, Britten, Burke, & O'Neill, 1982). Parents in the parent training group received 5 hours per week of training with their child until mastery for a total of approximately 25–50 hours; the clinic treatment group received 4½ hours of treatment per week for 1 year for a total of approximately 225 hours. The results indicated that children in both groups made similar gains when observed with the treatment provider, but children in the parent training group were more likely to respond appropriately to parent questions and directions in the home. This finding indicates that parent-implemented intervention leads to better generalization than therapist-implemented intervention and requires significantly fewer hours of therapist time. In addition, parents in the parent training group exhibited a significant increase in the amount of recreational/leisure activities they participated in, whereas parents in the clinic treatment group showed no change.

Parent-implemented interventions for young children with ASDs are compatible with recommendations from the NRC and the Individuals with Disabilities Education Act regarding teaching within the natural environment. More importantly, the research suggests that parent training is an effective intervention approach and can lead to better generalization than traditional therapist-delivered services. In addition, it has been shown to improve other aspects related to family functioning and allows for an increase in the number of hours of intervention a child receives per week, without an increase in the number of hours of direct intervention provided by professionals.

Given these findings, the NRC's Committee on Educational Interventions for Children with Autism concluded,

> As part of local educational programs and intervention programs for children from birth to age 3, families of children with autistic spectrum disorders should be provided the opportunity to learn techniques for teaching their child new skills and reducing problem behaviors. (NRC, 2001, p. 216)

OBSTACLES TO IMPLEMENTATION

Although parent training is now considered an essential component of successful early intervention programs for children with autism (NRC, 2001), formal parent training programs are still the exception rather than the rule in community-based ECSE settings for children with ASDs age 3–5 years (Hume et al., 2005). There are several obstacles that can prevent the inclusion of parent training programs in ECSE classrooms. The first obstacle involves the structure of most empirically based parent training programs, which are typically conducted individually with the parent, child, and parent educator once to twice per week over many months (Aldred et al., 2004; Kaiser et al., 2000; Mahoney & Perales, 2003; Wetherby & Woods, 2006). While this structure may be appropriate for private services or EI services delivered in the home, most publicly funded ECSE programs for children with ASDs older than 3 years are provided in a classroom setting that allows very little time for teachers to meet individually with a parent and child. This difference makes it difficult for most special educators serving children with ASDs in a classroom setting to envision using these models within their programs. To increase the likelihood that ECSE staff will include parent training in their curriculum, it is important to develop a parent training format that works within a classroom setting.

A second obstacle to the inclusion of parent training in community-based programs is the lack of quality parent training materials developed for families of children with ASDs. Many of the empirically based programs mentioned in the literature have developed materials for parent training; however, because they are typically conducted in a one-to-one setting, they lack many of the features necessary for providing training to a group of parents, such as slide presentations and video examples. Most ECSE teachers are unlikely to adapt materials designed for use in a one-to-one training program to a group program because of the amount of time necessary to develop group presentation materials.

A final obstacle to the provision of parent training is the lack of appropriate preparation for providers working with children with ASDs and their families. Most specialists—especially those who work with children ages 3 years and older—have been trained to work with children, not adults. In addition, they often are not trained to understand how adults learn or techniques for teaching parents specific skills (Mahoney et al., 1999). The lack of specific preparation activities for early childhood special educators in parent training is evident in the lack of courses available in this area in preparation programs in special education. To illustrate this point, McCollum (1999) reported her own cursory inspection of a variety of EI/ECSE textbooks revealed that, although the topic of families received a significant amount of attention, the topic of parent education was conspicuously absent. Thus, it is necessary to develop an effective teacher preparation protocol to encourage ECSE staff to provide parent-implemented intervention.

To address these issues, Ingersoll and Dvortcsak (2006, in press) developed Project ImPACT (Improving Parents As Communication Teachers), a parent training program designed specifically for use with children with ASDs and their families in ECSE classroom settings. The goal was to develop an evidence-based parent training curriculum using a format compatible with a classroom-based intervention model, including user-friendly materials, and incorporating an effective teacher preparation protocol.

PARENT TRAINING CURRICULUM

The parent training curriculum focuses on teaching families naturalistic intervention techniques to increase their child's social-communicative skills during daily activities and routines (Ingersoll & Dvortcsak, 2006). The specific intervention strategies have been drawn from a variety of evidence-based interventions shown to be effective for young children with ASDs and other developmental disorders. Parents are first taught strategies for setting up their home to ensure successful parent–child interactions. Subsequently, they are taught the intervention strategies (see Appendix 8.1). Project ImPACT is composed of developmental strategies (interactive techniques) to encourage parent responsiveness (e.g., Mahoney & Perales, 2003) and naturalistic behavioral strategies (direct teaching techniques) to teach specific social-communicative skills (e.g., Kaiser et al., 1992). Table 8.1 provides a description of the individual teaching techniques. The program

Table 8.1.   Intervention strategies

Topic 1: Set up your home for success

Parents are taught strategies for arranging their home to increase the likelihood of positive parent–child interactions, including having a well-defined play space, limiting distractions, rotating toys, and scheduling predictable play routines (Davis & Fox, 1999).

Topic 2: Follow your child's lead

In order to increase their child's motivation, parents are taught to follow their child's focus of attention and to provide teaching opportunities around the activities their child chooses. Parents are taught to provide a variety of highly motivating materials (e.g., toys, games, snacks), respond to their child's changing interests, and assist their child in his or her play. This technique is used in all naturalistic interventions and has been shown to increase parent responsiveness and child motivation (e.g., Kaiser et al., 1992).

Topic 3: Imitate your child

Parents are taught to imitate their child's vocalizations, actions with objects, and gestures. This strategy has been shown to increase child responsiveness and coordinated joint attention and is used to increase social engagement (Klinger & Dawson, 1992).

Topic 4: Animation

Parents are taught to exaggerate their gestures, facial expressions, and vocal qualities in order to increase their child's interest and to model appropriate nonverbal communication (Mahoney & MacDonald, 2007).

Topic 5: Modeling and expanding language

Parents are taught to use a variety of indirect language stimulation techniques (e.g., descriptive talk, conversational recast) to talk about their child's focus of interest. These techniques have been shown to be effective at increasing the rate and complexity of children's language skills (e.g., Camarata, Nelson, & Camarata, 1994; Ingersoll, Dvortcsak, Whalen, & Sikora, 2005; Kaiser et al., 1996).

Topic 6: Playful obstruction

Parents are taught to gain their child's attention during an interaction by playfully interrupting their child's activity. This technique is used to increase initiations from the child (Greenspan, Wieder, & Simons, 1998).

Topic 7: Balanced turns

Parents are taught to use balanced turns with their child to increase their reciprocity and to provide opportunities for child initiations (Mahoney & MacDonald, 2007).

Topic 8: Communicative temptations

Parents are taught to use a variety of communicative temptations (e.g., in sight, out of reach; assistance; inadequate portions; sabotage; protest; silly situations) to encourage their child to initiate communication (e.g., Kaiser, Ostrosky, & Alpert, 1993).

Topic 9: Prompting and reinforcement

Parents are taught prompting and reinforcement strategies to teach their child more complex social-communication skills, including the use of natural environment prompts and reinforcement. Parents are taught how to use prompting effectively, including providing clear and appropriate prompts, monitoring motivation, providing wait time, and moving from less to more supportive prompts to help the child respond correctly (e.g., Kaiser et al., 1992). Parents are also taught to use immediate reinforcement that is contingent on appropriate behavior, to provide praise, and to expand their child's response (e.g., Kaiser et al., 1992).

Topic 10: Teaching your child expressive language

Parents are taught to use a variety of prompts (e.g., physical prompt, gestural prompt, verbal model, verbal routines, choices, cloze procedure, questions, time delay) and reinforcement to teach their child new expressive language forms (e.g., Kaiser et al., 1992).

Topic 11: Teaching your child to understand and follow directions (receptive language)

Parents are taught to use clear and direct verbal instructions and to use a variety of prompts (e.g., physical prompt, visual prompt, verbal instruction) and reinforcement to teach their child to follow directions and increase receptive language (e.g., Kaiser et al., 1992).

(continued)

Table 8.1.   *(continued)*

Topic 12: Teaching your child social imitation

Parents are taught to use a number of strategies to encourage their child to imitate their play with toys and gestures in a reciprocal fashion (Ingersoll & Gergans, 2007).

Topic 13: Teaching your child play

Parents are taught to use a variety of prompts (e.g., physical prompt, gestural prompt, modeling, instruction, leading question, leading comment) to teach their child more complex play skills (Stahmer, 1995).

Topic 14: Putting it all together

Parents are taught how to use the *interactive* and *direct teaching* strategies together. In particular, parents are taught when to emphasize the interactive strategies (e.g., parents cannot control access to desired items or activities and/or the child is less motivated by the activity) and the direct teaching strategies (e.g., parents are able to control access to the desired item or activity and the child is highly motivated) and how to move back and forth between the two within an interaction.

includes a teacher's manual, which contains detailed procedures for conducting each session, PowerPoint presentations for the group sessions, a video with examples of parents using the intervention techniques with their children with ASDs, and coaching forms for the individual sessions. It also includes a manual for parents, which provides a description of each technique in parent-friendly language and homework (Ingersoll & Dvortcsak, in press).

PROGRAM FORMAT

The program is designed to be implemented over the course of 12 weeks. It is composed of six 2-hour group sessions and six 45-minute individual coaching sessions with the parent and child. Group and individual coaching sessions are alternated weekly, such that the parents receive instruction on the intervention techniques in a group format and then have an opportunity to practice the techniques with their child while receiving feedback individually (see Table 8.2).

Table 8.2.   Format of the parent training program

Week	Session	Topic
1	Group	Introduction to the program; set up your home for success (Topic 1)
2	Individual	Set up your home for success; goal development
3	Group	Make play interactive and modeling and expanding language (Topics 2–5)
4	Individual	Make play interactive and modeling and expanding language
5	Group	Create opportunities for your child to engage or communicate; overview of direct teaching (Topics 6–9)
6	Individual	Create opportunities for your child to engage or communicate
7	Group	Teaching your child expressive language and following directions (Topics 10–11)
8	Individual	Teaching your child expressive language and following directions
9	Group	Teaching your child social imitation and play (Topics 12–13)
10	Individual	Teaching your child social imitation and play
11	Group	Putting it all together (Topic 14)
12	Individual	Putting it all together

Group sessions are attended by parents only and consist of a didactic presentation, videotaped examples, group discussion and problem solving, and homework. Group sessions are designed to be conducted during the day or in the evening, depending on the needs of the teachers and families. The first session consists of an initial didactic presentation that reviews the research on parent training for children with ASDs, a description of the parent training program, an overview of the intervention techniques encompassed in the program, and strategies for setting up the home environment to encourage successful interactions. After the first session, subsequent sessions begin with a 20-minute discussion of the parents' use of the different intervention strategies in the home. The educator then introduces a new intervention strategy via didactic presentation, videotaped examples of parents using the techniques with children with ASDs, and group discussion. At the end of each group session, parents are instructed to write down one or two of their child's goals, activities they typically complete with their child, and the intervention techniques they would use to target the child's goals. Each parent is then instructed to go home and practice the techniques over the next week and to write down how their child responds.

The techniques are introduced in a specific sequence because they build on each other. The interactive techniques are introduced first to improve the child's initiations and engagement; the direct teaching techniques are then introduced to teach the child a specific skill.

Individual Coaching Sessions

The individual coaching sessions are attended by the parent and child and are typically conducted during the school day in the children's classrooms. Each parent coaching session is scheduled for 45 minutes, with 15 minutes between families so that the educator can see up to eight families per day. Similar to the group sessions, the individual coaching sessions begin with a review of the homework. In the first coaching session, the parent educator helps the parent develop goals for the child to target over the course of the program. In subsequent coaching sessions, the educator briefly reviews the technique and models use of the techniques with the child for 5–10 minutes; the parent then practices the techniques during play with the child while the parent educator provides feedback. For example, the parent might practice eliciting single words from the child while playing with cars by playfully obstructing the child's access to the cars and prompting him or her to say, "Car."

At the end of each session, the educator helps the parent brainstorm how to use the techniques in the home during daily routines to target the child's social-communicative goals. For example, the parent might be encouraged to use the same techniques practiced with the car to elicit language during meals. The educator then writes down the child's goals, home activities, and specific techniques to address the child's goals. The parent practices the techniques at home and writes down how the child responds.

TEACHER PREPARATION

Preparation for the program involves a combination of didactic training and hands-on technical assistance, totaling about 30 hours of direct training. At this

Table 8.3.   Parent training strategies

Developing individual and group rapport
Selecting appropriate treatment goals
Presenting the information
Demonstrating the intervention techniques with the child
Providing positive and corrective feedback to parents
Assigning and discussing homework
Building independence
Taking data

point, teacher preparation is conducted by the program developers. However, the goal is to disseminate the preparation training to specialists working in the schools.

Initial Workshop

The initial 2-day workshop provides an overview of parent training, research on the effectiveness of parent training for children with ASDs and their families, and the intervention strategies. The training then focuses on specific skills that are involved in presenting information in a group format and providing online feedback to parents during coaching sessions (see Table 8.3). This initial workshop consists of a combination of didactic presentation, group discussion, role play, and practice with students while receiving feedback from the instructors. In addition, attendees are shown a variety of video clips of parents working with their children and are asked to give online feedback based on the videotaped vignette.

After the initial training, participating staff receive onsite technical assistance to help them implement the program. Technical assistance is provided during the initial parent group session and during three or four of the coaching sessions. The trainer observes the teacher conducting the first group session and provides feedback to the teacher. During the individual coaching sessions, the trainer first demonstrates how to coach parents, then observes the teacher coaching parents and provides feedback. After each coaching session, the trainer meets with the teachers to answer any questions regarding parent coaching and provides feedback to the teachers on their coaching.

PROGRAM IMPLEMENTATION

As of the writing of this chapter, the parent training program has been implemented in 11 ECSE sites in Oregon as part of the Oregon Statewide Regional Program Autism Training Sites (RPATS). The RPATS were established as a collaborative effort between Portland State University, the Oregon State Department of Education, and Oregon Regional and Special Education programs in an effort to improve the quality of education for students with ASDs in the state. Several classrooms in each region have been selected as model sites. Teachers at these sites receive intensive, hands-on training in research-based practices for children with ASDs. After training, other teachers working with children with ASDs in the region can visit the model sites to learn how to implement the interventions in their own classrooms. All RPATS classrooms use the STAR curriculum with their students (Arick, Loos, Falco, & Krug, 2004), which is based on the principles of applied behavior analysis and includes three instructional formats: discrete trial training, PRT, and functional routines.

The number of staff who have received training in the parent training program per site has ranged from one to four, with the average being three per site. These staff members have included early childhood special educators, speech-language pathologists, occupational therapists, and autism specialists. The average number of participating families per site is 6 (with a range of 3–14). After receiving training in the parent program, participating sites are expected to offer the program one to two times per year.

PROGRAM EVALUATION

The feasibility of this program has been evaluated in several ways. With the first group of participating families, gains in parent knowledge of the intervention techniques were assessed via a pre-/postquiz and parents' satisfaction with the program (Ingersoll & Dvortcsak, 2006). These data suggested that parents increased their understanding of the intervention techniques substantially through the course of the program. Parents also reported a high rate of satisfaction with the program and felt that their children gained social-communicative skills as a direct result of it (for additional discussion of these data, see Ingersoll & Dvortcsak, 2006).

An anonymous web-based survey of participating teaching staff was also conducted 1–40 months posttraining to determine the teachers' assessment of the utility of the parent training model and their perception of parents' and children's response to the program. The survey was sent to 27 staff members, and 23 responded, yielding a high response rate (85%). Staff members were asked to rate their responses to a variety of questions on a 5-point scale (1 = strongly disagree, 5 = strongly agree), as well as to answer a number of open-ended questions.

To evaluate how easily the program could be integrated into the existing ECSE curriculum, the teachers were asked a number of questions regarding the appropriateness of the program in terms of content, format, materials, and preparation. Overall, the participating teachers found the parent training program to be very appropriate for use in ECSE settings and user friendly (see Figure 8.1).

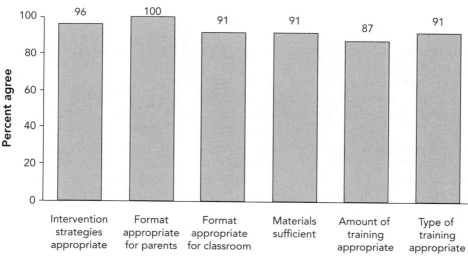

Figure 8.1.   Teachers' perceptions of the parent training curriculum, format, and teacher preparation protocol.

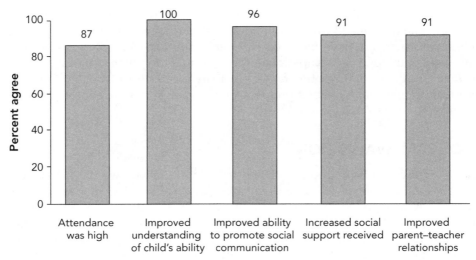

Figure 8.2.   Teachers' perceptions of participating parents' responses to the parent training program.

The teaching staff felt strongly that the intervention strategies used in the program were appropriate for use with young children with ASDs and their parents. They also reported that the format of the program was appropriate for training parents and for use in a classroom setting. The teachers reported that the program materials (session outlines, PowerPoint presentations, parent manual, and DVD) were sufficient for implementing the program. Finally, the majority felt that the amount and type of training they received would allow them to implement the program effectively. However, a number of teachers reported that they would have liked more training.

The teachers' perception of the parents' and children's response to the program was assessed to determine whether the teachers saw a benefit to including the program in their curriculum (see Figures 8.2 and 8.3). The teachers felt strongly that the program was beneficial for both the participating parents and their children. The teachers reported that parents improved their understanding of their child's skills and increased their ability to promote their child's social-communicative skills. They also reported that the children improved their social engagement and communication skills with their parents as a result of the program. Several additional benefits of the program were also endorsed, including increased social support for the parents and improved parent–teacher relationships. A smaller number of teachers also felt that the participating children generalized their improvement in social engagement and communication skills to the classroom. Finally, teachers were asked whether they felt that the program was a beneficial addition to the curriculum. A total of 100% of the teachers agreed with this statement, and 87% said that they would use the program in the future.

Through a series of open-ended questions, teachers were asked to report any concerns they had regarding the parent training program. A number of teachers suggested that, although attendance among participating families was high, overall participation among eligible families was more limited. Teachers suggested that the lack of participation was due to issues with child care, difficulty with scheduling, and the large number of non–English-speaking families in some

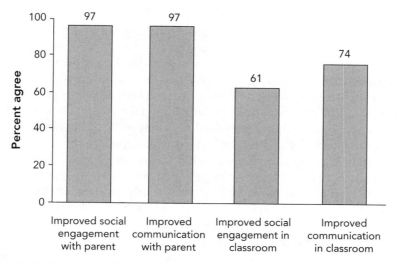

Figure 8.3.   Teachers' perceptions of participating children's responses to the parent training program.

programs. Teachers also reported concerns about the amount of time that the program took them to implement and difficulty receiving appropriate compensation for time spent on the program outside of the typical workday.

In sum, the participating teachers were very positive about the program and felt that it was a beneficial addition to the ECSE curriculum. More importantly, they were encouraged by the amount of progress they perceived the children to have made with their parents and in the classroom. As one teacher reported, "Children whose parents take this program tend to make much more progress than those who do not."

CONTRIBUTORS TO SUCCESS

Several factors that contributed to the success of this program were identified. First and foremost, strong administrative support greatly enhanced teachers' enthusiasm and commitment to the program. Administrative support involved commitment on the part of the administrator to the program in the form of help and flexibility with scheduling, securing teacher compensation (e.g., extra duty pay, comp time), and child care. In addition, teachers who were most successful implementing the program already had initial skill with the implementation of the treatment techniques in the program and a strong philosophical commitment to parent education. Finally, strong parent enthusiasm for the program helped deepen staff's commitment. Those staff who worked with parents who were outwardly appreciative of the teachers' efforts reported more success with the implementation of the program.

FUTURE DIRECTIONS

The initial evaluation of the parent training program appears promising in that teachers and parents find its content and format to be compatible with an ECSE intervention setting and perceive it to be effective for promoting social-communicative skills of young children with ASDs in the home. However, there are some limitations in its implementation, particularly in the ability of the ECSE classrooms to encourage maximal family participation. The addition of child care, flexibility in scheduling, and the use of interpreters for non–English-speaking families would likely have enhanced family involvement.

On the whole, the participating teachers expressed the view that the program led to improved child and family outcomes, as well as improved parent–teacher relationships. However, many of these same teachers felt that the program was time intensive and that they were not compensated for the time they spent outside of regular school hours. This fact seemed to lessen some of the teachers' enthusiasm for the program. For this reason, future research is needed to examine ways in which parent training can be more easily incorporated into the existing ECSE curriculum and/or ways to better compensate teachers for their efforts.

The next step is to empirically evaluate the effectiveness of the program on parent and child outcomes, both in the home and school settings. This evaluation will examine both the immediate and long-term outcomes of adding a parent training component to the ECSE curriculum on parent and child behavior. It will determine whether parents are able to maintain their use of the intervention strategies over time and whether gains in child skills maintain after the training program has ended. Furthermore, it will examine whether such a parent training program positively affects parents' satisfaction with their relationship with their child, as well as the parent–teacher relationship. This research is currently underway.

Given the fact that most other parent training programs for young children with ASDs are implemented on an individualized basis over many months, it will be important to compare individualized to group delivery formats to determine whether short-term group models, such as the one described here, are as effective as long-term, individualized models. If so, this less intense program may be more likely to be adopted by programs serving young children with ASDs in a group setting. Finally, it will be important to examine the effectiveness of the current teacher preparation protocol.

In summary, parent-implemented intervention is an effective method for promoting generalization in young children with ASDs. However, most parent training models for young children with ASDs are not compatible with classroom-based ECSE settings. The parent training program described in this chapter was designed specifically for use in such settings and our initial evaluation suggests that it can be effectively implemented within public ECSE classrooms. Future research is needed to determine the short- and long-term effectiveness of the program on parent and child outcomes.

REFERENCES

Aldred, C., Green, J. & Adams, C. (2004). A new social communication intervention for children with autism: A pilot randomized controlled treatment study suggesting effectiveness. *Journal of Child Psychology and Psychiatry, 45,* 1420–1430.

American Psychiatric Association. (2000). *Diagnostic and statistical manual of mental disorders* (4th ed., Text rev.). Washington, DC: Author.

Arick, J.R., Loos, L., Falco, R., & Krug, D.A. (2004). *The STAR Program: Strategies for teaching based on autism research, levels I, II, & III.* Austin, TX: PRO-ED.

Bagnato, S., Neisworth, T., Salvia, J.J., & Hunt, F.M. (1999). *Temperament and Atypical Behavior Scale (TABS): Early childhood indicators of developmental dysfunction.* Baltimore: Paul H. Brookes Publishing Co.

Bornstein, M.H., Tamis-LeMonda, C.S., & Haynes, O.M. (1999). First words in the second year: Continuity, stability, and models of concurrent and predictive correspondence in vocabulary and verbal responsiveness across age and context. *Infant Behavior & Development, 22,* 65–85.

Camarata, S.M., Nelson, K.E., & Camarata, M.N. (1994). Comparison of conversational-recasting and imitative procedures for training grammatical structures in children with specific language impairment. *Journal of Speech & Hearing Research, 37,* 1414–1423.

Carter, A.S., & Briggs-Gowan, M.J. (2000). *Manual of the Infant-Toddler Social-Emotional Assessment.* New Haven, CT: Yale University.

Charlop-Christy, M.H., & Carpenter, M. (2000). Modified incidental teaching sessions: A procedure for parents to increase spontaneous speech in their children with autism. *Journal of Positive Behavior Interventions, 2,* 98–112.

Davis, C.A., & Fox, J. (1999). Evaluating environmental arrangement as setting events: Review and implications for measurement. *Journal of Behavioral Education, 9,* 77–96.

Dawson, G., & Osterling, J. (1997). Early intervention in autism. In M. Guralnick (Ed.), *The effectiveness of early intervention* (pp. 307–326). Baltimore: Paul H. Brookes Publishing Co.

Delprato, D.J. (2001). Comparisons of discrete-trial and normalized behavioral intervention for young children with autism. *Journal of Autism and Developmental Disorders, 31,* 315–325.

Dunst, C., Hamby, D., Trivette, C., Raab, M., & Bruder, M.B. (2000). Everyday family and community life and children's naturally occurring learning opportunities. *Journal of Early Intervention, 23,* 151–164.

Fenson, L., Dale, P., Reznick, S., Thal, D., Bates, E., Hartung, J., et al. (1993). *MacArthur Communicative Development Inventory.* San Diego: Singular Publishing Group.

Gillett, J.N., & LeBlanc, L.A. (2007). Parent-implemented natural language paradigm to increase language and play skills in children with autism. *Research in Autism Spectrum Disorders, 1,* 247–255.

Greenspan, S.I., Wieder, S., & Simons, R. (1998). *The child with special needs: Encouraging intellectual and emotional growth.* Reading, MA: Addison-Wesley/Longman.

Hoff-Ginsberg, E., & Shatz, M. (1982). Linguistic input and the child's acquisition of language. *Psychological Bulletin, 92,* 3–26.

Hume, K., Bellini, S., & Pratt, C. (2005). The usage and perceived outcomes of early intervention and early childhood programs for young children with autism spectrum disorder. *Topics in Early Childhood Special Education, 25,* 195–207.

Individuals with Disabilities Education Act of 1990, PL 101-476, 20 U.S.C. §§1400 *et seq.*

Ingersoll, B., & Dvortcsak, A. (2006). Including parent training in the early childhood special education curriculum for children with autism spectrum disorders. *Journal of Positive Behavior Interventions, 8,* 79–87.

Ingersoll, B., & Dvorcsak, A. (in press). *Teaching social-communication: A practitioner's guide to parent training for children with autism.* New York: Guilford Press.

Ingersoll, B., Dvortcsak, A., Whalen, C., & Sikora, D. (2005). The effects of a developmental, social-pragmatic language intervention on rate of expressive language production in young children with autistic spectrum disorders. *Focus on Autism and Other Developmental Disabilities, 20,* 213–222.

Ingersoll, B., & Gergans, S. (2007). The effect of a parent-implemented imitation intervention on spontaneous imitation skills in young children with autism. *Research in Developmental Disabilities, 28,* 163–175.

Ingersoll, B., Lewis, E., & Kroman, E. (2007). Teaching the imitation and spontaneous use of descriptive gestures to young children with autism using a naturalistic behavioral intervention. *Journal of Autism and Developmental Disorders, 37,* 1446–1456.

Kaiser, A.P., Hancock, T.B., & Niefeld, J.P. (2000). The effects of parent-implemented enhanced milieu teaching on the social communication of children who have autism. *Early Education & Development, 11,* 423–446.

Kaiser, A.P., Hemmeter, M.L., Ostrosky, M.M., Fischer, R., Yoder, P., & Keefer, M. (1996). The effects of teaching parents to use responsive interaction strategies. *Topics in Early Childhood Special Education, 16,* 375–406.

Kaiser, A.P., Ostrosky, M.M., & Alpert, C.L. (1993). Training teachers to use environmental arrangement and milieu teaching with nonvocal preschool children. *Journal of The Association for Persons with Severe Handicaps, 18,* 188–199.

Kaiser, A.P., Yoder, P.J., & Keetz, A. (1992). Evaluating milieu teaching. In S.F. Warren & J. Reichle (Series & Vol. Eds.), *Communication and language intervention series: Vol. 1. Causes and effects in communication and language intervention* (pp. 9–48). Baltimore: Paul H. Brookes Publishing Co.

Klinger, L.G., & Dawson, G. (1992). Facilitating early social and communicative development in children with autism. In S.F. Warren & J. Reichle (Series & Vol. Eds.), *Communication and language intervention series: Causes and effects in communication and language intervention* (pp. 157–186). Baltimore: Paul H. Brookes Publishing Co.

Koegel, R.L., Bimbela, A., & Schreibman, L. (1996). Collateral effects of parent training on family interactions. *Journal of Autism and Developmental Disorders, 26,* 347–359.

Koegel, R.L., Schreibman, L., Britten, K.R., Burke, J.C., & O'Neill, R.E. (1982). A comparison of parent training to direct child treatment. In R.L. Koegel, A. Rincover, & A.L. Egel (Eds.), *Educating and understanding autistic children.* San Diego: College-Hill Press.

Laski, K.E., Charlop, M.H., & Schreibman, L. (1988). Training parents to use the Natural Language Paradigm to increase their autistic children's speech. *Journal of Applied Behavior Analysis, 21,* 391–400.

Lord, C., Risi, S., Lambrecht, L., Cook, E.H., Jr., Leventhal, B.L., DiLavore, P.C., et al. (2000). The Autism Diagnostic Observation Schedule-Generic: A standard measure of social and communication deficits associated with the spectrum of autism. *Journal of Autism & Developmental Disorders, 30,* 205–223.

Mahoney, G., Kaiser, A., Girolametto, L., MacDonald, J., Robinson, C., Safford, P., et al. (1999). Parent education in early intervention: A call for a renewed focus. *Topics in Early Childhood Special Education, 19,* 131–140.

Mahoney, G., & MacDonald, J. (2007). *Autism and developmental delays in young children: The Responsive Teaching curriculum for parents and professionals.* Austin, TX: PRO-ED.

Mahoney, G., & Perales, F. (2003). Using relationship-focused intervention to enhance the social-emotional functioning of young children with autism spectrum disorders. *Topics in Early Childhood Special Education, 23,* 77–89.

McCollum, J. (1999). Parent education: What we mean and what that means. *Topics in Early Childhood Special Education, 19,* 147–149.

McConachie, H., & Diggle, T. (2007). Parent implemented early intervention for young children with autism spectrum disorder: A systematic review. *Journal of Evaluation in Clinical Practice, 13,* 120–129.

McGee, G.G., Krantz, P.J., & McClannahan, L.E. (1985). The facilitative effects of incidental teaching on preposition use by autistic children. *Journal of Applied Behavior Analysis, 18,* 17–31.

Miranda-Linne, F., & Melin, L. (1992). Acquisition, generalization, and spontaneous use of color adjectives: A comparison of incidental teaching and traditional discrete-trial procedures for children with autism. *Research in Developmental Disabilities, 13,* 191–210.

National Research Council. (2001). *Educating children with autism.* Washington, DC: National Academies Press.

Ozonoff, S., & Cathcart, K. (1998). Effectiveness of a home program intervention for young children with autism. *Journal of Autism and Developmental Disorders, 28,* 25–32.

Pierce, K., & Schreibman, L. (1995). Increasing complex social behaviors in children with autism: Effects of peer-implemented pivotal response training. *Journal of Applied Behavior Analysis, 28,* 285–295.

Prizant, B., Wetherby, A., & Rydell, P. (2000). Communication intervention issues for children with autism spectrum disorders. In S.F. Warren & M.E. Fey (Series Eds.) & A.M. Wetherby & B.M. Prizant (Vol. Eds.), *Communication and language intervention series: Autism spectrum disorders: A transactional developmental perspective* (pp. 193–224). Baltimore: Paul H. Brookes Publishing Co.

Rocha, M., Schreibman, L., & Stahmer, A. (2007). Effectiveness of training parents to teach joint attention in children with autism. *Journal of Early Intervention, 29,* 154–172.

Sandall, S., Hemmeter, M.L., Smith, B.J., & McLean, M.E. (Eds.). (2005). *DEC recommended practices: A comprehensive guide for practical application in early intervention/early childhood special education.* Missoula, MT: Council for Exceptional Children, Division for Early Childhood.

Schreibman, L. (1988). *Autism.* Thousand Oaks, CA: Sage Publications.

Schreibman, L., Kaneko, W.M., & Koegel, R.L. (1991). Positive affect of parents of autistic children: A comparison across two teaching techniques. *Behavior Therapy, 22,* 479–490.

Schwartz, I.S., Anderson, S.R., & Halle, J.W. (1989). Training teachers to use naturalistic time delay: Effects on teacher behavior and on the language use of students. *Journal of The Association for Persons with Severe Handicaps, 14,* 48–57.

Shearer, M.S., & Shearer, D.E. (1977). Parent involvement. In J.B. Jordan, A.H. Hayden, M.B. Karnes, & M.M. Woods (Eds.), *Early childhood education for exceptional children* (pp. 208–235). Reston, VA: Council for Exceptional Children.

Smith, T., Groen, A.D., & Wynn, J.W. (2000). Randomized trial of intensive early intervention for children with pervasive developmental disorder. *American Journal on Mental Retardation, 105,* 269–285.

Stahmer, A.C. (1995). Teaching symbolic play skills to children with autism using pivotal response training. *Journal of Autism & Developmental Disorders, 25,* 123–141.

Thorp, D.M., Stahmer, A.C., & Schreibman, L. (1995). Effects of sociodramatic play training on children with autism. *Journal of Autism & Developmental Disorders, 25,* 265–282.

Walsh, S., Rous, B., & Lutzer, C. (2000). The federal IDEA natural environments provisions. Making it work. In S. Sandall & M. Ostrotsky (Eds.), *Young exceptional children monograph series 2: Natural environments and inclusion* (pp. 3–15). Denver, CO: Council for Exceptional Children, Division for Early Childhood.

Warren, S.F., Yoder, P.J., Gazdag, G.E., & Kim, K. (1993). Facilitating prelinguistic communication skills in young children with developmental delay. *Journal of Speech & Hearing Research, 36,* 83–97.

Wetherby, A., & Prizant, B. (2002). *Communication and Symbolic Behavior Scales Developmental Profile, first normed edition.* Baltimore: Paul H. Brookes Publishing Co.

Wetherby, A., & Prizant, B. (2003). *Communication and Symbolic Behavior Scales, normed edition.* Baltimore: Paul H. Brookes Publishing Co.

Wetherby, A., & Woods, J. (2006). Early social interaction project for children with autism spectrum disorders beginning in the second year of life: A preliminary study. *Topics in Early Childhood Special Education, 26,* 67–82.

Whalen, C.M., & Schreibman, L. (2003). Joint attention training for children with autism using behavior modification procedures. *Journal of Child Psychology and Psychiatry, 44,* 456–468.

Chapter 8
Appendix

Appendix 8.1.   Communicative temptations

Communicative Temptations

Use communicative temptations to increase opportunities for your child to inter-act with you and wait for a response. Your child can respond in any appropriate way (eye contact, affect, vocalization/words). If your child does not respond after several seconds, continue with the activity. These strategies are easy to implement during everyday activities such as meals and snacks, dressing, bath time, and bed-time. Plan extra time during these daily child care routines to use these strategies to enhance your child's communication. The following are suggestions for using these techniques during daily routines.

MEAL TIME

- Serve food whole that needs to be cut or diced for your child to eat it. (*Assistance*)

- Serve your child small portions of his or her favorite food items. Keep the rest of your child's meal in the middle of the table or in a sealed container. (*In sight and out of reach*)

- Pour small amounts of liquid from a larger pitcher into your child's cup. (*Inadequate portions*)

- If your child uses silverware, have certain necessary pieces of silverware miss-ing (e.g., no spoon with ice cream). (*Sabotage*)

- Offer your child food items that he or she does not like. (*Protest*)

- Pretend to eat a nonedible item (e.g., napkin). Make sure that you indicate that you are being silly by being animated, wait for a response, and then describe the correct way to do it (e.g., "Oh, I can't eat this. I need to eat the food!"). (*Silly situations*)

BATH TIME

- If your child likes water toys that wind up, have these available. Most young children will need assistance to operate them. (*Assistance*)

- Place all of your child's favorite bath time items (e.g., tub toys, bubble bath) on a shelf in the tub that he or she can see but cannot reach when sitting in the tub. (*In sight and out of reach*)

- Place your child's favorite bath time items in clear plastic containers with lids. When the lid is on, the containers should float, making the toys inside very attractive. (*In sight and out of reach*)

- If your child enjoys being washed, only wash one body part at a time. For example, wash one hand and then stop and wait for your child to indicate that you should continue washing. (*Inadequate portions*)

- If your child needs assistance undressing, only take off one item of clothes at a time, and wait for your child to indicate to you that you need to continue to help. (*Inadequate portions*)

- If your child has an established bath time routine that he or she enjoys, you can attempt to do certain steps out of order. For example, wash your child's feet before his or her head. (*Protest*)

BEDTIME

- If you read your child a book at bedtime, only read one page at a time. Wait for your child to indicate that he or she wants you to turn the page. (*Inadequate portions*)

- If you sing your child specific bedtime songs, only sing one or two lines at a time and wait for your child to indicate that he or she wants you to continue singing. (*Inadequate portions*)

- If you play certain music or videos at bedtime, stop the tape/CD or video periodically. Wait for your child to indicate that he or she wants you to continue to play it or give your child the tape/CD or video case without the tape/CD or video in it. (*Inadequate portions*)

- Offer your child a book, toy, music, or video that he or she does not like. (*Protest*)

DRESSING

- Only put on or take off one item of the child's clothing at a time. Wait for the child to request the next item. (*Inadequate portions*)

- Offer your child clothing items to wear that he or she does not like. (*Protest*)

- Try to put your child's clothes on incorrectly (e.g., put a shoe on his or her head, put your child's shirt on his or her feet). Make sure that you indicate that you are being silly by being animated, wait for a response, and then describe the correct way to do it (e.g., "Oh, your shirt goes over your head!). (*Silly situations*)

- Try to take your child's clothes off out of the correct order (e.g., try to take his or her sock off before you take off his or her shoe). Make sure that you indicate that you are being silly by being animated, wait for a response, and then describe the correct way to do it (e.g., "Oh, I need to take your shoe off first!). (*Silly situations*)

9

Generalization in School Settings

Strategies for Planning and Teaching

Ilene S. Schwartz, Carol Davis, Annie McLaughlin, and Nancy E. Rosenberg

Autism spectrum disorders (ASDs)[1] are seemingly everywhere these days: on the nightly news, in the paper, and on the radio. The number of books written by parents of children with ASDs and by people with ASDs themselves is burgeoning, as are professional books for teachers and parents about working with and raising children with ASDs. Of course, the information and potential misinformation about ASDs, causes, and potential treatments has proliferated most abundantly on the Internet. A recent Google search for *autism* produced 26,500,000 responses.

With all this attention to and concern about ASDs, one would think that public school teachers and administrators would be first to lead the charge to develop and implement effective, efficient, and sustainable interventions. Unfortunately, this has not been the case. In fact, when the Google search was expanded to the terms *autism* and *public schools*, only 895,000 hits were produced.

Public schools must play an integral role in the education of students with ASDs. This chapter presents characteristics of high-quality public school programs for students with ASDs, provides strategies for planning and facilitating generalization for students with ASDs in public school classrooms, and finally makes suggestions for how planning for and measuring generalization can begin with a student's individualized education program (IEP) and extend to daily communication between teachers and parents.

ROLE OF PUBLIC SCHOOLS

In the United States, politicians have realized that "a society is judged by how well we treat our most helpless and most vulnerable citizens" (Schwarzenegger, 2006). This lofty goal has been put into action by developing public school programs that not only welcome all children but also are mandated to provide a free appropriate public education to children regardless of ability or support needs.

Although the promise and ideal of a free appropriate public education was put into law in 1975 in the Education for All Handicapped Children Act (PL 94-

---

[1]The research reviewed and the recommendations made in this chapter also apply to students with disabilities other than ASDs that present the same or similar profile of strengths and support needs.

142), some states have even more protection and assurances for the education of all students. For example, in Washington, Article IX of the state constitution says, "It is the paramount duty of the state to make ample provision for the education of all children residing within its borders, without distinction or preference on account of race, color, caste, or sex." These political promises, public laws, and constitutional mandates ensure that every student living in the United States has a right to attend school—an entitlement that extends to children with ASDs. Not only do our public schools need to welcome all children with ASDs (hopefully alongside their typically developing peers), but they also are accountable for ensuring that these children make meaningful progress toward important educational outcomes.

This educational entitlement is especially important for children with ASDs. The cost of educating children with ASDs is staggering, but of course, the cost of not providing high-quality early intervention and educational services is even higher. Although the behavioral literature is replete with accounts of private schools and programs providing effective high-quality programs to children with ASDs, there are few reports of effective publicly funded programs for these children, especially as children move out of preschool.

If researchers and behavior analysts do not address the needs of children with ASDs in public schools, then one of the original dimensions of applied behavior analysis (ABA) is being violated—to study behaviors and work in settings that are of importance to the participants rather than convenient for study (Baer, Wolf, & Risley, 1968). In addition, if effective, high-quality public school programs are not created for children with ASDs, a double standard exists in the autism community. Children whose parents cannot afford to advocate, do not know how to advocate, or simply cannot successfully advocate for private services are put in double jeopardy: They are in educational jeopardy because of their ASD and once again because their families cannot afford the extraordinary costs of a home training program or private schooling (Cohen, 2002).

All school programs, however, are not created equally. Public school programs must step up to the challenge and provide programs for children with ASDs that provide adequate support and effective instruction. The characteristics of effective school programs have been described in detail elsewhere (Dawson & Osterling, 1997; Iovannone, Dunlap, Huber, & Kincaid, 2003; Schwartz & Davis, 2008) and are outlined next.

INDICATORS OF QUALITY PUBLIC SCHOOL PROGRAMS FOR CHILDREN WITH AUTISM SPECTRUM DISORDERS

Providing effective educational programming to students with ASDs is complex. Issues include where instruction should occur, who should provide the instruction, what should be taught, and how it should be taught. To organize the myriad of issues and decisions that are involved in planning a high-quality educational program, six characteristics that are common across these programs have been identified:

1.   Individualized supports and services based on student need

2.   Well-designed and normalized environments

3. Appropriate curricular content across domains

4. Systematic instruction and data-based decision making

5. Functional approaches to problem behavior

6. Family involvement and support

Individualized Supports and Services Based on Student Need

Since Evelyn Deno (1970) suggested a cascade of services, a goal of special education and school psychology has been to ensure that services provided for students with disabilities have been individualized to support and keep the child in the least restrictive environment. That is, the student's program (the goals and objectives developed for an individual student) dictates the placement rather than a preset district quota or preexisting program with an empty seat. It is clear that one type of program (e.g., inclusive, self-contained) for students with ASDs will not meet the needs of every child with ASD. It is up to the IEP team to determine where the best placement for each individual student should be, what services and supports are necessary, what objectives need to be addressed, and what instructional strategies will be most effective.

For students with ASDs, several aspects must be considered based on child preferences, learning characteristics, and family preferences:

1. Where instruction will occur (e.g., general education classroom, playground, computer lab, special education classroom)

2. Who will deliver the instruction (e.g., general education teacher, special education teacher, specialist)

3. What general supports will be necessary for the child to maintain a level of engagement that is likely to be intense enough to lead to better and generalized outcomes

Individual student characteristics are a critical part of determining the components of an individualized program. The needs and the curriculum will be developed based on an individual assessment for each student and revised frequently based on data from progress monitoring. Part of the progress monitoring must include probes for generalization. If a student with ASD can read fluently with a special education teacher in a resource room but not with his or her parents or general education teacher, then the teaching of that lesson is not complete. Learning is not accomplished until all four stages—acquisition, fluency, generalization, and maintenance—have been achieved (Wolery, Bailey, & Sugai, 1988).

Well-Designed and Normalized Environments

Well-designed and normalized environments are those environments that provide enough structure to adequately influence or promote the anticipated and appropriate student behavior. The benefits of highly structured environments in school settings are known. Simple arrangement of the environment can produce or facilitate many appropriate behaviors and can facilitate the generalization of newly acquired skills.

The environment plays a major role in the development and maintenance of both adaptive and maladaptive behavior. Environment in this sense consists not only of physical items such as chairs, materials, and square footage, but also of adult and peer interaction patterns, how teachers position themselves, and how teachers communicate with students. Providing students with an environment and interactions that support better child outcomes, discourage inappropriate behavior, and promote the generalization and maintenance of new skills is a critical component of any quality program.

Historically, however, educational interventions have focused less on development of a supportive environment and more on manipulating a single intervention. Physical arrangement of materials, proximity of adults to students, interspersing nonpreferred activities with preferred activities, and clearly defined transition periods are just some of the ways in which the environment of effective classrooms can influence the development of skills (i.e., communicative, social, and emotional skills) in students with ASDs. Other variables include keeping the length and expectations of an environment and activity within developmentally appropriate levels, embedding preferred materials, providing feedback to students regarding performance, and creating activities that keep students engaged. Finally, a supportive, consistent environment allows for easier interpretations when other types of instructional decisions are necessary.

Appropriate Curricular Content Across Domains

Discussing the specialized instruction that is necessary for skill acquisition for children with ASDs is premature without the assurance of high-quality programs in which to embed the specialized instruction. Schoolwide positive behavior support and response to intervention are two general education initiatives that provide an appropriate framework to construct effective public school programs for students with ASDs. These tiered approaches require educational teams to ensure that foundational components such as appropriate environments, instructional modifications, and adaptations are in place before more intrusive or restrictive instructional approaches are introduced. These approaches require schoolwide rules, routines, and consequences. This consistent approach across an entire school building will help to promote generalization for students across staff members and different parts of the school environment.

Systematic Instruction and Data-Based Decision Making

The literature provides educational teams with many evidenced-based instructional strategies to teach young children with ASDs. However, knowing the list of strategies is not sufficient. Systematic instruction is the process of identifying appropriate instructional procedures for teaching, matching them with what is being taught and where it is being taught, collecting ongoing evaluation data to monitor progress, and making decisions about instruction based on evaluation data.

To date, most of the systematic procedures validated for instruction of students with ASDs have been procedures that use ABA methods and principles. A range of strategies based on ABA principles have been empirically validated, including intense structured approaches or discrete trial training (e.g., Lovaas, 1987; Schwartz, Sandall, McBride, & Boulware, 2004), naturalistic strategies (McGee, Almeida, Sulzer-Azaroff, & Feldman, 1992; McGee, Krantz, & McClannahan, 1985), self-management (Koegel & Koegel, 1990; Koegel, Koegel, Hurley, & Frea, 1992), prompt fading, and modeling (Charlop & Milstein, 1989; Charlop, Schreibman, & Tryon, 1983; Ihrig & Wolchik, 1988; Jones & Schwartz, 2004). This is also true for the general education curriculum. Behavioral strategies often employed in general education include choice making (Foster-Johnson, Ferro, & Dunlap, 1994) and use of positive reinforcement during direct instruction (Stein & Davis, 2000).

Simply knowing and being able to implement a given strategy is not enough. Service providers need to identify under what conditions it is appropriate to use one strategy over another. Several factors should be considered when making a decision about which instructional strategy to use:

1. The instructional grouping (e.g., one to one, small group) of the students

2. The best context to teach the skill

3. The number of opportunities per day that the child needs to learn the skill

4. The schedule of reinforcement that is necessary for the child to learn the skill

Educational teams can only match the skills to be taught with the instructional strategies and context when data are collected and used to make instructional decisions. Data collection and then evaluation of the data to make changes in the instructional procedures are critical and necessary components of any program for children with ASDs. Without data collection, the team is unable to decide 1) the appropriate strategy and conditions to provide instruction and 2) whether or not those instructional procedures are effective. Moreover, Drasgow and Yell (2001) found that schools that used data to make decisions about instruction were more successful in due process hearings if the disagreement was about appropriate methodologies used for instruction.

Functional Approaches to Problem Behavior

Children with ASDs who exhibit challenging behaviors are more likely to be excluded and isolated from child care, preschool, and other early school settings. Given the nature of ASDs (i.e., deficits in communication and social skills), many children who are diagnosed with ASDs also exhibit challenging behavior. A lot of attention has been given to the use of positive behavior supports to manage behavior for children who exhibit challenging behavior. Positive behavior support is an approach to intervention that evolved from a call from advocates and the field to eliminate the use of highly punitive interventions to control behavior (Dunlap, Carr, Horner, Zarcone, & Schwartz, 2008). Positive behavior support is grounded in the concept that all behavior is communicative and serves a purpose; thus, to successfully design an intervention that is effective, it is necessary to identify the purpose (i.e., function) of the behavior.

The use of functional behavioral assessment to identify the purpose of the behavior is critical to better matching an intervention that will serve the purpose and teach the child a new skill to replace the existing challenging behavior. For example, if a boy drops to the floor when asked to wash his hands, the teacher may allow him to go to the snack table without washing his hands, thus allowing the child to escape the task. Subsequently, the next time that the child is asked to wash his hands, he may again drop to the floor and have a tantrum. When planning an intervention, the child could instead be taught to request help—thus reducing the challenging behavior.

The literature is very clear: a functional approach to challenging behavior includes the systematic examination of variables through the use of indirect (e.g., interviews, scales, review of existing documents) and direct (e.g., scatterplot, ABC analysis, environmental manipulation) measures to develop a hypothesis about the conditions under which the challenging behavior is likely to occur and be maintained. The real emphasis of a function-based approach to challenging behavior is on prevention and teaching alternative skills that serve the same function, while also examining the ways in which people respond to the behavior.

Positive behavior support plans are typically designed by using a combination of strategies that are likely to reduce challenging behavior while increasing appropriate alternative skills. In addition, a positive behavior plan should be a good fit with the context and service providers who will be implementing the plan. That is, the plan should consist of strategies that are known to be effective with students with ASDs and are acceptable and doable to those who will be implementing the plan (Albin, Lucyshyn, Horner, & Flannery, 1996).

Family Involvement and Support

Research has demonstrated that family participation in a child's school program has a positive impact on a child's learning (Dunlap, 1999). Children with ASDs provide more of a challenge, often exhibiting difficulties generalizing skills from one environment to another or from the presence of one person to another, thus making skill acquisition difficult. Research has shown that for children with special needs, parent participation leads to a number of positive outcomes, including greater generalization and maintenance gains, as well as more continuity in intervention programs. Given the importance of parent participation and these unique learning and behavioral needs of children with ASDs, it is critical that schools partner with families to provide the best learning opportunities for children with ASDs.

STRATEGIES TO PROMOTE GENERALIZED RESPONDING IN SCHOOLS

Although there is a large and ever-growing body of literature describing instructional strategies for students with ASDs that have been conducted in public schools, few studies have carefully examined the characteristics that support or may interfere with the generalization of newly learned behavior across settings, materials, and people. Instead, much of the research is similar to our own work: an instructional strategy was carefully implemented and then measured to see if the effects generalized to additional settings or individuals (e.g., Apple, Billingsley, & Schwartz, 2005; Garfinkle & Schwartz, 2002; McBride & Schwartz, 2003). Although many of these studies demonstrated generalized behavior change, their purpose was not to study the process of generalization. Three areas of research are notable exceptions in the careful analysis of success in demonstrating generalized behavior change: peer-mediated instruction, general case programming, and naturalistic

Table 9.1.   Research on generalization at school

Strategies to promote generalized responding
Multiple exemplars
General case programming
Pivotal Response Training (Koegel & Koegel, 2006)
Use of effective and efficient instructional strategies
Interspersed instruction
Naturalistic instruction
Peer-mediated instruction
Team planning and collaboration
Avoiding multiple settings, which can interfere with staff communication
Dedicating time to planning and team meetings for consistency across settings (Donegan, Ostrosky, & Fowler, 1996)
Using a matrix to plan for efficient instruction

instructional strategies. (See Table 9.1 examples for research on generalization at school.)

Peer-Mediated Instruction

In a systematic program of research spanning more than 30 years, Strain and others (e.g., Kohler & Strain, 1997; McEvoy, Twardosz, & Bishop, 1990) demonstrated that peers are effective in promoting the acquisition and generalized use of social skills in preschool children with ASDs. This research demonstrated that typically developing peers can be taught to be effective prompters for children with ASDs and that the effects of these interventions are durable and socially valid.

Peer-mediated instruction can also be implemented at the classwide level, teaching many children the skill at the same time. For example, one study (Laushey & Heflin, 2000) trained an entire class in play skills to enhance the social skills of kindergarten children with ASDs, using the "stay, play, and talk" procedure (English, Goldstein, Kaczmarek, & Shafer, 1996). The entire class received instruction on how to play with an assigned buddy, then the buddies were rotated to increase the number of students with whom the student with ASD played. By training the entire class to be peer tutors and not singling out one child, the student with ASD will have more opportunities across the day to practice the skill.

General Case Programming

The use of general case programming requires the intentional selection of a variety of stimuli to use during instruction in order to teach a broad range of responses across settings, people, and materials (Engelmann & Carnine, 1982). For example, O'Neill, Faulkner, and Horner (2000) used general case programming to teach communication skills to two students with autism. The students learned how to request specific items or help with the items. First, the teachers identified the teaching and generalization probes. For one of the students, the teaching probes included five different categories: food packaging, out-of-reach food, out-of-reach toys, movement of doors, and dressing (see Table 9.2). Each category included two to five teaching examples, and each generalization test included four or five different

Table 9.2.   Categories of teaching probes

Category	Training examples	Generalization testing examples
Food packaging	Ice-cream bar (lunch table in cafeteria)	Jar with cookies (snack table in classroom)
	Carton of milk (lunch table in cafeteria)	Bag of chips/nuts (lunch table in cafeteria)
	Banana (snack table in classroom)	Box of cereal (snack table in classroom)
	Box of crackers (snack table in classroom)	Carton of juice (lunch table in cafeteria)
	Container of yogurt (snack table in classroom)	Container with cookies (snack table in classroom)
Out of reach (food)	Glass of water (sink in classroom)	Cookies on plate (snack table in classroom)
	Carton of milk (snack table in classroom)	Bowl of yogurt (counter in classroom)
	Toaster pastries (counter in classroom)	Bag of chips/nuts (snack table in classroom)
	Applesauce (snack table in classroom)	Ice cream (lunch table in cafeteria)
		Carton of juice (lunch table in classroom)
Out of reach (toys)	Keyboard (shelf in classroom)	Hand lotion (sink in classroom)
	Trampoline (floor in classroom)	Kaleidoscope (table in classroom)
		Empty cup (lunch table in cafeteria)
		Bubbles (shelf in classroom)
		Slinky (table in classroom)
Movement (doors)	In restroom door in cafeteria (doorknob)	In classroom door (doorknob)
		Out building exit door (push bar)
	Out classroom door (doorknob)	In door to office (doorknob)
	Out playground door (push bar)	In playground door (pull handle)
	In front door (pull handle)	In music room door (doorknob)
Dressing	Coat off (in arrival area in classroom)	Apron off (by sink in classroom)
	Pull pants down (in restroom)	Remove extra shirt (at table in cafeteria)
	Apron on (by sink in classroom)	Put on coat (in classroom for recess)
	Put on extra shirt (at table in cafeteria)	Pull pants up (in restroom)

With kind permission from Springer Science+Media: *Journal of Developmental and Physical Disabilities*, The effects of general case training of manding responses on children with severe disabilities, 12(1), 2000, pp. 43–60, O'Neill, Faulkner, & Horner.

probes that were not included in the teaching examples. This particular student was able to demonstrate target responses in an average of 94% of the generalization examples.

Naturalistic Instructional Strategies

Since Hart and Risley (1968) documented the effectiveness of incidental teaching with children attending Head Start programs, researchers have developed and documented a number of naturalistic strategies to address the language needs of children with ASDs and related disorders (for a review, see Hall, 2008; Koegel, 2000). In addition to incidental teaching, these strategies include mand modeling, choice making, time delay, the natural language paradigm, and Pivotal Response Training (PRT).

All of these naturalistic strategies take advantage of items and activities that are motivating to the student to teach a wide variety of important skills and behaviors. In addition, because the instruction is dispersed across naturally occurring and interesting activities, this type of instruction has been extremely successful in producing generalized and durable behavior change. For example, Harper, Symon, and Frea (2008) used PRT to improve the social interactions of students with ASDs while on the playground. Peers were trained in PRT strategies including gaining attention, varying activities, narrating play, reinforcing attempts, and turn taking. The students with ASDs increased their specific target behaviors of gaining peer attention and initiating play.

ACTIVITIES AND TIPS

It is axiomatic to say that planning, teamwork, and coordination are required to facilitate the generalization of newly acquired and highly valued skills and behaviors. However, it is often surprising to see how little time and energy is truly spent by the educational team to plan for and promote generalization. This section presents a framework for thinking more productively about the strategies used to facilitate generalization and presents some concrete strategies (including sample data sheets) that teams can use to facilitate generalization.

In 1977, Stokes and Baer published a seminal review of the current practices to facilitate generalization in the ABA literature. The nine categories that they developed to describe the strategies are still considered to be the most comprehensive review of this literature. Interestingly, and somewhat distressing, the strategy that appeared most frequently was actually a nonstrategy—train and hope. That is, interventionists taught skills but did not do anything else to facilitate the generalization of the target skill. The following activities and tips can help educational teams to move beyond training and hoping to planning and coordinating.

When planning for and promoting generalization, practitioners should focus on four primary questions:

1. Is this an important and highly valued skill or behavior?

2. Is the initial instruction being conducted in the most efficient, effective, culturally relevant, and socially valid manner?

3. Does the student have opportunities to demonstrate, practice, and be reinforced for the skill or behavior frequently and across a variety of settings?

4. Are members of the educational team (including family members) working together to plan and promote the generalization of the target skill and behavior?

Is This an Important and Highly Valued Skill or Behavior?

Every student, teacher, and family has a limited amount of time—and therefore a limited number of objectives—that can be addressed at any one time. This requires practitioners to be judicious in selecting skills and behaviors to teach. Skills and behaviors can be important because of family preferences, because of state guidelines, because they help children become more independent and successful in a less restrictive environment, or because they are keystone skills

(Wolery, 1991) that enable students to gain access to important lessons that are available in the classroom or community environment.

The bottom line for this question is relatively simple: If a skill or behavior is not valued, do not make it a priority. Skills that are valued are more likely to generalize because students will be more likely to have the opportunity and motivation to demonstrate them outside of the training setting. These valued skills are said to have a high level of social validity (Schwartz & Baer, 1991; Wolf, 1978). Spend those limited minutes of instructional time on skills and behaviors that are priorities.

Is the Initial Instruction Being Conducted in the Most Efficient, Effective, Culturally Relevant, and Socially Valid Manner?

Wolery et al. (1988) proposed a four-level model of learning—acquisition, fluency, generalization, and maintenance—suggesting that a skill or behavior cannot be generalized if some degree of fluency has not been achieved. Therefore, the efficiency with which a student acquires a skill can influence how quickly and thoroughly he or she will be able to demonstrate generalized use of that skill over time. It is beyond the scope of this chapter to review the instructional strategies for students with ASDs (see Hall, 2008, for a review of a number of approaches). However, it is essential that data are taken frequently while teaching new skills and behaviors; these data should be analyzed and used to make decisions that affect the efficiency of teaching and learning.

Does the Student Have Opportunities to Demonstrate, Practice, and Be Reinforced for the Skill or Behavior Frequently and Across a Variety of Settings?

Recall the old adage, "Practice makes perfect." Although perfection is not the goal for generalization of new skills, nothing will happen without opportunities to practice the target skill or behavior. Teaching a skill that the student will not have an opportunity to perform and be reinforced for (ideally by the natural contingencies supporting that behavior) will surely inhibit generalization and increase the irrelevance of a student's educational program. Skills that enable children to obtain reinforcers in the environment (e.g., requesting preferred activities) have a high likelihood of generalizing and maintaining.

Are Members of the Educational Team (Including Family Members) Working Together to Plan and Promote the Generalization of the Target Skill and Behavior?

Because, by definition, generalization requires that a student demonstrates the target skill or behavior across people, materials, or places, it makes sense to borrow one more proverb: It takes a village to facilitate generalization for students with

ASDs. Although it may not take an entire village, a teacher or parent certainly cannot do it alone. All members of the educational team must work together to plan, promote, and measure generalization. Appendices 9.1–9.3 provide examples of how members of the educational team—at school and at home—can work together to plan for and document the generalization of highly valued skills.

Appendix 9.1 is a School–Home Communication and Data Sheet. The purpose of this form is twofold. First, it provides a simple and efficient manner to provide the information that parents request on a daily basis (these questions should be tailored to meet the needs of individual families and students). It also provides a format for school staff and family members to work together on a valued skill. In this case, it answers questions about events that happened in the recent past (i.e., how to answer the dreaded question "What did you do at school today?"). Appendix 9.2 is a simple datasheet that can be used either at school across providers and settings or at home and school to collect data on the acquisition and generalization of a targeted skill. Appendix 9.3 is a planning matrix to facilitate instruction and the assessment of acquisition and generalization of new skills.

All of these forms share a common purpose: planning for generalization—the take-home message. The most important component of facilitating generalization is planning for it. However, planning alone is not sufficient; rather, it is a necessary and often neglected foundational step.

FUTURE DIRECTIONS

Issues of the generalization and durability of behavior change are essential to achieving meaningful outcomes for students with ASDs. To achieve generalized outcomes, planning for generalization must occur at the initial stages of intervention and continue throughout the intervention process. Promoting generalization is a team effort; participants from every aspect of a student's community need to be enlisted to help identify the appropriate goals to teach and promote the generalization and maintenance of the newly acquired skills. Finally, researchers need to study how the process of generalization can coexist with efforts to scale up implementation of evidence-based practices.

To ensure that all students with ASDs experience programs with more efficient generalization planning, educational teams (including family and community members) should engage in collaborative planning and goal setting. Two strategies may be especially useful in this planning process: using environmental inventories and person-centered planning. The purpose of an environmental inventory is to assess the skills necessary to help the student be as successful and independent as possible in the environments in which he or she spends time (e.g., school, home, community settings). Future research and tool development are needed to provide environmental inventories that are relevant and user friendly.

The environments to be included in these assessments can be determined by a person-centered plan (O'Brien & O'Brien, 2002). A person-centered plan is a comprehensive planning process that involves the student with disabilities and the people who care about and support him or her. The goal of this process is for the team to identify hopes and dreams, then put a plan in place to ensure that these positive outcomes come to fruition, while ensuring that any nightmares identified during the process are avoided.

Planning a relevant and meaningful course of study for a student with ASD is the first step in facilitating generalized and durable outcomes. The best program plan, however, depends on state-of-the-art teaching to translate the planned objectives into meaningful changes that affect a student's quality of life. A state-of-the-art teaching program includes staff who are adequately trained and supported, implementation of the programs with fidelity and intensity, data-based decision making, high-quality motivational and reinforcement systems, and meaningful family support.

School programming that results in generalized and durable behavior change is a promise that our country has made to every student with ASD and his or her family. Through continued research, teacher training, and involvement of families in the planning process, progress can be made towards this important and meaningful accomplishment.

REFERENCES

Albin, R.W., Lucyshyn, J.M., Horner, R.H., & Flannery, K.B. (1996). Contextual fit for behavior support plans. In L.K. Koegel, R.L. Koegel, & G. Dunlap (Eds.), *Positive behavioral support: Including people with difficult behaviors in the community* (pp. 81–92). Baltimore: Paul H. Brookes Publishing Co.

Apple, A.L., Billingsley, F., & Schwartz, I.S. (2005). Effects of video modeling alone and with self-management on compliment-giving behaviors of children with high functioning ASD. *Journal of Positive Behavior Interventions, 7*, 33–46.

Baer, D.M., Wolf, M.M., & Risley, T.R. (1968). Some current dimensions of applied behavior analysis. *Journal of Applied Behavior Analysis, 1*, 91–97.

Charlop, M.H., & Milstein, J.P. (1989). Teaching autistic children conversational speech using video modeling. *Journal of Applied Behavior Analysis, 22*(3), 275–285.

Charlop, M.H., Schreibman, L., & Tryon, A.S. (1983). Learning through observation: The effects of peer modeling on acquisition and generalization in autistic children. *Journal of Abnormal Child Psychology, 11*(3), 355–366.

Cohen, S. (2002). *Targeting autism*. Berkeley: University of California Press.

Dawson, G., & Osterling, J. (1997). Early intervention in autism. In M. Guralnick (Ed.), *The effectiveness of early intervention* (pp. 307–326). Baltimore: Paul H. Brookes Publishing Co.

Deno, E. (1970). Special education as developmental capital. *Exceptional Children, 37*(3), 229–237.

Donegan, M.M., Ostrosky, M.M., & Fowler, S.A. (1996). Children enrolled in multiple programs: Characteristics, supports, and barriers to teacher communication. *Journal of Early Intervention, 20*, 95–106.

Drasgow, E., & Yell, M. (2001). Functional behavioral assessments: Legal requirements and challenges. *School Psychology Review, 30*, 239–251.

Dunlap, G. (1999). Consensus, engagement, and family involvement for young children with autism. *Journal of The Association for Persons with Severe Handicaps, 24*, 222–225.

Dunlap, G., Carr, E., Horner, R., Zarcone, J., & Schwartz, I. (2008). Positive behavior support and applied behavior analysis: A familial alliance. *Behavior Modification, 32*(5), 682–698.

Education for All Handicapped Children Act of 1975, PL 94-142, 20 U.S.C. §§ 1400 *et seq.*

Engelmann, S., & Carnine, D. (1982). *Theory of instruction: Principles and applications*. New York: Irvington Publishers.

English, K., Goldstein, H., Kaczmarek, L., & Shafer, K. (1996). "Buddy skills" for preschoolers. *Teaching Exceptional Children, 23*(3), 62–66.

Foster-Johnson, L., Ferro, J., & Dunlap, G. (1994). Preferred curricular activities and reduced problem behaviors in students with intellectual disabilities. *Journal of Applied Behavior Analysis, 27*, 493–504.

Garfinkle, A.N., & Schwartz, I.S. (2002). Peer imitation: Increasing social interactions in children with autism and other developmental disabilities in inclusive preschool classrooms. *Topics in Early Childhood Special Education, 22*(1), 26–38.

Hall, L. (2008). Autism spectrum disorders: From theory to practice. New York: Prentice-Hall.

Harper, C.B., Symon, J.B.G., & Frea, W.D. (2008). Recess is time-in: Using peers to improve social skills of children with autism. *Journal of Autism and Developmental Disorders, 38*, 815–826.

Hart, B.M., & Risley, T.R. (1968). Establishing use of descriptive adjectives in the spontaneous speech of disadvantaged preschool children. *Journal of Applied Behavior Analysis, 1*, 109–120.

Ihrig, K., & Wolchik, S.A. (1988). Peer versus adult models and autistic children's learning: Acquisition, generalization, and maintenance. *Journal of Autism and Developmental Disorders, 18*(1), 67–79.

Iovannone, R., Dunlap, G., Huber, H., & Kincaid, D. (2003). Effective educational practices for students with autism spectrum disorders. *Focus on Autism and Other Developmental Disabilities, 18*, 150–165.

Jones, C.D., & Schwartz, I.S. (2004). Siblings, peers, and adults: Differentiated effects of models for children with autism. *Topics in Early Childhood Special Education, 24*, 187–198.

Koegel, L.K. (2000). Interventions that facilitate communication in autism. In Treatments for people with autism and other pervasive developmental disorders: Research perspectives [Special issue]. *Journal of Autism and Developmental Disorders, 30*(5), 383–391.

Koegel, L.K., Koegel, R.L., Hurley, C., & Frea, W.D. (1992). Improving social skills and disruptive behavior in children with autism through self-management. *Journal of Applied Behavior Analysis, 25*(2), 341–353.

Koegel, R.L., & Koegel, L.K. (1990). Extended reductions in stereotypic behavior of students with autism through a self-management treatment package. *Journal of Applied Behavior Analysis, 23*(1), 119–127.

Koegel, R.L., & Koegel, L.K. (2006). *Pivotal response treatments for autism: Communication, social, and academic development.* Baltimore: Paul H. Brookes Publishing Co.

Kohler, F., & Strain, P.S. (1997). Combining incidental teaching and peer-mediation with young children with autism. *Journal of Autism and Related Disorders, 12*, 196–206.

Laushey, K.M., & Heflin, L.J. (2000). Enhancing social skills of kindergarten children with autism through the training of multiple peers as tutors. *Journal of Autism and Developmental Disorders, 30*, 183–193.

Lovaas, O.I. (1987). Behavioral treatment and normal educational and intellectual functioning in young autistic children. *Journal of Consulting and Clinical Psychology, 55*, 3–9.

McBride, B.J., & Schwartz, I.S. (2003). Effects of teaching early interventionists to use discrete trials during ongoing classroom activities. *Topics in Early Childhood Special Education, 23*(1), 5–18.

McEvoy, M., Twardosz, S., & Bishop, N. (1990). Activities for encouraging young children with handicaps to interact with their peers. *Education and Treatment of Children, 13*(2), 159–167.

McGee, G.G., Almeida, M., Sulzer-Azaroff, B., & Feldman, R.S. (1992). Promoting reciprocal interactions via peer incidental teaching. *Journal of Applied Behavior Analysis, 25*(1), 117–126.

McGee, G.G., Krantz, P.J., & McClannahan, L.E. (1985). The facilitative effects of incidental teaching on preposition use by autistic children. *Journal of Applied Behavior Analysis, 18*(1), 17–31.

O'Brien, C.L., & O'Brien, J. (2002). The origins of person-centered planning: A community of practice perspective. In S. Holburn & P.M. Vietze (Eds.), *Person-centered planning: Research, practice, and future directions.* Baltimore: Paul H. Brookes Publishing Co.

O'Neill, R.E., Faulkner, C., & Horner, R.H. (2000). The effects of general case training of manding responses on children with severe disabilities. *Journal of Developmental and Physical Disabilities, 12*(1), 43–60.

Sandall, S.R., & Schwartz, I.S. (2008). *Building blocks for teaching preschoolers with special needs* (2nd ed.). Baltimore: Paul H. Brookes Publishing Co.

Schwartz, I.S., & Baer, D.M. (1991). Social-validity assessments: Is current practice state-of-the-art? *Journal of Applied Behavior Analysis, 24,* 189–204.

Schwartz, I.S., & Davis, C.A. (2008). Effective services for young children with autistic spectrum disorders (ASD). Best practices in school psychology. In A. Thomas & J. Grimes (Eds.), *Best practices in school psychology V*. Washington, DC: National Association of School Psychology.

Schwartz, I.S., Sandall, S.R., McBride, B.J., & Boulware, G.L. (2004). Project DATA (Developmentally Appropriate Treatment for Autism): An inclusive, school-based approach to educating children with autism. *Topics in Early Childhood Special Education, 24,* 156–168.

Schwarzenegger, A. (2006, September 22). *Transcript of Governor Arnold Schwarzenegger signing legislation to protect foster youth.* Retrieved September 19, 2008, from http://gov.ca.gov/speech/4108/

Stein, M., & Davis, C.A. (2000). Direct instruction as a positive behavioral support. *Beyond Behavior, 10,* 7–12.

Stokes, T.F., & Baer, D.M. (1977). An implicit technology of generalization. *Journal of Applied Behavior Analysis, 10,* 349–367.

Wolery, M. (1991). Instruction in early childhood special education: "Seeing through a glass darkly. . . knowing in part." *Exceptional Children, 58,* 127–135.

Wolery, M., Bailey, D.B., & Sugai, G. (1988). *Effective teaching: Principles and procedures of applied behavior analysis with exceptional students.* New York: Allyn & Bacon.

Wolf, M.M. (1978). Social validity: The case for subjective measurement or how applied behavior analysis is finding its heart. *Journal of Applied Behavior Analysis, 11,* 203–214.

Chapter 9
Appendices

School–Home Communication and Data Sharing Sheet

Student: _____ Teacher: _____ Date: _____

Parent requested information

Number of questions your child answered correctly this morning: _____

Toilet accidents: _____

How much lunch did my child eat?: _____

What was today's standout behavior?: _____

Overall behavioral rating for the day:

1 (We need to talk)　　　2　　　3 (Average)　　　4　　　5 (Outstanding)

Questions for you to ask your child at home (we worked together to answer these before the end of the school day). Circle the plus sign if child answers correctly.

Who did you play with at recess today?: _____ + −

What did we discuss at class meeting today?: _____ + −

What was the best thing that you did at school today?

_____ + −

Information so that we can ask your child about what happened at home:

What did you do last night?_____

What books did you read last night? _____

What TV show did you watch last night?_____

Other:_____

_____

Comments: _____

_____

Training and Generalization Data at a Glance

Date: _____

Child's name: _____   Teacher's name: _____

Target skill: _____

Circle correct responses; slash (/) incorrect responses

Training data Date										
Where did you conduct training?	5	5	5	5	5	5	5	5	5	5
	4	4	4	4	4	4	4	4	4	4
	3	3	3	3	3	3	3	3	3	3
	2	2	2	2	2	2	2	2	2	2
	1	1	1	1	1	1	1	1	1	1
	0	0	0	0	0	0	0	0	0	0
Criteria:	ND	ND	ND	ND	ND	ND	ND	ND	ND	ND

Generalization data Date										
Where did you assess for generalization?	5	5	5	5	5	5	5	5	5	5
	4	4	4	4	4	4	4	4	4	4
	3	3	3	3	3	3	3	3	3	3
	2	2	2	2	2	2	2	2	2	2
	1	1	1	1	1	1	1	1	1	1
	0	0	0	0	0	0	0	0	0	0
Criteria:	ND	ND	ND	ND	ND	ND	ND	ND	ND	ND

Comments, questions, or issues to discuss with the team: _____

_____

_____

APPENDIX 9.3.

Training and Generalization Activity Planning Matrix

Child's name: _____   Date: _____

Teacher/classroom: _____

Circle correct responses; slash (/) incorrect responses

Objective/target behavior	Training setting and data	Generalization setting and data
	1 2 3 4 5	1 2 3 4 5
	1 2 3 4 5	1 2 3 4 5
	1 2 3 4 5	1 2 3 4 5
	1 2 3 4 5	1 2 3 4 5
	1 2 3 4 5	1 2 3 4 5
	1 2 3 4 5	1 2 3 4 5
	1 2 3 4 5	1 2 3 4 5

Comments: _____

_____

_____

Adapted from Sandall & Schwartz (2008).
In *Real Life, Real Progress for Children with Autism Spectrum Disorders*, edited
by Christina Whalen. Copyright © 2009 Brookes Publishing Co. All rights reserved.

10

Generalizing In-Home Treatment Gains

Sabrina D. Daneshvar, William D. Frea, and Ronit M. Molko

Kevin, a 5-year-old boy with autism, has been receiving 20 hours per week of in-home applied behavior analysis (ABA) therapy for the past 8 months. He has made great progress in many areas, including being able to follow directions, play with a variety of toys, use utensils when eating, and label and request many common objects using one- or two-word phrases. His parents are thrilled that he has been spontaneously greeting his two therapists when they arrive in the home for the daily therapy sessions. Kevin's parents were excited for his grandmother, who lives out of state, to see him and how much progress he had made when they went to visit her over Thanksgiving. Imagine their shock and embarrassment when Kevin did not speak at all during Thanksgiving dinner and barely uttered a few words during the entire trip. Kevin had done extremely well during therapy, making gains in many areas. These gains seemed futile, however, when he was unable to use what he had learned in other environments and with other people.

Similar to Kevin's situation, Sarah's family and therapists practiced turn taking and how to initiate with peers at home during therapy sessions for weeks before a big birthday party Sarah was going to attend. At home, she was able to approach her therapists, say, "Let's go play," and take turns appropriately while playing a wide variety of games. Sarah's parents were filled with anticipation as the party approached, hoping that she would be able to play with her friends and have a good time. Unfortunately, despite the hours spent practicing and preparing for the party, Sarah spent the entire time spinning in circles in the backyard, refusing to even look at any of her peers. Her parents were so disappointed that the hours of therapy she had received did not translate into improved social skills. They had hoped Sarah would at least have an increased interest in other children or a better ability to take part in what they were doing. Sarah's situation is another example of the importance of identifying meaningful treatment goals and making sure those goals generalize to new situations and people.

The use of in-home behavior therapy as the intervention of choice for the treatment of individuals with autism spectrum disorders (ASDs) has become more prevalent. There is always a challenge in developing in-home programs that will effectively generalize acquired skills. With the growing expectation of in-home treatment comes the urgency to train therapists in how to program for generalization and maintenance of learned skills.

The general consensus among researchers and treatment providers is that an optimal in-home program for children with ASDs includes intensive early intervention (a minimum of 20–25 hours per week) based on the principles of ABA (Anderson, Avery, DiPietro, Edwards, & Christian, 1987; Howard, Sparkman, Cohen, Green, & Stanislaw, 2005). In fact, studies have consistently documented the efficacy of home-based ABA intervention in improving language skills, cognitive functioning, and academic performance, while decreasing disruptive behaviors (e.g., Anderson et al., 1987; Smith, Groen, & Wynn, 2000; Weiss, 1999), as described in the cases of Kevin and Sarah.

STRENGTHS OF IN-HOME PROGRAMS

In-home programs have several strengths. First and foremost, in-home programs allow for access to a significantly greater number of treatment hours than clinic-based programs. In-home ABA programs result in fast acquisition of skills and have been proven effective in yielding rapid gains in various domains (e.g., Howard et al., 2005). Tight stimulus control, precise teaching, opportunities for many learning trials, and objective data collection all promote the development of new skills (e.g., Elliot, Hall, & Soper, 1991).

Other advantages of in-home ABA programs are the opportunity for parent education and involvement, as well as the ability to teach in the natural environment. It is expected that parent education is part of any ABA program, as parental involvement is critical to its success. Parent education results in increased teaching time and teaching opportunities, improved generalization of skills, overall satisfaction, and improvements in a family's quality of life (e.g., Anderson et al., 1987; Brookman-Frazee, 2004; Smith et al., 2000). Researchers have demonstrated that parent-implemented interventions have resulted in greater generalization and maintenance of skills than when parents rely solely on therapist-implemented interventions (Koegel, Schreibman, Britten, Burke, & O'Neill, 1982). Research has also found that parents' incidental teaching of skills such as speech and play in the home complements and reinforces those skills taught during intensive one-to-one ABA intervention (e.g., Charlop-Christy & Carpenter, 2000; Laski, Charlop, & Schreibman, 1988; McGee, Krantz, & McClannahan, 1985). Caregivers have been successfully taught both to manage challenging behavior and to teach adaptive skills (e.g., Brookman-Frazee, 2004; Harris, 1982; Koegel, Bimbela, & Schreibman, 1996; Malmberg, 2008). In general, a strong parent education program seeks to identify activities that increase parent–child interactions, teach parents typical developmental milestones, and provide the opportunity to practice skills learned in a one-to-one setting. Most importantly, parent education programs improve parents' abilities to apply behavioral strategies to naturally occurring family routines throughout the day in multiple settings, when interventionists are not present. It is important that parents are included as active participants to ensure that the goals and strategies most important to the family are incorporated in intervention.

Indeed, parents whose children have received intensive early ABA intervention reported higher satisfaction and reduced stress as compared to parents whose children did not receive intensive intervention (Howard et al., 2005). In-home ABA programs are able to focus on typically occurring family routines, such as feeding, bedtime routines, and playtime. A successful program will build teaching opportunities within existing routines in addition to building new routines. Parents are a stable part of a child's life; therefore, parents can consistently use ABA interventions to target routines and behaviors throughout a child's development (Mullen & Frea, 1995).

GENERALIZATION CONCERNS

Despite the clear benefits of in-home programming, there are some concerns with regards to generalization, as described in the cases of Kevin and Sarah. When most people consider risks to generalization, they probably think of a clinical environment where the child is seen by a therapist in a treatment room. They might recall some of the steps that are taken to promote generalization in that environment, such as parent training or using a simulated living room. One would think that providing services in the child's home would solve most of the problems that result in a lack of generalization, but that is not always the case. Many therapists fail to appreciate that children with ASDs will struggle to generalize language and social goals when a tightly structured teaching environment is established, regardless of the setting. The risks to generalization are more related to *how* skills are taught than *where* they are taught (Horner, Dunlap, & Koegel, 1988; Stokes & Baer, 1977).

Limiting teaching to in-home settings may result in less exposure to multiple exemplars of new behaviors. Introducing multiple exemplars into teaching ensures that learning is not too focused and uses multiple teachers, stimuli, and settings (Stokes & Baer, 1977). New tasks should be taught using multiple and diverse exemplars so that after a sufficient range of new behaviors are successfully mastered, the child is able to perform new behaviors without direct teaching of all new concepts.

The tight stimulus control and presentation of discriminative stimuli that encourage fast acquisition within the home can also limit the generalizability and spontaneity of new skills. Teaching conditions should be flexible and less predictable by allowing a variation in teaching, presentations of trials, and varying positive reinforcers and feedback. Another limitation of in-home programming is the difficulty with bringing other stimuli, such as peers, into the home. Playdates are challenging because they require intensive facilitation and organization. However, they are a critical aspect of an in-home program. Programming common stimuli involves presenting salient stimuli in both the training and generalization settings; ideally, a peer would be able to interact with a child at home and across other settings (e.g., playground, school, birthday party) for optimal generalization (Stokes & Baer, 1977). The importance and utility of playdates is discussed in more detail later in this chapter.

TRADITIONAL DISCRETE TRIAL TRAINING

Based on principles of ABA, discrete trial training (DTT) is the most structured behavioral intervention for teaching children with ASDs (e.g., Lovaas, 1987) and is a popular approach commonly used in many in-home programs (e.g., Lindsley, 1996; Smith et al., 2000). DTT involves repetitive exercises in which a child is given a discriminative stimulus and reinforced each time he or she responds correctly.

Trials are described as *discrete* because there is a clear beginning (i.e., discrimina-tive stimulus), middle (i.e., response), and end (i.e., consequence) to each. Whereas DTT results in fast acquisition of new skills, it has been criticized for its limited generalizability; in particular, DTT programs often do not incorporate pro-gramming for generalization of skills (Koegel & Koegel, 1995; Scott, Clark, & Brady, 2000). New skills are learned under certain stimulus conditions that may not generalize to other situations. Additional criticisms of strict DTT programs are that children become cue or prompt dependent, they do not learn to initiate behavior, and they tend to respond in a rote manner (Elliot et al., 1991). Because DTT programs remain popular, it is important to examine how skills are taught, evaluate the generalizability of skills learned, and actively program for lasting behavior change in the natural environment (Koegel & Koegel, 2006).

WORKING WITH THE FAMILY TO ESTABLISH GENERALIZATION GOALS AND PLANNING

Intensive in-home programming is becoming the "gold standard" of early inter-vention for young children with ASDs. The greatest strengths of the in-home program come from the access to and utility of teaching during natural family routines and the involvement of parents in teaching opportunities. Although one would think that generalization is inherent for in-home programs, this has not been the case. Parent education and teaching in natural environments do promote children's generalization and maintenance of skills (Koegel et al., 1982; Lovaas, Koegel, Simmons, & Long, 1973; McClannahan, Krantz, & McGee, 1982), but steps still need to be taken to ensure that program gains will transfer to other settings and other communication partners. Generalization is no longer an after-thought but should be planned from the onset. Parents are taught concepts such as prompt dependency, the risks of tight stimulus control, and the tendency for children with ASDs to promote sameness in their environment. The mantra of *functional skills* should be repeated whenever reviewing the child's progress. This mantra focuses the team on the future and on what opportunities need to be cre-ated to ensure that everything the child is learning in the home is taught and maintained at school, in the community, and during playdates.

Recognize the Importance of Family Routines

Anchoring communication and social goals to family routines increases the likeli-hood that the goals will be meaningful to the family and that the family will have increased input as to what program success should look like. The sustainability of goals within family routines has been seen as a critical unit of analysis for pro-gram success (Lucyshyn, Albin, & Nixon, 1997; Moes & Frea, 2000, 2002).

While embedding communication goals into family routines facilitates fam-ily involvement and commitment to the program, it can also serve to limit multi-ple exemplars. ABA instruction should not become routine. For ideal generaliza-tion programming, the goal is to vary the teaching environment and the discrim-inative stimuli associated with instruction (Koegel, Koegel, & McNerney, 2001). Therapists should always strive toward the ultimate goal of effective communi-cation and socialization in progressively less predictable environments (e.g., playground, mall, birthday party). Referencing the family routine ensures successful family participation, input, and sustainability (i.e., maintenance); however, referencing less predictable environments allows for a stronger gauge of generalization.

Identify Generalization Goals

A failure to generalize can be seen when the child simply does not demonstrate any newly learned skills outside of the home or when a parent or primary caregiver/interventionist is not present. This level of program failure can be common when the program relies too heavily on discrete trial methods and pushes toward rapid acquisition of many skills without considering the generalization of those skills. A failure to generalize can also be seen, however, when a specific new skill does not generalize despite the overall program being successful. Often, these surprises can be avoided through clear communication early in the program, with the family considering their expectations for success outside the home environment. In the same way that it is wise to anchor in-home successes to identified home routines, it is important to reference generalization successes to activities and people outside of the teaching routines.

One way of ensuring that the team communicates generalization expectations regularly is to schedule that communication. It is a good idea to include generalization as an agenda item during monthly clinical team meetings. That is, when the team meets to review goals and outcomes, the family should be asked to give input on potential generalization targets associated with each goal. This method allows the team to probe those targets either with therapists running generalization sessions or parents reporting back generalization progress in the targeted activity.

Test for Generalization

Ultimately the skills in the home program have to serve the child wherever he or she goes. The best way of knowing how the program is proceeding is to gather information in as many environments as possible. The practitioner needs to ask as many people as possible, "How is the child doing?" Playdates are also a great way to gauge how things are going; however, targeting generalization can be hard and emotional. It may be scary and sad for the parents to watch their child struggle during a playdate. Therefore, it is important that the therapist prepares the parent for failure. Failure informs the program; it is baseline, and improvement is targeted from an understanding of baseline. If the child struggles for long periods with minimal success, then we know the program needs major revision. However, if the child struggles and improves with our efforts, then we have an opportunity to expand the program by building on these successes.

Ultimately, long-term success will rely on the child successfully integrating into typical classrooms and multiple community environments (McEachin, Smith, & Lovaas, 1993; National Research Council, 2001). This will not likely happen all at once when someone decides, "It's time to start generalizing skills." Instead, generalization goal identification will start the moment therapy begins and may continue through most of childhood.

GENERALIZATION OF PARENT SKILLS RELATING TO CHALLENGING BEHAVIOR

ABA programs are not only concerned with generalization of child skills but also address the parents' abilities to transfer what they have learned to different situations. Parents need to be able to use their assessment and intervention skills outside of the home as well. This is especially true when challenging behaviors arise in new community settings and activities. The ability to assess the cause of challenging behavior will be required for years and in many different situations (Lucyshyn, Kayser, Irvin, & Blumberg, 2002). It is important for parents to work with their behavior analyst in multiple settings, demonstrating both teaching skills and assessment skills.

The basic functions of challenging behavior and how to develop hypotheses should be taught to the family. Many practical resources are available to teach and support families in this process (Carr et al., 1994; Glassberg, 2006; Lucyshyn, Dunlap, & Albin, 2002; O'Neill et al., 1997). Parents will need to have multiple opportunities to assess behavior outside of the home environment and develop plans to teach functional alternatives.

Without a focus on generalization and sustainability, a behavioral program will ultimately be unsuccessful. The family needs skills that will follow them wherever they go. Only recently has the field of behavior analysis confronted its failure to promote generalization and maintenance (Horner et al., 1988; Scotti, Evans, Meyer, & Walker, 1991). It is now an expectation that new research includes generalization data and follow-up data to demonstrate true effectiveness. There is also a better understanding that tightly controlled treatment sessions pose a risk to generalization. Indeed, a quality ABA program will actively program for generalization from the onset of therapy and track and monitor generalization throughout treatment and during follow-up.

The goal tracking datasheet (Appendix 10.1) is a sample used at Autism Spectrum Therapies. On this datasheet, target behaviors are first taught and tracked in a highly structured environment. The behaviors are then generalized to play-based settings, and assessments of generalization are also scheduled on a weekly and monthly basis. The first row of the datasheet shows the example of tracking the target behavior of a child's ability to wait for 7 seconds for access to a toy across a variety of increasingly natural environments.

It is important for professionals to understand that more natural, play-based intervention approaches not only promote generalization but also reduce challenging behaviors (Koegel, Koegel, & Surrat, 1992). Behavioral interventions should be fun for the child and produce broad gains in communication and socialization.

GENERALIZATION OF LANGUAGE SKILLS

The most critical skills taught within an intensive ABA program are in the area of language. The ability to communicate effectively opens up new socialization opportunities, reduces challenging behaviors as needs get met, and forms the foundation for almost every new skill set that will be added to the child's future program. The language skills must generalize if the program is to be considered successful. For this to happen, language goals must move to additional partners and additional settings as soon as successes are achieved.

The tight stimulus control that is often present when moving from vocal imitation to words presents a risk to generalization if it remains for too long. Words should not be treated as successful imitation responses but rather requests that are rewarded with the item that the child is vocalizing. The lack of this functional relationship (e.g., say "ball," get ball) is often the first threat to generalization. For example, if the child is repeating toy names and being reinforced with pretzels, the program may take much longer to reach functional, generalized language.

As with any new skill, the family should be included in generalization planning early on to identify environments where new vocabulary can be tested. Often this begins with trips to the store or playdates with a familiar friend or relative. Ultimately, the more people who are providing natural and functional reinforcers, the stronger the generalization is.

GENERALIZING PLAY AND SOCIAL SKILLS

While it may seem like a theoretical distinction, in truth many social skills are merely communicative responses unless they are actually used, *unprompted*, in social environments with peers and other untrained social partners. Social skills such as greetings, asking questions, or commenting on someone's behavior can be communicated without the intention of having a social interaction. Depending on how these skills are taught, they may never be viewed by the learner as skills to use outside of the teaching environment. Most families assume that the social skills being taught in their child's program are intended to benefit him or her socially. In other words, they are not simply another set of communication goals to be used in the home. If the family is not being engaged in the discussion of how to make these skills truly social in the child's life, then it is likely that the skills being learned will not become social skills.

Too often, the social skills in an ABA program are not actually social. Rather, they are responses that are taught exclusively in structured trials and seldom make it into natural social routines. For example, the critical goal of social initiations often terminates at the level of approaching a therapist or sibling with one of several practiced questions (e.g., "Look at this!" or "Do you want to play?"). These requests are not necessarily social requests; they may not function to initiate a preferred social interaction for the child. When such an initiation happens unprompted in a natural social environment (e.g., playground, cousin's house) to generate a rewarding social exchange, it is more clearly social. Because the generalization of social skills is unpredictable for many children with ASDs, it is important to select pivotal social skills (e.g., initiations) and prompt them in as many different social environments as possible (Koegel, Carter, & Koegel, 2003).

The term *social* is often used broadly when categorizing goals in the child's program. It is critical that social skills are defined as part of true social interactions and their functional use is an outcome measure. Core socials skills should be well defined. For example, if pointing is being taught as an initiation, then all members of the family should understand the expectations for how pointing is being taught to begin an interaction. Broad social skills (e.g., initiating, responding) should be a primary topic of the team's generalization discussions. Social skills should lead to conversational skills that maintain and extend interactions. Thus, as social skills develop—particularly during play-based ABA sessions in the home—plans should be in place on how to extend those treatment gains into peer interactions.

Social skills must have reference points outside of the home environment that identify them as true social goals. It is reasonable that social skills will be taught with a peer component (Goldstein, English, Shafer, & Kaczmarek, 1997). Thus, greetings need to be extended into the preschool and selected community environments. Question asking needs to be taught broadly, with meaningful social reinforcers, and practiced in as many opportunities outside of the home as possible; objective data also must be collected. Generalization of mastered skills across different people, places, and stimuli needs to be tracked and monitored.

Another sample datasheet used at Autism Spectrum Therapies (Appendix 10.2) keeps the team accountable for measuring generalization of mastered goals and ensures that the child is successfully using new behaviors in a variety of contexts. As will be discussed next, social validity is the critical measure of whether the family achieved what they expected from the program. Often, social skills outcomes have the weakest social validity.

A primary risk of teaching social skills in the home program is that it is a safe and predictable environment. Social situations outside of the home are seldom predictable and are often feared by the child with ASD. Often the bridges to success in unpredictable environments are planned social skills sessions that focus on the child's preferred activities and topics. As the child becomes ready to practice social skills in more unstructured settings, he or she is introduced to those settings with opportunities to demonstrate social skills within familiar and preferred activities so that initial success is likely.

SOCIAL VALIDITY

What happens when a child does generalize new skills but the parent is disappointed with the outcome? Or, what happens when the family's quality of life does not improve after treatment? Take the example of Jacob.

Jacob's parents were thrilled when he started receiving in-home ABA services. Prior to therapy, Jacob only spoke a few words. His inability to successfully communicate resulted in violent tantrums during which Jacob would often bite himself and hit other people. These tantrums were particularly embarrassing for Jacob's parents when they occurred in public, such as at his favorite toy store when he could not appropriately communicate what he wanted.

Jacob's therapists immediately set about teaching him words. He learned to label almost 50 different objects with a variety of discriminative stimuli such as "What is this?" or "What do you see?" He was able to label objects on flashcards, as well as while looking at books and actual three-dimensional objects. He labeled objects with his sister, his parents, and both of his therapists in a variety of places, such as at home, in his classroom, and in the community. Jacob's treatment team was very pleased with his generalization of his new language. The team expected that because Jacob had learned the labels for many items, he would now be able to express his needs; therefore, his number of tantrums would go down.

However, Jacob's tantrums continued at the same levels, despite the fact that he had a new repertoire of words. Jacob's team eventually came to realize that he was not using the words functionally or spontaneously as a way to get his needs met. The quality of life for Jacob and his family did not improve, as he continued to have violent tantrums. The goal of teaching Jacob words to communicate ended up not being meaningful for him or resulting in positive changes in the family's life. His parents were extremely disappointed with the amount of time and money they had invested in Jacob's therapy because his challenging behaviors still had such a negative impact on the family's life.

At the heart of understanding the importance of generalization is the concept of social validity. Social validity represents the therapist's understanding of what the family's expectation is of treatment and their satisfaction with the results. Strong social validity, in a nutshell, means that the parents view the treatment successes as aligned with what matters to them. In Jacob's example, the outcomes of treatment were not in alignment with what was important to the family. Instead of Jacob learning functional language that would reduce his frustration in natural social environments, he was taught words in isolation. What the therapist thought were critical language goals actually were not what the family was expecting at all and did not alleviate the significant behavior challenges facing this family.

As discussed, social skills do not necessarily equate to being social. Talking does not always mean communicating. Furthermore, outcomes are not always successes in the parents' eyes. Social validity is an ongoing analysis of the meaningfulness of the program, and the targeted outcomes should not be a surprise.

Many Eyes

It is always a good idea to have many significant people look at the program, including family members, teachers, family friends, and specialists. Although too many treatment providers can pose a major problem, having input on how the program looks can only help formulate questions for the family. It is important that the family be able to inquire about the direction of the program in an informed way so that they can be part of the programming and outcomes.

As people understand the goals of the program, they can be part of generalization planning. While social validity is the process of ensuring that the outcomes are valued, generalization planning involves making sure those outcomes are functional across settings and people. There is the question of what is being learned and the question of how it is being learned. The goal is for meaningful skills to be learned and to make sure that those skills generalize to meaningful settings and contexts.

Playdates

An important referent is how well the child is doing with peers. Within a motivating play environment, one hopes that language and social skills will generalize to peer interactions. Scheduling multiple playdates early on and throughout the intervention helps anchor goals to the real world. This is true not only for peer play but for any critical outcome that the family values.

It is common for parents to state that succeeding in preschool or kindergarten is an important goal. Playdates are extremely revealing about how the program is teaching the child to relate to peers. The playdates should be structured in a way to directly probe the skills that have been taught in the home program. In addition to providing information on the success of the program, playdates are an excellent way of generating new meaningful goals. Often during a playdate, the parent or therapist will be surprised that the child was unable to perform a basic social skill. That observation directly informs the child's program and can result in an immediate change that will have enormous impact on future success.

It is often in observing failures, whether they occur during play or in the community, that therapists truly know how well a program is succeeding in specific areas. They learn the most during these observations. There will always be generalization targets, and those targets should never be set randomly. As stated previously, significant risk is associated with a program that teaches outside of the natural environment. For some goals, the home is not the most natural environment. When that is the case, it can only be known how well those skills generalize in their most natural contexts. Within those struggles, generalization goals are identified.

PRACTICAL APPLICATIONS

Parents have to be informed and ready to ask the right questions when selecting an in-home treatment program for their child. As it has been reiterated throughout this chapter, treatment goals and new skills lose their value if there is not a widespread change in a child's behavior and the quality of life for the family. Generalization needs to be planned from the onset of treatment, and children need to able to perform behaviors in systematically less predictable and safe environments. Communication between key players on the team (e.g., parents, therapists, teachers) needs to be clear from the beginning so that everyone has the same expectations for the program and the outcomes.

The most challenging areas for children with ASDs are language and social skills. An appropriate treatment program does not teach rote language or social behaviors; rather, the idea is that a child will learn to truly enjoy social interactions and understand the utility of communicating. The ultimate goal of any educational program should be successful integration into typical classrooms and multiple community environments (National Research Council, 2001), with the child being able to respond to natural and functional reinforcers. With the expectation that research in the field of behavior analysis actively addresses generalization (Horner et al., 1988), there is no reason why the same expectation should not be placed on in-home ABA programs. Indeed, receiving a diagnosis of ASD is life changing for a family; it is up to treatment providers to ensure the highest-quality programming and long-lasting, meaningful behavior change so that each child will be able to live up to his or her potential.

REFERENCES

Anderson, S.R., Avery, D.L., DiPietro, E.K., Edwards, G.L., & Christian, W.P. (1987). Intensive home-based early intervention with autistic children. *Education and Treatment of Children, 10,* 352–366.

Brookman-Frazee, L. (2004). Using parent/clinician partnerships in parent education programs for children with autism. *Journal of Positive Behavior Interventions, 6,* 195–213.

Carr, E.G., Levin, L., McConnachie, G., Carlson, J.I., Kemp, D.C., & Smith, C.E. (1994). *Communication-based intervention for problem behavior: A user's guide for producing positive change.* Baltimore: Paul H. Brookes Publishing Co.

Charlop-Christy, M.H., & Carpenter, M.H. (2000). Modified incidental teaching sessions (MITS): A procedure for parents to increase spontaneous speech in their children with autism. *Journal of Positive Behavior Interventions, 2,* 98–112.

Elliot, R.O., Hall, K., & Soper, H.V. (1991). Analog language teaching versus natural language teaching: Generality and retention of language learning for adults with autism and mental retardation. *Journal of Autism and Developmental Disorders, 21,* 433–447.

Glassberg, B.A. (2006). *Functional behavior assessment for people with autism: Making sense of seemingly senseless behavior.* Bethesda, MD: Woodbine House.

Goldstein, H., English, K., Shafer, K., & Kaczmarek, L. (1997). Interaction among preschoolers with and without disabilities: Effects of across-the-day peer intervention. *Journal of Speech, Language, and Hearing Research, 40,* 33–48.

Harris, S.L. (1982). A family systems approach to behavioral education with parents of autistic children. *Child and Family Behavior Therapy, 4,* 21–35.

Horner, R.H., Dunlap, G., & Koegel, R.L. (1988). *Generalization and maintenance: Life-style changes in applied settings.* Baltimore: Paul H. Brookes Publishing Co.

Howard, J.S., Sparkman, C.R., Cohen, H.G., Green, G., & Stanislaw, H. (2005). A comparison of intensive behavior analytic and eclectic treatments for young children with autism. *Research in Developmental Disabilities, 26,* 359–383.

Koegel, L.K., Carter, C.M., & Koegel, R.L. (2003). Teaching children with autism self-initiations as a pivotal response. *Topics in Language Disorders, 23,* 134–145.

Koegel, R.L., Bimbela, A., & Schreibman, L. (1996). Collateral effects of parent training on family interactions. *Journal of Autism and Developmental Disorders, 26*(3), 347–359.

Koegel, R.L., & Koegel, L.K. (1995). *Teaching children with autism: Strategies for initiating positive interactions and improving learning outcomes.* Baltimore: Paul H. Brookes Publishing Co.

Koegel, R.L., & Koegel, L.K. (2006). *Pivotal Response Treatments for autism: Communication, social, and academic development.* Baltimore: Paul H. Brookes Publishing Co.

Koegel, R.L., Koegel, L.K., & McNerney, E.K. (2001). Pivotal areas in intervention for autism. *Journal of Clinical Psychology, 30,* 19–32.

Koegel, R.L., Koegel, L.K., & Surrat, A. (1992). Language intervention and disruptive behavior in preschool children with autism. *Journal of Autism and Developmental Disorders, 22,* 141–153.

Koegel, R.L., Schreibman, L., Britten, K.R., Burke, J.C., & O'Neill, R.E. (1982). A comparison of parent training to direct clinic treatment. In R.L. Koegel, A. Rincover, & A.L. Egel (Eds.), *Educating and understanding autistic children* (pp. 260–280). San Diego: College-Hill Press.

Laski, K.E., Charlop, M.H., & Schreibman, L. (1988). Training parents to use the natural language paradigm to increase their autistic children's speech. *Journal of Applied Behavior Analysis, 21,* 391–400.

Lindsley, O.R. (1996). The four free-operant freedoms. *The Behavior Analyst, 19,* 199–210.

Lovaas, O.I. (1987). Behavioral treatment and normal educational and intellectual functioning in young autistic children. *Journal of Consulting and Clinical Psychology, 55,* 3–9.

Lovaas, O.I., Koegel, R.L., Simmons, J.Q., & Long, J.S. (1973). Some generalization and follow-up measures on autistic children in behavior therapy. *Journal of Applied Behavior Analysis, 6,* 131–166.

Lucyshyn, J.M., Albin, R.W., & Nixon, C.D. (1997). Embedding comprehensive behavioral supports in family ecology: An experimental, single-case analysis. *Journal of Consulting and Clinical Psychology, 65,* 241–251.

Lucyshyn, J.M., Dunlap, G., & Albin, R.W. (2002). *Families and positive behavior support: Addressing problem behavior in family contexts.* Baltimore: Paul H. Brookes Publishing Co.

Lucyshyn, J.M., Kayser, A.T., Irvin, L.K., & Blumberg, R. (2002). Functional assessment and positive behavior support at home with families. In J.M. Lucyshyn, G. Dunlap, & R.W. Albin (Eds.), *Families and positive behavior support: Addressing problem behaviors in family contexts* (pp. 97–132). Baltimore: Paul H. Brookes Publishing Co.

Malmberg, D.B. (2008). Assessment of a collaborative parent education program targeting the rigid and ritualistic behaviors of children with autism. *Dissertation Abstracts International: Section B: The Sciences and Engineering, 68,* 7-B.

McClannahan, L.E., Krantz, P.J., & McGee, G.G. (1982). Parents as therapists for autistic children: A model for effective parent training. *Analysis and Intervention in Developmental Disabilities, 2,* 223–252.

McEachin, J.J., Smith, T., & Lovaas, O.I. (1993). Long-term outcome for children with autism who received early intensive behavioral treatment. *American Journal of Mental Retardation, 97,* 359–372.

McGee, G.G., Krantz, P.J., & McClannahan, L.E. (1985). The facilitative effects of incidental teaching on preposition use by autistic children. *Journal of Applied Behavior Analysis, 18,* 17–31.

Moes, D.R., & Frea, W.D. (2000). Using family context to inform intervention planning for the treatment of a child with autism. *Journal of Positive Behavior Interventions, 2,* 40–46.

Moes, D.R., & Frea, W.D. (2002). Contextualized behavior support in early intervention for children with autism and their families. *Journal of Autism and Developmental Disorders, 32,* 519–533.

Mullen, K.B., & Frea, W.D. (1995). A parent–professional consultation model for functional analysis. In R.L. Koegel & L.K. Koegel (Eds.), *Teaching children with autism: Strategies for initiating positive interactions and improving learning opportunities* (pp. 175–188). Baltimore: Paul H. Brookes Publishing Co.

National Research Council. (2001). *Educating children with autism.* Washington, DC: National Academies Press.

O'Neill, R.E., Horner, R.H., Albin, R.W., Sprague, J.R., Storey, K., & Newton, J.S. (1997). *Functional assessment and program development for problem behavior* (2nd ed.). Pacific Grove, CA: Brooks/Cole Publishing.

Scott, J., Clark, C., & Brady, M. (2000). *Students with autism: Characteristics and instructional programming.* San Diego: Singular Publishing.

Scotti, J.R., Evans, I.M., Meyer, L.H., & Walker, P. (1991). A meta-analysis of intervention research with problem behavior: Treatment validity and standards of practice. *American Journal on Mental Retardation, 96,* 233–256.

Smith, T., Groen, A.D., & Wynn, J.W. (2000). Randomized trial of early intervention for children with pervasive developmental disorder. *American Journal on Mental Retardation, 105,* 269–285.

Stokes, T.F., & Baer, D.M. (1977). An implicit technology of generalization. *Journal of Applied Behavior Analysis, 10,* 349–367.

Weiss, M. (1999). Differential rates of skill acquisition and outcomes of early intensive behavioral intervention for autism. *Behavioral Interventions, 14,* 3–22.

Chapter 10
Appendices

APPENDIX 10.1

Sample Goal Tracking Datasheet

MT: Errorless trials with prompt fading until 3 independent responses from child. If appropriate, start with field of 2. **ET:** ET1 through ET6. 80% ET6 with field of 4-5 across 2 days. **RR:** 80% across 2 days across minimum of 3 skill areas (e.g., expressive labels, gross motor imitation, receptive labels). **Acquired:** 80% across 2 days in RR. **Mastered in play-based:** Skill demonstrated across 2 people, 2 environment, 2 stimulus. **Note:** Movement through each level to be determined by the supervisor

Target area: _____

Month: _____

Target behavior	Date introduced	MT	ET	RR	Acquired in DTT	Introduced in play-based	Mastered in play-based	Follow-up		
								Generalization schedule—1x/week	Generalization schedule—2x/month	Generalization schedule—3x/month
Waiting 7 seconds for access to a toy	9/1/08	9/5/08	9/12/08	9/14/08	9/17/08	9/25/08	9/28/08	10/12/08	11/1/08	12/3/08

(continued)

(continued)

Target behavior	Date introduced	MT	ET	RR	Acquired in DTT	Introduced in play-based	Mastered in play-based	Generalization schedule— 1x/week	Generalization schedule— 2x/month	Generalization schedule— 3x/month

APPENDIX 10.2.

Sample Mastered Skills Generalization Datasheet

Child: Susy

Therapist: Bobby

Date	Target	Activity	Location	Materials	Response	Notes
10/1/08	Turn taking	Don't Break the Ice game	Neighbor's house	Don't Break the Ice game	+	Susy took turns 5 times. Great waiting and sharing!
10/12/08	Turn taking	Video game	Susy's living room	Video game, controller, television	+	Susy did great taking turns with her brother; no behaviors.
12/15/08	Greetings	Morning cirle time	Susy's classroom	None	+	Susy greeted her teacher independently.

Index

Page numbers followed by *f* indicate figures; those followed by *t* indicate tables.